# WISCONSIN MODEL EARLY LEARNING STANDARDS
## WITH INTRODUCTION

2003 Edition
2008 Edition
2011 Edition
2013 Edition
2017 Edition (Updates to the 2013 Edition)

**The Wisconsin Model Early Learning Standards Steering Committee**
Wisconsin Department of Public Instruction
Wisconsin Department of Children and Families
Wisconsin Department of Health Services
Wisconsin Head Start State Collaboration Office
Wisconsin Early Childhood Collaborating Partners
Wisconsin Early Childhood Association
Wisconsin Division of Exceptional Children

**Funding for the 2003, 2008, 2011, 2013, and 2017 Editions are from:**
Wisconsin Head Start State Collaboration Project
Wisconsin Department of Public Instruction
Wisconsin Department of Health Services
Braided Funding Initiative
Wisconsin Early Childhood Collaborating Partners
Great Lakes Head Start Quality Network (QNet)
Wisconsin Department of Children and Families
Race to the Top- Early Learning Challenge Grant

**This publication is available from**
Wisconsin Child Care Information Center
2109 South Stoughton Road
Madison, WI 53716
608-224-5388 or 1-800-362-7353

Or order online at *dcf.wisconsin.gov/ccic/wmels*

The Wisconsin Model Early Learning Standards (WMELS) are published in English, Spanish, and Hmong. All versions are available on the Wisconsin Early Childhood Collaborating Partners (WECCP) web page and can be downloaded in a PDF format: **www.collaboratingpartners.com/wmels-documents.php**. This website also has related documents including: frequently asked questions, training materials, training calendars, alignment with Wisconsin Academic Standards, as well as information about curriculum and assessment.

**For more information on the
Wisconsin Model Early Learning Standards initiative contact:**

**Katherine McGurk**
Wisconsin Department of Children and Families
608-266-7001
kathy.mcgurk@wisconsin.gov

**Sherry W. Kimball**
Wisconsin Department of Public Instruction
608-267-9625
sherry.kimball@dpi.wi.gov

October 2017
Wisconsin Department of Public Instruction
Tony Evers, PhD, State Superintendent
ISBN 978-1-57337-166-7

The Wisconsin Department of Public Instruction does not discriminate on the basis of sex, race, color, religion, creed, age, national origin, ancestry, pregnancy, marital status or parental status, sexual orientation, or disability.

Printed on Recycled Paper

# Acknowledgements

## WMELS State and Regional Steering Committee, 2013 & 2017 Leadership Team

Arlene Wright, WMELS Statewide Coordinator, Office of Early Learning, Wisconsin Department of Public Instruction (2013)

Jill Haglund, Office of Early Learning, Wisconsin Department of Public Instruction

Julie Betchkal, Early Childhood Program Support, CESA 11 (2017)

Wendy Bowe, Head Start Technical Assistance Center

Abbe Braun, Supporting Families Together Association

Amy Carriere, Early Childhood Program Support, CESA 10 (2017)

Glenna Carter, WI Child Care Information Center (2017)

Penny Chase, Supporting Families Together Association (2013)

Ruth Chvojicek, WI Birth-3 RESource (2017)

Bridget Cullen, Division for Early Childhood Care and Education, Wisconsin Department of Children and Families

Catharine Daentl, WECCP Website Manager, CESA 5 (2017)

Jenny Giles, Special Education Consultant, Wisconsin Department of Public Instruction

Jill Hoiting, Supporting Families Together Association

Carrie Holden, WECCP Regional Collaboration Coach-Milwaukee (2017)

Heather Jordan, Great Lakes Inter-Tribal Council (2017)

Sherry W. Kimball, UW Waisman Center (2017)

Linda Leonhart, Head Start Collaboration Office, Wisconsin Department of Public Instruction (2013)

Kathy McGurk, Division for Early Childhood Care and Education, Wisconsin Department of Children and Families

Joanna Parker, Office of Early Learning, Wisconsin Department of Public Instruction

Jeanette Paulson, Wisconsin Early Childhood Association

Mary L. Peters, Waisman Center, UW Madison

Michelle Ogorek, Statewide Early Childhood Coordinator, Wisconsin Department of Public Instruction (2017)

Nicole Lopez, The Registry, Wisconsin (2017)

Ann Ramminger, Office of Early Learning, Wisconsin Department of Public Instruction

Waisman Center, UW Madison (2013)

Katie Roberts, Wisconsin Technical College System

Pamela Torres, Great Lakes Inter-Tribal Council (2013)

## Research and Development

**The 2003 edition of the Wisconsin Model Early Learning Standards was researched and written by Diane Jenkins, Jenkins and Associates, Madison, Wisconsin.**

**The 2008/2011/2013 edition of the Wisconsin Model Early Learning Standards was researched and written by the following team:**

Arlene Wright, WMELS Coach and 2008/2013 Lead Coordinator; Independent Education Consultant, Chippewa Falls

Ruth Chvojicek, OSEP Outcome Grant Coordinator; Early Education Program Support, CESA 5

Linda Hurst, WMELS Coach; Early Childhood Consultant

Ann Ramminger, Southern Region Community Collaboration Coach; Early Childhood Professional Dev., UW Waisman Center

Vikki Lane Kunstman, Retired, Curriculum and Instruction Coordinator and Early Learning Consultant, CESA 6

**The following people advised on the 2003 and/or 2008/2011/2013/2017 editions of the standards**

Barbara Chaney, UW-LaCrosse

Ya-Fang Cheng, UW-Madison

Christine Enockson, Watertown Unified School District

Beth Graue, UW-Madison

Kathy Hartjes, Wisconsin Kindergarten Teachers Association

Sally Jansen, Green Bay Public Schools Head Start

Patricia Kielpinski, Milwaukee Area Technical College

Sherry W. Kimball, Waisman Center, UW-Madison

Joan Laurion, UW-Extension – Dane County and Family Child Care

Julie Lennon, Green Bay Public Schools Early Childhood Special Education

Mary McLean, Ph.D., UW-Milwaukee

Lana Nenide, Wisconsin Alliance for Infant Mental Health

Barb Novak, Wisconsin Department of Public Instruction

Casey O'Keefe, MS/CCC-SLP Cardinal Stritch University

Elizabeth Olsen, CESA 5/ Dane County Parent Council

Teressa Pellett, Children's Trust Fund

Mary L. Peters, Waisman Center, UW-Madison

Pence Revington, Parents Plus Wisconsin (PIRC)

Mary Roach, Ph.D., UW-Extension

Connie Robers, Rock-Walworth CFS Head Start

Paul Sandrock, Wisconsin Department of Public Instruction

Elaine Strom, Dane County Parent Council, Inc.

Ann Terrell, Early Childhood Council and Milwaukee Public Schools

Gaye Tylka, Early Childhood Response to Intervention Statewide Coordinator, CESA 4

Paula Wainscott, Eau Claire Schools Head Start

Sheila Weihert, Heritage Elementary School, De Pere

Christopher Weinhold, Wisconsin Rapids Public Schools

Christina Wen, Waisman Center, UW-Madison

## 2008/2011/2013 Editions Layout, Editing, Proofing, and Cover Design

Original Layout: Fernando Hernandez, CESA 5

Original Editing and Layout: Neldine Nichols, Wisconsin Department of Public Instruction

Revision Editing: Arlene Wright and Laura Paella, Wisconsin Department of Public Instruction; Glenna Carter, Child Care Information Center

Proofing: Roslyn Wise, WI Department of Public Instruction

Cover Design: Cynthia Hoffman Meldorf at Mercury Communication in conjunction with the Think Big Start Small: Invest in a Child's Future public awareness campaign

Greetings!

The Wisconsin Model Early Learning Standards (WMELS) have played a significant role in improving the quality of early childhood programs in Wisconsin. Since they were first published in 2004, these standards have had a positive impact on the many child care, Head Start, early childhood special education, and kindergarten programs that have embraced them. They have played a critical role in communities that have worked in partnership to establish shared expectations among these programs. Throughout these years, the Departments of Children and Families and Public Instruction have championed a unique collaboration across state agencies and related associations, as well as with early childhood educators and child care providers, to promote our common commitment to excellence in early childhood education and care services for Wisconsin's young children and their families.

The WMELS are based upon research conducted into all aspects of children's early learning and development, and encompass guiding principles, developmental expectations, and performance and program standards for the delivery of high-quality education and care to young children. The standards include a broad description of children's growth, to ensure a holistic approach to creating positive early childhood environments. To guide programs serving children from birth to first grade, the WMELS address approaches to learning, health and physical development, social and emotional development, language development and communication, and cognition and general knowledge development.

The knowledge and skills described are designed to provide support and information to families, caregivers, and educators concerning children's development within certain age spans, rather than dictate exactly when or how each child should progress. Also of importance is that the standards acknowledge and are responsive to variations in culture, language, and ability. By including the full scope of children's early development, addressing diversity, and aligning content across all early childhood settings, the WMELS are intended to effect greater collaboration and consistency across early childhood systems in Wisconsin.

Thank you for your commitment to providing high-quality early childhood experiences to the children of Wisconsin. Through collaboration and with common reference points, we can create positive early childhood environments that lay a critical foundation for our young children's future success.

Sincerely,

Eloise Anderson
Secretary
Department of Children and Families

Tony Evers, PhD
State Superintendent
Department of Public Instruction

# Wisconsin Model Early Learning Standards
## Table of Contents

Acknowledgements .................................................................................................... iii

Introduction ................................................................................................................ 1

    I. **Health and Physical Development** ........................................................... 12
        A. Physical Health and Development ................................................... 14
        B. Motor Development ........................................................................ 20
        C. Sensory Organization ..................................................................... 23

    II. **Social and Emotional Development** ......................................................... 26
        A. Emotional Development ................................................................. 28
        B. Self-concept .................................................................................... 32
        C. Social Competence ........................................................................ 35

    III. **Language Development and Communication** ........................................ 42
        A. Listening and Understanding ......................................................... 44
        B. Speaking and Communicating ....................................................... 47
        C. Early Literacy .................................................................................. 54

    IV. **Approaches to Learning** .......................................................................... 66
        A. Curiosity, Engagement, and Persistence ....................................... 68
        B. Creativity and Imagination ............................................................. 71
        C. Diversity in Learning ...................................................................... 73

    V. **Cognition and General Knowledge** ......................................................... 78
        A. Exploration, Discovery, and Problem Solving ................................. 80
        B. Mathematical Thinking ................................................................... 85
        C. Scientific Thinking .......................................................................... 96

**Interest Areas: Children Learn from Play** ............................................................ 102

## Appendixes

Appendix A: Alignment of Wisconsin Model Early Learning Standards with Wisconsin Academic Standards for English Language Arts and Mathematics and Wisconsin Essential Elements ................................. 107

Appendix B: Wisconsin Model Early Learning Standards and IDEA Early Childhood Outcomes ........................................................ 114

Appendix C: References and Resources .............................................................. 116

Appendix D: Early Care and Education Resource Listing .................................... 124

# Wisconsin Model Early Learning Standards
## Introduction

*The Wisconsin Model Early Learning Standards provide a common language and guidance for families, professionals, and policymakers around early childhood education and care.*

Why do we have model early learning standards? Based on research and supported by evidence-based practices, the Wisconsin Model Early Learning Standards (WMELS) provide a framework for families, professionals, and policymakers to:

- Share a common language and responsibility for the well-being of children from birth to first grade;
- Know and understand developmental expectations of young children; and
- Understand the connection among the foundations of early childhood, K-12 educational experiences, and lifelong learning.

With the inclusion of the birth-to-3 age range, the revised WMELS also includes developmental continuums, sample behaviors of children, and sample strategies for adults.

The development of the standards was guided by research in the field and supported by content experts from institutions of higher education in the state. Aligned to the Wisconsin Academic Standards (kindergarten through grade 12), the WMELS are intended to provide early learning opportunities that support children's continued success in school and future life.

The basis for the development of the WMELS is a set of guiding principles that specify beliefs and values about young children in Wisconsin. The primary principles are as follows:

- All children are capable and competent.
- Early relationships matter.
- A child's early learning and development is multidimensional.
- Expectations for children must be guided by knowledge of child growth and development.
- Children are individuals who develop at various rates.
- Children are members of cultural groups that share developmental patterns.
- Children exhibit a range of skills and competencies within any domain of development.
- Children learn through play and the active exploration of their environment.
- Parents are children's primary and most important caregivers and educators.

A more detailed description of the WMELS Guiding Principles is located on page 10 of the Introduction Section.

# Wisconsin Model Early Learning Standards
## Framework

*The Wisconsin Model Early Learning Standards specify developmental expectations for children from birth through entrance to first grade. The Wisconsin Model Early Learning Standards reflect attention to all the domains of a child's learning and development. Each domain is divided into sub-domains. Each sub-domain includes developmental expectations, program standards, performance standards, and developmental continuum. Samples of children's behavior and adult strategies are also provided. The framework is described below in a narrative and on the following page as a chart.*

### Developmental Domains
Discrete area of the child's development. The areas are interrelated and include:
- Health and Physical Development
- Social and Emotional Development
- Language Development and Communication
- Approaches to Learning
- Cognition and General Knowledge

### Sub-Domains
Developmental domains are further divided into sub-domains. The sub-domains are labeled with letters "A, B, and C." For example, in the domain of Health and Physical Development the sub-domains are:
- A. Physical Health and Development
- B. Motor Development
- C. Sensory Organization

### Developmental Expectation
Broad general statement of what the child should know and be able to do within the expected wide variability of development that occurs in the early childhood period.

### Performance Standard
Statement that represents the specific information, skills, or both that a child should know and be able to do. The performance standards are designed "forward" from birth to first grade and are aligned with the Wisconsin Academic Standards.

### Learning Expectations
Subcomponent of a performance standard that translates the standard into what a child should know and be able to do at a specific developmental age level. Learning Expectations are not included in this document. Determining local age/grade level learning expectations are local district and community decisions.

### Curriculum and Assessment
Each program/service can determine their own curriculum and assessment based on the standards and local age/grade level expectations that apply to their particular setting. Selection of curriculum and assessment is a local decision.

### Developmental Continuum
Predictable but not rigid sequence of accomplishments which describes the progressive levels of performance in the order in which they emerge in most children, based on current research. The developmental continuums begin at an early developmental level and continue through developmental levels that would be typical through the completion of kindergarten (to first grade).

### Sample Behaviors of Children
Observable "samples" of what children might do as they demonstrate accomplishments at each level of the developmental continuum are included for each of the developmental continuums linked to each performance standard. The samples are "only samples," they are not meant to be inclusive of all children's behaviors or adult strategies that are associated with the developmental continuum and performance standard.

### Sample Strategies for Adults
"Samples" of what adults might do to assist the child to gain knowledge or learn skills at each level of the developmental continuum. The adult samples are not a definitive list or an exhaustive inventory.

### Program Standard
Refers to what programs must do to ensure children have the opportunities and experiences needed to meet developmental expectations.

### Note
**Learning Expectations, Curriculum, and Assessment** are not included in the framework; however, they are critical to "understanding the big picture."

# Framework for Wisconsin Model Early Learning Standards Document

**DEVELOPMENTAL DOMAINS**
- Health and Physical Development
- Social and Emotional Development
- Language Development and Communication
- Approaches to Learning
- Cognition and General Knowledge

**Sub-Domains**
Labeled with A, B, C, etc.

**Developmental Expectations**
What child should know
and should be able to do

**Performance Standards**
Specific information and/or
skills child should know
and should be able to do

**Program Standards**
What programs must
do for children

LOCAL DECISIONS
**Learning Expectations, Curriculum, Assessment**

**Developmental Continuum**
Progressive levels of performance

**Sample Behaviors of Children**     **Sample Strategies for Adults**

# Wisconsin Model Early Learning Standards
## Design

*The Wisconsin Model Early Learning Standards were designed to reflect the shared values and commitments of the citizens of Wisconsin to prepare young children for success in school and later life. Designed for all children, they create a common language among the families and the various programs and services within the early childhood community. They set the stage for the development of appropriate curriculum and the use of assessment practices that support and promote children's learning and development.*

### Why are early learning standards necessary and important?

Families, early care and education professionals, communities, and policymakers all share accountability for the optimal development and well being of young children. The Wisconsin Model Early Learning Standards provide a framework of developmentally appropriate expectations for young children that can guide the creation, evaluation, and improvement of conditions necessary for children's optimal development and create a common language. As a result of the combined efforts of families, early care and education professionals, communities, and policymakers, young children will have expanded opportunities for positive development and learning experiences.

### Why is a common language important?

Young children grow and learn best when all of the adults in their lives understand child development and are consistent with each other. Because the Wisconsin Model Early Learning Standards create common language and address all aspects of development, they can become the basis for conversation and learning opportunities in a variety of settings and situations. The Wisconsin Model Early Learning Standards recognize that parents are the child's primary and most important nurturers/teachers and therefore support partnerships between parents and the programs and settings they choose for their children.

The Wisconsin Model Early Learning Standards provide opportunities for promoting dialogue across settings and strengthening the early care and education system. Careful articulation of early learning standards can provide a common vision and common vocabulary to unite early care and education programs. The Wisconsin Model Early Learning Standards provide an opportunity to further dialogue with the K-12 system and establish more clearly the important role of early care and education in children's success later in school which will result in a more integrated education system.

### Are the Wisconsin Model Early Learning Standards appropriate for all children?

The Wisconsin Model Early Learning Standards reflect expectations for a typically-developing child; adapting and individualizing learning experiences accommodates optimal development for all children. The Wisconsin Model Early Learning Standards recognize that children are individuals who develop at individual rates. While children generally develop in similar stages and sequences, greatly diverse patterns of behavior and learning emerge as a result of the interaction of several factors, including genetic predisposition and physical characteristics, socio-economic status, and the values, beliefs, and cultural and political practices of their families and communities. Because brain development and social-emotional development are most active in the early years of a child's life, all of the child's experiences are of critical importance to the child and our society. As such, these standards support the development of optimal learning experiences that can be adapted in response to the individual developmental patterns of children.

### How can the Wisconsin Model Early Learning Standards be used for children with disabilities?

The Standards are designed to address individual differences and will serve as the foundation for individualized programming decisions for children with disabilities. While the vast majority of students with disabilities should be expected to work toward and achieve these Standards, accommodations and modifications to help these students reach the achievement goals will need to be individually identified and implemented. For children with disabilities, these decisions are made as part of their Individualized Education Program (IEP) plans developed by the school district's IEP team. This team could include school personnel as well as child care and Head Start personnel and the child's parent. Persons working with children with disabilities will need to pay special attention to the IEP and how curriculum adaptations and special education services can be provided to meet each child's individually identified developmental needs. Some accommodations and/or modifications may be necessary as young children with disabilities master the skills and competencies related to the Standards. Adapting and individualizing learning experiences can help assure that each child is exposed to activities that can help him or her reach his/her optimal development.

### How do the Wisconsin Model Early Learning Standards relate to the assessment of the development of young children?

By setting appropriate expectations for young children in the five domains of early learning and development, the Wisconsin Model Early Learning Standards set the stage for the development of appropriate curriculum and the use of assessment practices that support and promote children's learning and development. Assessment practices are a component of program standards. Appropriate assessment practices for young children take into account the following considerations:

- Young children learn in ways and at rates different from older children.
- Young children come to know things through doing as well as through listening and often represent their knowledge better by showing than by telling.
- Young children's development and learning is rapid, uneven, and episodic, so that point-in time assessments do not give a complete picture of their learning.
- Young children's achievements are the result of a complex mix of their ability to learn and their past learning opportunities. Resources on appropriate assessment practices for young children are listed in the resource section.

### What is the difference between the Wisconsin Model Early Learning Standards and curriculum?

The Wisconsin Model Early Learning Standards are guidelines that reflect widely held expectations about what children should know and be able to do from birth to the beginning of first grade. The performance standards further outline how children may demonstrate that they meet expectations. The program standards are general statements for teachers and caregivers to guide in providing the opportunities and experiences children need to meet developmental expectations. The Wisconsin Model Early Learning Standards provide a guideline for curriculum decisions and development. Curriculum is determined based on the Standards that provide guidelines for what children should know and be able to do. Curriculum reflects the practices, interactions, and instruction that are implemented to support children's early learning and development. The National Association for the Education of Young Children's position statement "Where We Stand on Curriculum, Assessment and Program Evaluation," recommends the following: "Implement curriculum that is thoughtfully planned, challenging, engaging, developmentally appropriate, culturally and linguistically responsive, comprehensive, and likely to promote positive outcomes for all young children."

### How do the Wisconsin Model Early Learning Standards relate to the Wisconsin Academic Standards?

The Wisconsin Model Early Learning Standards align with the Wisconsin Academic Standards in their comprehensive focus on developmentally appropriate expectations for children birth to first grade. Research indicates that children who meet expectations in these developmental domains will be successful in mastering academic standards. As such, the Wisconsin Model Early Learning Standards provide a foundation for the Wisconsin Academic Standards.

### Where can I find more information about the design of the Wisconsin Model Early Learning Standards?

- Frequently Asked Questions are available on the Collaborating Partners web site at www.collaboratingpartners.com/wmels-faq.php.
- More information about alignment of the Wisconsin Model Early Learning Standards and the Wisconsin Academic Standards can be found in Appendix A of this document as well as at www.collaboratingpartners.com/wmels-model-academic-standards.php.
- More information about OSEP Child Outcomes can be found in Appendix B as well as www.collaboratingpartners.com/disabilities-about.php.

# Wisconsin Model Early Learning Standards (WMELS)

**WMELS intended use**
- Improve the quality of all early learning environments.
- Guide professional development activities and investments.
- Inform educators and caregivers in their decisions regarding approaches to curriculum development across all early learning environments.

**WMELS document IS NOT intended to be used as**
- A tool for program assessment.
- A tool for program curriculum.

**WMELS document contains**
- Developmental domains, developmental expectations, program standards, performance standards, developmental continuums, sample behaviors of children, and sample strategies for adults.
- Performance standards that connect (align) to the Wisconsin Academic Standards.

**WMELS document DOES NOT contain**
- Age/grade level learning expectations.
- Curriculum or an assessment tool.

**WMELS designed to reflect**
- A developmental sequence of abilities demonstrated by typically developing children between the ages of birth to first grade.
- Expectations for the critical knowledge and skills that children learn during the early years.

**WMELS IS NOT designed to reflect**
- A rigid sequence of developmental abilities typical of young children birth to first grade.
- A comprehensive list of every skill or piece of knowledge that a particular child may exhibit.
- An age-referenced continuum.

**WMELS domains presented**
- As integrated knowledge and skills.
- As interconnected domains; the development of skills in one area is related to and influences development in other areas.

**WMELS domains ARE NOT presented**
- To be used separately as discrete knowledge and skill sets.

**WMELS developmental continuum and sample behaviors**
- Show how the skills and knowledge demonstrated at very early ages provide the foundation for more complex skills at a later age.
- Are a general guide to help early care and education professionals and parents to observe a continuum of development recognizing that children are unique and develop at individual rates.

**WMELS developmental continuum and sample behaviors ARE NOT intended to be**
- Used as age markers.
- Used as a prescriptive listing.
- A comprehensive or exhaustive set of sample behaviors of children and sample strategies for adults.

**WMELS guides communities**
- To consider the determination of local age/grade level expectations at the district and community level. The local age/grade level learning can be used to make decisions about curriculum and assessment that will determine instructions, activities, and interactions.

**WMELS document IS NOT intended to be used as**
- Age/grade level learning expectations that further define each performance standard for each age (grade) level.

# Wisconsin Model Early Learning Standards
## One Tapestry, Many Threads

*Young children learn and grow best in the context of relationships and community. This context is made up of a variety of people, programs, and experiences. Widespread use of the Wisconsin Model Early Learning Standards will form a tapestry of common understanding and support. Everyone who is interested in providing quality care and education for all children will find common uses for these standards. The individual threads of this tapestry will each be used in their own unique way.*

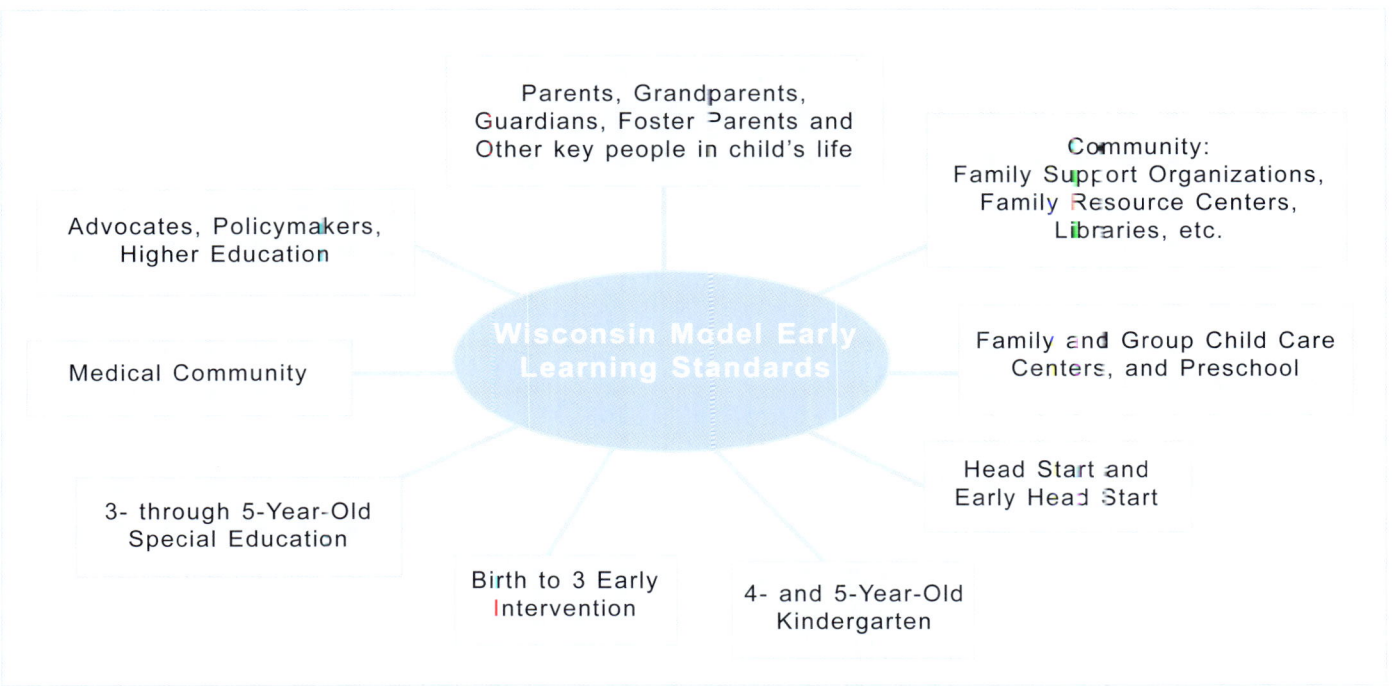

**THE EARLY CHILDHOOD COMMUNITY WILL HAVE COMMON USES FOR WISCONSIN MODEL EARLY LEARNING STANDARDS**

Everyone can use these standards as a
- Guide in creating a unifying vision for young children in Wisconsin, based upon the guiding principles.
- Resource for creating quality early learning opportunities.
- Resource for creating a common language across all settings and programs for young children and their families.
- Guide in the selection and implementation of curriculum and assessment.
- Source of example adult strategies to use as a guide for interacting with children in a positive way.
- Tool to support collaborative conversations and professional development with others in the early care and education system.
- Tool to help parents understand child development, how it is individual to each child, and how learning is influenced by our everyday interactions.
- Tool to help communities understand the importance of the early years from birth to first grade and the link with further educational and life success.
- Validation of the critical nature of early development and the role that adults play to help children progress toward optimal development based upon their individual capacities and needs.

**INDIVIDUAL PROGRAM THREADS WILL HAVE DIFFERENT USES FOR WISCONSIN MODEL EARLY LEARNING STANDARDS**

**Parents, Grandparents, Foster Parents, Guardians, and other key people in a child's life can use the WMELS as a**

- Resource on child development and early learning.
- A reminder that children's skills, abilities, and behaviors fluctuate along the developmental continuum because each person learns as an individual.
- Guide for the language and expectations used in conversations with others involved in the lives of their children.

**Community: Family Support Organizations, Libraries, Family Resource Centers, etc., can use the WMELS as a**

- Guide to provide training and programs that are grounded in solid child development for young children, their families, and others who impact their lives.
- Source in understanding performance standards for ALL children and the continuum of development for each performance standard birth to first grade.
- Tool to assist in finding and identifying children who may benefit from early childhood services.

**Family and Group Child Care Centers and Preschools can use the WMELS as a**

- Source to understand performance standards for ALL children and the continuum of development for each performance standard birth to first grade.
- Resource for enhancing quality educational programs and services through staff training and development.
- Resource to understand child development in the five domains and how they interrelate.
- Tool for making decisions regarding curriculum development and activity planning.
- Tool to assist in finding and identifying children who may benefit from early childhood services.

**Head Start and Early Head Start can use the WMELS as a**

- Tool to align with the Head Start Child Outcomes Framework so that a common language is created with parents, collaborative programs, and other stakeholders.
- Resource to complement Head Start performance standards and to facilitate smooth transitions for children between settings.

**Four-Year-Old and Five-Year-Old Kindergartens (4K and 5K) can use the WMELS as a**

- Resource for enhancing quality educational programs and services through staff training and development.
- Resource to understand child development in the five domains and how they interrelate.
- Tool for making decisions regarding curriculum development.
- Tool to develop, review, and align local age/grade level learning expectations which align to the Wisconsin Academic Standards.
- Resource to aid in communication and dialogue regarding the continuum of developmental and learning expectations between early childhood and first grade.

**Birth to 3 Early Intervention Services can use the WMELS as a**

- Source in understanding performance standards for ALL children and the continuum of development for each performance standard birth to first grade.
- Resource to understand child development in the five domains and how they interrelate.
- Tool to support the development of the Individual Family Service Plan (IFSP) with families and other members of the IFSP team.

**3- through 5-Year-Old Special Education can use the WMELS as a**

- Source to understand performance standards for ALL children and the continuum of development for each performance standard birth to first grade.
- Resource to understand child development in the five domains and how they interrelate.
- Tool to support the development of the Individualized Education Program (IEP) with families and other members of the IEP team.

**Medical Communities can use the WMELS as a**

- Source to understand performance standards for ALL children and the continuum of development for each performance standard birth to first grade.
- Tool to assist in finding and identifying children who may benefit from early childhood services.

**Advocates, Policy Makers, Higher Education can use the WMELS as a**

- Resource to guide efforts to assure the optimal learning and development of young children by making a commitment to support early childhood education and care efforts.
- Resource to support and strengthen the resources available to support families with young children.
- Resource to build stronger connections among the various programs and services that impact the lives of young children and their families.
- Resource to design educational programs for professionals who work with children birth to first grade and their families.

# Wisconsin Model Early Learning Standards
## Training and Professional Development

*Training for the Wisconsin Model Early Learning Standards (WMELS) is taking place throughout the state of Wisconsin. The purpose of the training is to assist all those who are committed to providing quality education and care, to use the WMELS as a guide for providing quality services for young children birth to first grade. During the training, participants become familiar with the components of the WMELS, e.g., developmental domains, developmental expectations, program standards, performance standards, developmental continuum, and sample behaviors for children and adults. The Teaching Cycle (pictured below) is used throughout the training as a means of applying the components of the WMELS to learning and instruction.*

*Wisconsin Model Early Learning Standards*

## Teaching Cycle

### Assessment
Gathering information to determine the current developmental level of the child.
- *Data Collection*
- *Data Analysis*

### Implementation
Providing meaningful, experiential activities that support individual and group goals guided by supportive interactions and relationships.

### Planning and Curriculum Goals
Deciding what should be done to promote development and what we want children to learn.

This Teaching Cycle aligns with the Wisconsin Department of Public Instruction's *Framework for Personnel Development for Special Education*

For information about the Wisconsin Model Early Learning Standards and trainings happening in your area go to: *www.collaboratingpartners.com/wmels-training-opportunities.php.*

# Wisconsin Model Early Learning Standards
## Guiding Principles

*The Wisconsin Model Early Learning Standards Steering Committee has established nine Guiding Principles to inform the development and application of the Wisconsin Model Early Learning Standards in Wisconsin. These guiding principles reflect the knowledge base in scientific research, our values, and our commitment to young children and families.*

### All children are capable and competent.
Development and learning begins at birth for all children in all settings. The Wisconsin Model Early Learning Standards support practices that promote development and protect young children from the harm that results from inappropriate expectations. In this they are aligned with ethical principles of the early childhood profession.

### Early relationships matter.
Beginning at birth, a child forms relationships with adults who will guide their learning and development. Especially during the earliest years of a child's life from birth to age 3, a child's growth and development is shaped within the context of those relationships. Positive relationships are essential for the development of personal responsibility, capacity for self-regulation, for constructive interactions with others, and for fostering academic functioning and mastery. Warm, sensitive, and responsive interactions help children develop a secure, positive sense of self and encourage them to respect and cooperate with others.

### A child's early learning and development is multidimensional.
Developmental domains are highly interrelated. The Wisconsin Model Early Learning Standards reflect the interconnectedness of the domains of children's development: social and emotional development, approaches to learning, language development and communication, health and physical development, and cognition and general knowledge.

### Expectations for children must be guided by knowledge of child growth and development.
The Wisconsin Model Early Learning Standards are based on research about the processes and sequences of young children's learning and development and the conditions under which children develop to their fullest potential.

### Children are individuals who develop at various rates.
The Wisconsin Model Early Learning Standards recognize that there are individual rates of development and learning across any age range.

### Children are members of cultural groups that share developmental patterns.
The Wisconsin Model Early Learning Standards acknowledge that children's development and learning opportunities reflect the cultural and linguistic diversity of children, families, and environments.

### Children exhibit a range of skills and competencies within any domain of development.
The Wisconsin Model Early Learning Standards support the development of optimal learning experiences that can be adapted for individual developmental patterns.

### Children learn through play and the active exploration of their environment.
The Wisconsin Model Early Learning Standards reflect the belief that children should be provided with opportunities to explore, and apply new skills through child-initiated and teacher-initiated activities, and through interactions with peers, adults, and materials. Teachers and families can best guide learning by providing these opportunities in natural, authentic contexts. Positive relationships help children gain the benefits of instructional experiences and resources.

### Parents are children's primary and most important caregivers and educators.
Families, communities, and schools all have significant roles to play in terms of what opportunities are available to children, and how well a child is able to take advantage of those learning opportunities. Children who see themselves as highly valued are more likely to feel secure, thrive physically, get along with others, learn well, and feel part of a community.

# Wisconsin Model Early Learning Standards
## Section One

| DEVELOPMENTAL DOMAIN | Page |
|---|---|
| I. HEALTH AND PHYSICAL DEVELOPMENT | 12 |
| A. PHYSICAL HEALTH AND DEVELOPMENT | 14 |
| B. MOTOR DEVELOPMENT | 20 |
| C. SENSORY ORGANIZATION | 23 |

# Wisconsin Model Early Learning Standards

## I. HEALTH AND PHYSICAL DEVELOPMENT

Health encompasses emerging knowledge and practices related to health, safety, and nutrition that promote physical well-being. Physical development encompasses rate of growth and muscle control (motor development). Fine or small motor control refers to such abilities as manipulation of materials and tools, hand dominance, and eye-hand coordination. Gross or large motor control refers to such characteristics as balance, coordination, purposeful control, locomotion, and stability of body movements and functions. Sensory integration is the neurological process of organizing the information received from the three main sensory systems—tactile, proprioceptive, and vestibular. The tactile sense provides information to the brain primarily through the surface of the skin about the texture, shape, and size of objects in the environment. The proprioceptive sense provides information to the brain from the joints, muscles, and ligaments about where the body is in space and what they are doing. The vestibular sense provides information through the inner ear about balance and movement. When the brain integrates or organizes sensory information efficiently a child learns to respond appropriately and automatically.

### Rationale

Children's future health and well being are directly related to the development and strengthening of their large and small muscles, involvement in sensory experiences, and the practicing of healthy behavior. Good physical health and motor development allows for full participation in learning experiences. While engaging in active movement and exploration and encountering a variety of situations and new challenges, the child's brain and body are learning to work together smoothly. When children take an active role in caring for their bodies, make appropriate food choices, and participate in physical activity, they feel a sense of pride and accomplishment in their independence and develop a sound foundation for healthy growth in all other areas of development.

---

### A. PHYSICAL HEALTH AND DEVELOPMENT

*Developmental Expectation*

*Children in Wisconsin will be physically healthy and will be able to effectively care for their own physical needs.*

**Performance Standard**

During the early childhood period, children in Wisconsin will show evidence of developmentally appropriate abilities in the following areas:

A.EL.1a   Demonstrates behaviors to meet self-help and physical needs. *Sleep*

A.EL.1b   Demonstrates behaviors to meet self-help and physical needs. *Dressing*

A.EL.1c   Demonstrates behaviors to meet self-help and physical needs. *Toileting*

A.EL.1d   Demonstrates behaviors to meet self-help and physical needs. *Eating*

A.EL. 2   Demonstrates behaviors to meet safety needs.

A.EL. 3   Demonstrates a healthy life style.

**Program Standard**

Early care and education programs in Wisconsin will provide developmentally appropriate, increasingly complex and diverse opportunities for children to understand and care for their physical well-being.

# I. HEALTH AND PHYSICAL DEVELOPMENT (continued)

## B. MOTOR DEVELOPMENT

*Developmental Expectation*

*Children in Wisconsin will develop and refine their use of small and gross motor skills.*

**Performance Standard**

During the early childhood period, children in Wisconsin will show evidence of developmentally appropriate abilities in the following areas:

B.EL.1a  Moves with strength, control, balance, coordination, locomotion, and endurance.
*Purpose and Coordination*

B.EL.1b  Moves with strength, control, balance, coordination, locomotion, and endurance.
*Balance and Strength*

B.EL. 2  Exhibits eye-hand coordination, strength, control, and object manipulation.

**Program Standard**

Early care and education programs in Wisconsin will provide increasingly complex and diverse opportunities for children to develop their fine and gross motor skills.

## C. SENSORY ORGANIZATION

*Developmental Expectation*

*Children in Wisconsin will integrate input from all sensory systems and learn to respond appropriately and automatically within their environment.*

**Performance Standard**

During the early childhood period, children in Wisconsin will show evidence of developmentally appropriate abilities in the following areas:

C.EL. 1  Uses senses to take in, experience, integrate, and regulate responses to the environment.

**Program Standard**

Early care and education programs in Wisconsin will provide increasingly complex and diverse opportunities for children to integrate input from all sensory systems and learn to respond appropriately and automatically within their environment.

---

### Important Reminders

The Wisconsin Model Early Learning Standards recognize that children are individuals who develop at individual rates. While they develop in generally similar stages and sequences, greatly diverse patterns of behavior and learning emerge as a result of the interaction of several factors, including genetic predisposition and physical characteristics, socio-economic status, and the values, beliefs, and cultural and political practices of their families and communities. The Wisconsin Model Early Learning Standards reflect expectations for a typically developing child; adapting and individualizing learning experiences accommodates optimal development for all children.

The Wisconsin Model Early Learning Standards developmental continuum and sample behaviors ARE NOT intended to be used as age markers, a prescriptive listing of development with every first item in a continuum starting at birth, nor as a comprehensive or exhaustive set of sample behaviors of children and sample strategies for adults.

## A. Physical Health and Development

**PERFORMANCE STANDARD:** A.EL. 1a DEMONSTRATES BEHAVIORS TO MEET SELF-HELP AND PHYSICAL NEEDS

### SLEEP

| Developmental Continuum | Sample Behaviors of Children | Sample Strategies for Adults |
|---|---|---|
| Engages in periods of sleep and wakefulness varying in length and time of day or night. | • Child sleeps for short periods of time that could vary from minutes to hours in length and wakes when hungry or uncomfortable.<br>• Child may have day and night mixed up and may have longer periods of being awake and alert during the night.<br>• Child may suddenly cry or make vocal noises during sleep. | • When child wakes, watch for signs of hunger such as rooting with the mouth or putting hands near the mouth.<br>• Allow child to follow own pattern of waking and sleeping. He or she will gradually begin to sleep more at night and less during the day.<br>• It is normal for the child to make noises or even cry for short periods of time—even when asleep. If the child cries harder or for more than a few seconds he/she is indicating the need for something else (hunger or the need to be held). |
| Begins to follow predictable sleeping pattern. | • Child becomes calm and falls asleep when rocked.<br>• Child sleeps through the night.<br>• Child falls asleep and wakes at approximately the same time each day/night. | • Watch child for signs of tiredness such as rubbing eyes or crying and gently rub back or rock to help fall asleep.<br>• Be alert to the time of day or routine of child's sleep pattern and begin to put child in his/her crib when it is time to sleep. Assist him/her to calm self by playing soft, rhythmic music, providing comfort object, such as a pacifier, or gently patting back. |
| Rests for periods throughout the day with assistance of adult. | • Child may nap for 1-3 hours and be active and alert during wake hours.<br>• Child may delay sleeping by demanding things such as a drink or to play longer.<br>• Child may be tired and grumpy during the day after a sleepless night. | • Create a consistent time of day for child to lie down and rest for several hours.<br>• Set a naptime routine such as reading a short book, darkening the child's sleeping area, and playing quiet music.<br>• Parents and caregivers should communicate together to establish evening and morning routines that calm children.<br>• If child resists rest when showing signs of tiredness, calmly say things such as, "You are acting like you are tired—you are crying and your eyes look tired—you will feel better after you rest for awhile." |
| Recognizes physical need for rest/sleep and cares for own needs. | • Child gradually eliminates naps.<br>• Child chooses quiet activity such as looking at a book when feeling physically tired.<br>• Child says, "I'm tired" and lies down to rest. | • As child begins to show signs of needing less rest during the day, provide quiet activities such as reading books together or putting together a puzzle rather than forcing him/her to sleep.<br>• Allow child to rest when he/she expresses the need—he/she is learning to care for his/her physical needs in an appropriate manner. |

Listed above are *sample* behaviors of children and *sample* strategies for adults, they are not a definitive list or an exhaustive inventory. They start from an early developmental level and continue through older ages to the completion of kindergarten.

## A. Physical Health and Development (continued)

**PERFORMANCE STANDARD:** A.EL. 1b Demonstrates behaviors to meet self-help and physical needs

### DRESSING

| Developmental Continuum | Sample Behaviors of Children | Sample Strategies for Adults |
|---|---|---|
| Depends on adult to care for dressing needs. | • Child relies on adult to dress him/her appropriately for the environment. | • Dress child appropriately for the temperature of his/her surroundings and in clothing comfortable for sleeping.<br>• The child's preference for being kept warm or cool varies. Determine child's comfort level by watching his/her physical reactions. The child may show that he/she is too hot or cold by squirming, getting red cheeks, or crying. |
| Cooperates with dressing by extending arm or leg. | • Child holds arm out so that shirt can be pulled over his/her head. | • Talk to the child as you dress him/her telling the child what you are doing. For example, "We're going to put your shirt on—first we put your head in, now your arms, and now we pull it down."<br>• Provide clothing for child that is easy to pull on/off—such as pants with elastic. Point out to the child that the tag in the clothing goes in the back. |
| Undresses/dresses self with assistance. | • Child delights at removing clothing such as hat, socks, shoes.<br>• Child helps adult when pulling on and off clothing such as pants, socks, shirt, and coat.<br>• Child pulls shirt or pants up awkwardly at first then with more skill with purpose of dressing/undressing self.<br>• Child begins to use simple fasteners such as Velcro, zippers (if zipper is started for them), or tying shoes. | • Allow child to physically help you take clothing off—letting them feel what it's like to pull off of arms and legs.<br>• Show the child how to pull a zipper up and down, how to put Velcro together, and how to button large buttons.<br>• Help the child practice using fasteners using toys or dolls with fasteners.<br>• Talk to the child while you are working together so he/she begins to also understand the names of clothing articles. |
| Dresses self with minimal assistance. | • Child is able to put on all articles of clothing including shirts with buttons or pants with zippers. He/she will require assistance at first to align buttons or start zippers on coats.<br>• Child ties own shoes with skill.<br>• Child selects clothes to wear by himself/herself. | • Teach child how to do things such as start zippers or fasten small buttons or snaps. If the child becomes frustrated, calmly and gently assist him/her and praise attempts. For example, "Great job—you zipped the zipper up and down—or—you got your coat on all by yourself!"<br>• If child becomes frustrated and unwilling to try, gently help him/her rather than taking over the task. Even though it takes more time than just doing it yourself, it will help the child learn to do it by himself/herself. |

Listed above are *sample* behaviors of children and *sample* strategies for adults, they are not a definitive list or an exhaustive inventory. They start from an early developmental level and continue through older ages to the completion of kindergarten.

## A. Physical Health and Development (continued)

**PERFORMANCE STANDARD:** A.EL. 1c Demonstrates behaviors to meet self-help and physical needs

### TOILETING

| Developmental Continuum | Sample Behaviors of Children | Sample Strategies for Adults |
|---|---|---|
| Depends on adult to care for diapering needs. | • Child may become fussy or try to get adult attention when diaper is dirty or wet. | • Change child's diaper at regular intervals to prevent diaper rash. |
| Seeks assistance with diapering and toileting. | • Child may vocalize or hide when he/she has a soiled diaper.<br>• Child verbalizes need to use toilet and rushes to toilet—has occasional accidents.<br>• Child pulls down pants (with assistance) and sits. | • Help child begin to use the toilet when it appears he/she is aware of a soiled diaper, is uncomfortable with it, and is able to physically get to the bathroom and pull down own pants.<br>• Help child become aware of when he/she needs to use the toilet by asking on a regular basis. |
| Takes responsibility for toileting. | • Child anticipates need to use the bathroom and asks to "go."<br>• Child may need assistance to manipulate pant's fasteners.<br>• Child may need reminders and/or assistance with personal hygiene during toileting. | • When away from home, such as a car trip, plan regular bathroom stops to help the child learn to plan for his/her toileting needs.<br>• During this period of learning, avoid clothing with tough to manipulate fasteners so that the child can easily care for his/her own needs.<br>• Teach child how to properly clean himself/herself and how to properly wash hands following toileting. |
| Takes full responsibility for toileting during day and night. | • Child uses the bathroom with no reminding or assistance.<br>• Child may occasionally have "accidents"—particularly at night. | • It is normal for the child to have toileting accidents through the age of six or seven years. It is important not to punish but to remind child to use the bathroom earlier the next time he/she needs to "go." |

Listed above are *sample* behaviors of children and *sample* strategies for adults, they are not a definitive list or an exhaustive inventory. They start from an early developmental level and continue through older ages to the completion of kindergarten.

## A. Physical Health and Development (continued)

**PERFORMANCE STANDARD:** A.EL.1d DEMONSTRATES BEHAVIORS TO MEET SELF-HELP AND PHYSICAL NEEDS

### EATING

| Developmental Continuum | Sample Behaviors of Children | Sample Strategies for Adults |
|---|---|---|
| Physically and verbally indicates need for food. | • Child cries or roots mouth near nipple when hungry.<br>• Upon sight of the bottle child makes a noise or reaches for it.<br>• If not hungry, child doesn't eat when given bottle. | • Learn to recognize child's signals for hunger and respond promptly. The child is born with an internal signal for hunger and by responding promptly you are confirming that need in an appropriate fashion. This is also a critical time for building a trusting relationship with the child.<br>• Provide a calm environment in which to feed the young child. Talk, hum, or sing to him/her during feeding time.<br>• Never force a child to eat. It's possible the child's cry or fussiness (that you thought meant hunger) is actually a need for something else, such as to be held and comforted. |
| Feeds self with adult assistance. | • Child uses fingers to feed self cereal or crackers.<br>• Child assists adult in feeding by placing hand on spoon or adult's hand.<br>• Child makes noises or points to refrigerator or kitchen cupboard indicating desire for food.<br>• Child feeds self by using utensils such as small spoon or fork, awkwardly at first but becomes more skilled with practice. | • Put simple foods such as cereal or crackers on tray in front of child. This will give the child practice using his/her fingers to pick up food and get it to his/her mouth.<br>• Allow the child to assist you in feeding—allowing him/her to hang onto spoon if desired. This is how the child learns to do it by himself/herself. Be prepared for the messiness that happens by using large washable bibs, a covering on the floor, and having a wet washcloth available!<br>• When child indicates he/she is hungry through pointing or gestures, say, "You're hungry" or "You're thirsty." This will help him/her learn the language needed to get food. |
| Feeds self with proficiency. | • Child recognizes feeling of physical hunger and says, "I'm hungry." (Not just at sight of food)<br>• Child is able to pour liquid from small pitcher without spilling.<br>• Child becomes skilled at using spoon and fork and using table knife for cutting softer foods.<br>• Child selects food he/she is hungry for and serves self the appropriate amount on plate. Recognizes feeling of fullness and says, "I'm done." | • The child naturally selects foods that his/her body needs. Provide healthy choices and allow the child to choose which foods and how much of each. Let the child serve himself/herself.<br>• Help the child to put appropriate amounts of food on his/her plate. The child will have a tendency to put a large amount of food on his/her plate when feeling really hungry. Assure the child that he/she can take more if still hungry when finished with what's on the plate.<br>• Never force the child to eat. Be a role model in encouraging the child to try new foods. |
| Uses appropriate table etiquette or manners during mealtimes. | • Assists adult in setting table with plates, silverware, napkin, and cup.<br>• Asks to have food passed. For example, "Please pass the rice." | • Teach child to set the table by using a placemat with tableware drawn in the appropriate spot.<br>• Model or practice asking for food to be passed at the table or asking to be excused from the table. The child learns quickly and it's a good time to teach behavior he/she will be expected to use the rest of his/her life. |

Listed above are *sample* behaviors of children and *sample* strategies for adults, they are not a definitive list or an exhaustive inventory. They start from an early developmental level and continue through older ages to the completion of kindergarten.

## A. Physical Health and Development (continued)

**PERFORMANCE STANDARD:** A.EL. 2 Demonstrates behaviors to meet safety needs

| Developmental Continuum | Sample Behaviors of Children | Sample Strategies for Adults |
|---|---|---|
| Shows preference for parent(s) or primary caregiver. | • Child turns head to parent's voice.<br>• Child becomes calmer more quickly when being comforted by parent or primary caregiver. | • Life-long bonds between parent and child are formed in the first hours/days of life. Spend time holding and talking to your child as much as possible. |
| Shows awareness of new/uncomfortable situations or strangers. | • Child clings to parent or familiar adult when entering a new situation or when strangers are present.<br>• Child may cry at the sound of angry voices or loud toys. | • Help the child feel safe when entering new situations or meeting new people by holding his/her hand securely or telling them softly that you are there.<br>• The child may respond to fear and other threatening emotions from the adults around him/her. Remain calm and talk to the child in a reassuring voice to help him/her feel safe. |
| Shows awareness of danger in harmful situations and begins to recognize simple rules. | • Child walks in swimming pool area when told to walk by lifeguard.<br>• While playing in a sandbox together, child tells playmate, "You're not supposed to throw sand."<br>• Child does not respond when a stranger asks a question. | • When it appears child is beginning to understand rules, give child simple rules to follow. Tell him/her what you want him to do. For example, say "Walk by the pool;" not "Don't run."<br>• Teach the child what a stranger is and that he/she should not talk to or go with strangers.<br>• Help child recognize figures of authority that can help him/her such as police officers, fire fighters, or crossing guards. |
| Follows rules with little supervision. | • Child doesn't touch matches or electrical plugs, and is able to tell another child not to touch because, "It is dangerous!"<br>• Child stops and looks both ways before crossing the street.<br>• Child follows fire drill procedure without reminder or direction from adult. | • Tell and model consistent, clear rules to follow regarding health and safety, such as staying away from matches or what to do if a stranger approaches them when they are not with an adult.<br>• Praise child when you witness him/her observing safety rules. For example, "You are doing a good job stopping and looking both ways before crossing the street!"<br>• Every home or child care program should have a plan for what to do in case of a fire. Practice your plan with the child so that he/she will know what to do in case of an emergency. |

Listed above are *sample* behaviors of children and *sample* strategies for adults, they are not a definitive list or an exhaustive inventory. They start from an early developmental level and continue through older ages to the completion of kindergarten.

## A. Physical Health and Development (continued)

**PERFORMANCE STANDARD:** A.EL. 3 Demonstrates a healthy life style

| Developmental Continuum | Sample Behaviors of Children | Sample Strategies for Adults |
|---|---|---|
| Depends on adult to care for personal hygiene and exercise needs. | • Child relies on adult to wipe nose (but may fuss mildly at the action).<br>• Child relies on adult to clean body on a regular basis.<br>• Child displays need to move or change positions — such as changing from sitting in an infant chair to lying on back on blanket. | • Bath time can be a fun time between child and adult. Talk and sing to the child during bath time—telling him/her what you are doing as you do it. Remember to always check the water temperature before placing child in the water.<br>• If child has been fed and is rested but still indicating a need for something, he/she may just want to be moved—either to be held or have his/her position changed. Responding to the child's behavior will help him/her learn to communicate needs to you.<br>• Well-child check-ups at the child's regular health-care provider are an important way of keeping track of the child's health status. Discussion of the child's height/weight, eating, sleeping, and exercise patterns are very important right from birth. |
| Shows awareness of need for personal hygiene and exercise. | • Child may make a face or point at his/her stuffy nose - indicating a need to have it wiped.<br>• Child stands on adult's lap while adult holds hands.<br>• Child says "ucky" and points to hands that need to be washed. | • While caring for child's hygiene needs, talk to the child about what you are doing. For example, say "Your nose is runny, we need to wipe it with a tissue." This will help him/her learn to use the words associated with the actions.<br>• Play simple games with the child to help him/her stretch and get physical movement. Place child on a blanket on floor with toys to reach.<br>• Make a regular practice of brushing child's teeth allowing child to hold on to the toothbrush with you to help. |
| Begins to take responsibility for personal hygiene and exercise needs. | • Child reaches for tissue and attempts to wipe own nose.<br>• Child washes and dries own hands—when reminded.<br>• Child brushes own teeth—with reminding.<br>• Child expresses need to get up and run after sitting for a length of time. | • Help the child to develop a routine for washing hands (especially before and after meals) and brushing teeth.<br>• The young child needs exercise to be healthy. Create times for children to run and stretch and move. Do things such as go to the park, go for walks, go swimming, and play physical games together.<br>• Model healthy exercise habits. The more the young child sees the adults exercising and using their bodies the more likely it is that the child will choose to exercise his/her body.<br>• Regular visits to the dentist help children become accustomed to this. |
| Cares for personal health, hygiene, and exercise needs independently. | • Child washes hands regularly and as needed without prompting from adult.<br>• Child understands that brushing teeth and exercising regularly is needed to remain healthy.<br>• Child understands the role of the dentist and doctor in helping him/her to remain healthy. | • Continue to encourage and praise child for engaging in healthy practices such as regular hand washing, brushing teeth, and using a tissue to wipe a runny nose.<br>• Talk to child about the role of doctors and dentists to help us stay healthy and that they are not just people that care for us when we are sick.<br>• Support young child in participating in community youth activities such as swimming lessons, theater, art classes, etc. |

Listed above are *sample* behaviors of children and *sample* strategies for adults, they are not a definitive list or an exhaustive inventory. They start from an early developmental level and continue through older ages to the completion of kindergarten.

## B. Motor Development

**PERFORMANCE STANDARD:** B.EL. 1a MOVES WITH STRENGTH, CONTROL, BALANCE, COORDINATION, LOCOMOTION, AND ENDURANCE

**PURPOSE AND COORDINATION**

| Developmental Continuum | Sample Behaviors of Children | Sample Strategies for Adults |
|---|---|---|
| Manipulates objects with hands. | • Child reaches for and grabs rattle or toy of interest.<br>• Child takes cracker or cereal from high chair tray and puts in mouth.<br>• Child locates, grabs, and mouths toys and/or any small object within reach. | • While child is sitting, shake a rattle to encourage him/her to reach for and grab it.<br>• Put cereal or pieces of graham crackers on child's high chair tray within reach so the child can practice picking up small objects with the hands and fingers. |
| Rolls over. | • While lying on stomach child rolls awkwardly to back (usually by accident the first several times).<br>• Child becomes stronger and faster at rolling both front to back and back to front.<br>• Child may occasionally roll body purposefully numerous times to reach another location. | • Place child on tummy on a blanket on the floor and watch for signs that he/she is beginning to move his or her body in a way that could lead to rolling over.<br>• In the beginning it may help to gently take the child's legs and push to assist rolling all the way over.<br>• Put toys that the child really enjoys just out of reach so that he/she will be encouraged to roll body over to get the toy. |
| Crawls. | • Child uses either arms or legs to move body forward or backward a short distance, often without realizing he/she is moving.<br>• Child scoots body forward or backward with more strength using either arms or legs—sometimes both—with purpose of reaching object or person.<br>• Child is able to raise body onto hands and knees and move in all directions in coordinated fashion (often with considerable speed). | • Provide lots of opportunities for children to move arms and legs by placing on a large blanket or rug and placing toys of interest nearby, encouraging him/her to move to get the toys.<br>• A young child learning to crawl can be surprisingly fast and can maneuver his/her body into small, unexpected spaces such as under TV's or small tables. Make sure the environment is safe for the child to move around in without having things topple over onto them if bumped. |
| Walks and climbs on low objects. | • Child uses furniture or people to pull self up.<br>• Child stands up and moves around furniture (while hanging onto furniture for support)—often in an attempt to reach desired object on top of furniture (such as toy, food, or a pet).<br>• Child stands up and climbs onto furniture or small playground equipment such as slide—sometimes to reach on object and sometimes "just to climb." | • As child is learning to get body up onto furniture or people, offer a hand of support at first to maneuver getting up and down.<br>• Be very aware of furniture with sharp edges or corners and/or breakable items that could be fallen on. As the child is learning to use the muscles in his/her arms, legs, and bodies the child will fall often. It's best to have a safe (and relatively soft) environment in which to learn.<br>• Provide low objects to crawl onto such as toddler size slides or small boxes. The child will love simply going up and down for long periods of time, and this gives the child's muscles lots of good exercise. |
| Walks up and down stairs with alternating steps. | • Child walks up and down stairs one step at a time, with adult assistance.<br>• Child walks up and down stairs, holding onto railing, one step at a time.<br>• Child walks up and down stairs, holding onto railing, alternating feet. Child walks on a variety of surfaces without assistance. | • Hold onto child's hand securely while he/she is learning to walk up and down stairs. Child will begin by placing feet together one step at a time.<br>• Allow child opportunity to practice moving up stairs then gradually become secure in also going down stairs. Provide close supervision to prevent accidents. |

Listed above are *sample* behaviors of children and *sample* strategies for adults, they are not a definitive list or an exhaustive inventory. They start from an early developmental level and continue through older ages to the completion of kindergarten.

## B. Motor Development (continued)

**PERFORMANCE STANDARD:** B.EL. 1b MOVES WITH STRENGTH, CONTROL, BALANCE, COORDINATION, LOCOMOTION, AND ENDURANCE

**BALANCE AND STRENGTH**

| Developmental Continuum | Sample Behaviors of Children | Sample Strategies for Adults |
|---|---|---|
| Sits independently with balance. | • Child sits upright on adult's lap.<br>• Child remains upright when placed in sitting position on floor.<br>• Child sits upright on floor while playing with toys without assistance of adult or infant chair. | • Set child on blanket on floor—at first with some support of a nearby large pillow. Make sure there are no hard or sharp objects nearby if child tips over.<br>• Set child on blanket on ground or floor placing a favorite toy between child's legs—encouraging child to balance and sit upright to play with toy. |
| Stands without support. | • Child lets go of table and remains standing for a few seconds.<br>• Child stands in a wide stance after letting go of adult's hand or finger.<br>• Child becomes increasingly more stable when standing on own without support of object or person. | • Observe child as he/she maneuvers around low furniture. Watch for signs that the child is starting to stand without support for a few seconds.<br>• Help child to stand with support of two fingers and gently remove fingers, but stay close, encouraging child to stand alone. |
| Squats without falling. | • Child squats down to pick up toy without falling.<br>• Child squats down to look under table or inside a play tunnel to look inside. | • Peek under one end of a small table such as a coffee table and call child's name. Encourage child to bend or squat down to peek back at you.<br>• Hold a toy down low to encourage child to squat while reaching for it. |
| Walks, runs, climbs, jumps, skips, and hops with control. | • Child can walk for sustained periods of time without reaching for objects or falling.<br>• Child runs across room after pet or another child.<br>• Child can hop on two feet, at first hopping in place and gradually hops and moves forward with skill.<br>• Child stands and balances on one foot without assistance for more than a few seconds. | • Provide opportunity for child to run, hop, jump, etc., by going to the park, playing outside, or going to the gym and playing together.<br>• Provide a swing set, slide, riding toys, tricycle, or climbing structure in your home, school, or child care center and provide opportunity every day to play on it.<br>• Create fun things to climb on indoors such as big boxes, piles of pillows, or even small step stools. |
| Throws objects with strength and control. | • Child pushes large ball forward along the floor with both arms.<br>• Child throws a large playground ball underhand, reaching up from knees and throwing without a lot of direction at first.<br>• Child throws a small ball or beanbag overhand to a target (such as aiming for a basket or box). | • Sit or kneel on the floor near child and roll a large ball back and forth to the child.<br>• Play "catch" with child by throwing and catching a large soft ball such as beach ball. You will be doing more catching at first than throwing.<br>• Give child tennis balls, beanbags, or soft, squishy balls (such as Koosh balls), and a big box or basket to throw the balls into. You can extend it into a math activity by counting how many balls the child gets into the basket successfully. |

Listed above are *sample* behaviors of children and *sample* strategies for adults, they are not a definitive list or an exhaustive inventory. They start from an early developmental level and continue through older ages to the completion of kindergarten.

## B. Motor Development *(continued)*

**PERFORMANCE STANDARD:** B.EL. 2 EXHIBITS EYE-HAND COORDINATION, STRENGTH, CONTROL, AND OBJECT MANIPULATION

| Developmental Continuum | Sample Behaviors of Children | Sample Strategies for Adults |
|---|---|---|
| Tracks objects visually and focuses on an object or person. | • Child turns head and visually follows objects and familiar faces.<br>• Child focuses on the movement of a ceiling fan or leaves blowing in the breeze.<br>• Child purposefully focuses eyes on a toy, familiar person, or area of interest (such as a colorful light or leaves moving in a tree) for a sustained period of time.<br>• Child watches items of interest or a nearby child for longer periods of time as attention span increases. | • Provide toys and moving objects in the environment, e.g., mobiles, activity center, books, mirrors, and rattles.<br>• Smile and look into the child's eyes as you talk with him/her.<br>• Position child on the floor or in infant seat so that he/she can see objects of interest easily without needing to turn body uncomfortably. |
| Reaches for and grasps objects. | • Child moves both arms toward dangling toy.<br>• Child can transfer an object purposefully from hand to hand.<br>• Child can feed self a cookie or cracker. | • Hold rattle or interesting toys in front of child to reach for.<br>• Hand child crackers or small cookies. |
| Coordinates eyes with hands and uses both hands with intention and purpose. | • Child uses thumb and forefinger to pick up pieces of cereal.<br>• With supervision child drops two or three beads into a container before dumping them out and starting over.<br>• Child scribbles on paper holding crayon or marker with different kinds of grasps but beginning to use thumb and fingertips. | • Hold cereal or small crackers in front of child in your hand so that he/she can pick them out of your hand (or off of high chair tray).<br>• Give child bowl and plastic beads to put in and out of bowl.<br>• Give child large crayon or marker (with supervision) and a large piece of paper to mark on. |
| Performs simple fine motor skills and manipulates smaller objects with increasing control. | • Child draws a line with a crayon or marker on drawing paper.<br>• Child fits together a wide variety of manipulatives such as large stringing beads, large puzzle pieces, play dough and cookie cutters, or large Legos.<br>• Child makes snips on paper with a scissors. | • Help child learn how to hold marker or large crayon and together make marks on paper. Gradually lessen your assistance until child is holding marker correctly and using it to mark paper.<br>• Provide fit-together toys, 2-4 piece puzzles for child to play with under your supervision.<br>• Sit on floor with child and play along side child modeling how to put objects together, string beads, make shapes with play dough, etc. |
| Uses strength and control to perform complex fine motor tasks. | • Child can control a marker, crayon, or pencil to create some shapes.<br>• Child can cut lines and curves with scissors.<br>• Child can use small tools such as staplers or paper punches.<br>• Child uses a spoon, fork, and small table knife at mealtimes.<br>• Child can button and zip clothing and may tie shoestrings.<br>• Child puts together small manipulatives such as small stringing beads and small building blocks. | • Put together a "writing" box containing a variety of writing utensils and a variety of papers. Get it out for child to play when you are able to "play along side" the child.<br>• Teach child how to use fork and spoon to serve self and how to cut soft foods (e.g., green beans or large pasta) with a table knife. Allow him/her to spread butter or jelly on toast "all by himself."<br>• Teach child how to manipulate buttons and zippers. Praise child for doing it "all by himself."<br>• Include toys with small manipulatives in child's assortment of toys. Be aware of toys with small pieces that might be a choking hazard in case little ones are nearby. |

Listed above are *sample* behaviors of children and *sample* strategies for adults, they are not a definitive list or an exhaustive inventory. They start from an early developmental level and continue through older ages to the completion of kindergarten.

## C. Sensory Organization

**PERFORMANCE STANDARD:** C.EL.1 USES SENSES TO TAKE IN, EXPERIENCE, INTEGRATE, AND REGULATE RESPONSES TO THE ENVIRONMENT

| Developmental Continuum | Sample Behaviors of Children | Sample Strategies for Adults |
|---|---|---|
| Exhibits responses to physical stimuli. | • Child explores objects such as toys or hands with the mouth.<br>• Child will anticipate and imitate facial expressions of parent(s) or trusted caregivers.<br>• Child tolerates and shows enjoyment of touch to body, arms, legs, and face.<br>• Child may turn head away from bright light or loud sounds. | • Child receives much sensory information in the area around his or her mouth. Provide a variety of safe, clean toys for the child to explore with his/her mouth.<br>• A child receives visual cues from the facial expressions of those he/she trusts and is around most often. By smiling, talking, and providing positive feedback to the child, you are teaching him/her to use the information he/she is receiving from the senses in the development of a positive self image.<br>• Touch is an important way for the child to develop a feeling of security and to learn about his/her own body. Gently massaging or rubbing the infant's back, arms, or legs will help the child's sensory system begin to learn to take in information from all parts of his/her body.<br>• A child's cries don't always mean the child is hungry or needs a diaper changed—it could mean the child is trying to adjust to the messages he is receiving from the environment around him. Observe child's reaction to noise or light. If child seems agitated if light is bright—try adjusting to see if this makes a difference to child's behavior. |
| Exhibits body awareness and begins to move in intentional fashion. | • Child intentionally sucks hand or uses pacifier to calm self.<br>• Child intentionally reaches for a toy or colorful object and passes it from hand to hand.<br>• Child turns toward object or rolls over to reach object while lying on his/her back.<br>• Child tolerates and is able to adjust reaction to being swung, rocked, or spun. | • As the child develops, he/she will become more skilled at calming himself/herself when tired or when his/her senses are overloaded. It is healthy for the child to learn to start to regulate his/her own behaviors and not rely on adults to always care for his/her needs. Adults can support the child to do this by allowing the child to have the opportunity to do it himself/herself. He/she may need a little help with things such as putting the pacifier back in his mouth.<br>• Both sides of the child's brain are becoming more coordinated at working together. This is supported by giving the child objects to manipulate in his/her hands, or objects to visually track overhead.<br>• A child learns to move his muscles intentionally by experiencing his/her body moving in different ways. Place toys to attract the child's attention nearby to motivate him/her to turn from side to side and eventually roll over. The child's brain and muscles are learning to operate together through this practicing.<br>• Discuss with your pediatrician if child cries, or shows unusual discomfort or distress by various types movement. This might be an indication of child's sensitivity to sensory input. |
| Skills become more refined; acts and moves with increased intention and purpose. | • Child is becoming more skilled at eye-hand coordination and can successfully draw with a crayon, pour from a small pitcher, button a shirt, or string beads.<br>• Child negotiates simple obstacle course.<br>• Child seeks and plays in enclosed areas, e.g., cloth tunnel or boxes.<br>• Child is able to transition from one activity to another without becoming anxious or upset. | • Provide lots of materials for child to manipulate and practice coordinating his/her eye and hand movements together such as large crayons, markers, stacking blocks, stringing beads, puzzles, etc.<br>• By running "around" or "through" objects on a playground or a simple obstacle course set out in the house, the child is learning to problem solve and do spatial planning that are important in the development of future math concepts.<br>• The child is increasing awareness of his/her body in space by seeking out enclosed spaces where he/she experiences boundaries closer to the body.<br>• Giving warning before moving to a new activity may help the child cope with change, e.g., "In a few minutes we are going to pick up toys and get ready to go in the car." |

Listed above are *sample* behaviors of children and *sample* strategies for adults, they are not a definitive list or an exhaustive inventory. They start from an early developmental level and continue through older ages to the completion of kindergarten.

## C. Sensory Organization (continued)

**PERFORMANCE STANDARD:** C.EL.1 Uses senses to take in, experience, integrate, and regulate responses to the environment (continued)

| Developmental Continuum | Sample Behaviors of Children | Sample Strategies for Adults |
|---|---|---|
| Anticipates and adjusts behavior efficiently and engages in complex skills and abstract thinking. | • Child selects appropriate clothing for the weather or adjusts water temperature appropriately.<br>• Child uses words to express a need to get up and run after sitting for 20 minutes or longer.<br>• Child's large and small muscle ability is quickly becoming more refined, and the child is able to do things such as use a pencil and use the appropriate amount of pressure in writing.<br>• Child is able to tolerate or suppress "reflexive responses" to sensations such as an itchy tag on clothing or walking on wet grass. | • Help child learn to anticipate changes in the environment by saying things like, "It is cold out today, what will you have to put on before you go outside?" Or, "The library is a quiet place, we have to use our soft voices."<br>• As children get older they are able to tolerate sitting quietly for longer periods. But, if children are tired or if they have already been sitting and not moving for a long time, help them get some of the energy out of their muscles by running or playing on play equipment for a short time.<br>• Children learn to integrate their senses through experiencing different situations and using a variety of materials. Provide many different kinds of experiences for the child that engages his or her large and small muscles and thinking skills.<br>• If a child shows exaggerated responses to things such as clothing tags, changes in walking surfaces, etc., it is recommended to discuss this behavior with the child's pediatrician or teacher. This type of reaction may indicate sensitivity to various sensory inputs. |

Listed above are *sample* behaviors of children and *sample* strategies for adults, they are not a definitive list or an exhaustive inventory. They start from an early developmental level and continue through older ages to the completion of kindergarten.

# Wisconsin Model Early Learning Standards
## Section Two

| DEVELOPMENTAL DOMAIN | Page |
|---|---|
| II. SOCIAL AND EMOTIONAL DEVELOPMENT | 26 |
|     A. EMOTIONAL DEVELOPMENT | 28 |
|     B. SELF-CONCEPT | 32 |
|     C. SOCIAL COMPETENCE | 35 |

## II. SOCIAL AND EMOTIONAL DEVELOPMENT

This domain includes children's feelings about themselves and others, their ability to form relationships, interest in and skills needed to maintain positive relationships with adults and children, ability to understand the perspective and feelings of others, and skills needed to succeed in a group setting. Social and emotional competence is developed from infancy, through the toddler and preschool years, and beyond. Children's early relationships are the foundation for social and emotional competence and affects all other developmental domains. Social competence is the ability to achieve personal goals in social interactions while maintaining positive relationships with others.

### Rationale

Social and emotional development is an ongoing process of skills acquisition and mastery, involving emotions, perception, cognition, and language. There is a direct relationship between a child's social and emotional well being and overall success in school and life. Emotional development is a complex process, involving a range and intensity of emotional reactions, perception of emotions in self and others, emotional self-regulation, and behavioral expressions of emotions. Emotional development occurs through the interactions of a child's temperament in the context of relationship and experience. Self-concept refers to a child's developing awareness of self in relation to others, sense of well being, and trust that he or she has a right to a place in the world. Children depend upon their interactions with adults and peers to construct a sense of self. Social competence is a culturally determined construct that includes the self-regulation needed to succeed in social settings.

---

### A. EMOTIONAL DEVELOPMENT

*Developmental Expectation*

*Children in Wisconsin will demonstrate emotional competence and self regulation.*

**Performance Standard**

During the early childhood period, children in Wisconsin will show evidence of developmentally appropriate abilities in the following areas:

A.EL. 1   Expresses a wide range of emotions.

A.EL. 2   Understands and responds to others' emotions.

**Program Standard**

Early care and education programs in Wisconsin will provide the environment, context, and opportunities for children to develop emotional competence and self-regulation.

---

### B. SELF-CONCEPT

*Developmental Expectation*

*Children in Wisconsin will have a personal sense of well being.*

**Performance Standard**

During the early childhood period, children in Wisconsin will show evidence of developmentally appropriate abilities in the following areas:

B.EL. 1   Develops positive self-esteem.

B.EL. 2   Demonstrates self-awareness.

**Program Standard**

Early care and education programs in Wisconsin will provide the environment, context, and opportunities for children to develop a personal sense of well-being.

## II. SOCIAL AND EMOTIONAL DEVELOPMENT (continued)

**C. SOCIAL COMPETENCE**

*Developmental Expectation*

*Children in Wisconsin will form and maintain secure relationships and gain understanding of social systems.*

**Performance Standard**

During the early childhood period, children in Wisconsin will show evidence of developmentally appropriate abilities in the following areas:

C.EL. 1  Demonstrates attachment, trust, and autonomy.

C.EL. 2  Engages in social interaction and plays with others.

C.EL. 3  Demonstrates understanding of rules and social expectations.

C.EL. 4  Engages in social problem solving behavior and learns to resolve conflict.

**Program Standard**

Early care and education programs in Wisconsin will provide the environment, context, and opportunities for children to develop social competence.

### Important Reminders

The Wisconsin Model Early Learning Standards recognize that children are individuals who develop at individual rates. While they develop in generally similar stages and sequences, greatly diverse patterns of behavior and learning emerge as a result of the interaction of several factors, including genetic predisposition and physical characteristics, socio-economic status, and the values, beliefs, and cultural and political practices of their families and communities. The Wisconsin Model Early Learning Standards reflect expectations for a typically developing child; adapting and individualizing learning experiences accommodates optimal development for all children.

The Wisconsin Model Early Learning Standards developmental continuum and sample behaviors ARE NOT intended to be used as age markers, a prescriptive listing of development with every first item in a continuum starting at birth, nor as a comprehensive or exhaustive set of sample behaviors of children and sample strategies for adults.

## A. Emotional Development

**PERFORMANCE STANDARD:** A.EL. 1 EXPRESSES A WIDE RANGE OF EMOTIONS

| Developmental Continuum | Sample Behaviors of Children | Sample Strategies for Adults |
|---|---|---|
| Uses facial expressions and body movements to express comfort or discomfort. | • Child cries to express needs for food, sleep, diaper change, position change, or holding.<br>• Child exhibits mutual gaze with adult during routine care giving or play activities.<br>• Child begins to smile<br>• Child signals over-stimulation by looking away.<br>• Child molds and relaxes body when held and cuddled.<br>• Child adopts a rigid posture when upset. | • Respond promptly and consistently to crying to meet needs while talking in a pleasant and caring way.<br>• Tune in to the child's cues to determine when he/she is receptive to social play and when he/she needs a break.<br>• Talk to the child while changing diaper, feeding, and dressing. Use daily activities as natural opportunities to shape emotional development.<br>• Experiment with many ways to hold a child to provide comfort.<br>• Communicate with other adults to provide consistent and positive interactions for the child.<br>• Learn to read the child's signals.<br>• Anticipate and plan activities according to the child's needs.<br>• Respond promptly to the child's cues.<br>• Experiment to determine what works and when it works. |
| Displays a variety of emotions: interest, pleasure, anger, surprise, anxiety, sadness, joy, excitement, disgust, and disappointment. | • Child smiles and giggles when adults play with him/her.<br>• When he/she cannot have something from the store, the child falls down and cries.<br>• Child shows signs of jealousy, such as crawling to and raising his/her arms to an adult who is holding another child.<br>• Child uses many emotional gestures, such as pouting, whining, and crying to convey desire for objects.<br>• Child actively shows affection for familiar person: hugs, smiles at, runs toward, leans against, etc. | • Acknowledge and name/label the emotion that the child may be feeling based on behavior he/she exhibits. For example, "It looks like you might be angry because you can't use that toy."<br>• Use calm and understanding voice tones and body language in response to the child showing emotion.<br>• Communicate with the child at eye level so he/she can see your facial expressions.<br>• Set aside times every day to have fun with the child and point out the many emotions involved in everyday life. |
| Uses words and gestures to express more complex emotions. | • Child shakes head for "no" and runs away from caregiver.<br>• Child may start to bite or hit because he/she does not have words to express his/her emotions yet.<br>• Child may hit another and say "that's mine" to show anger/frustration when another child takes a toy away.<br>• Child jumps up and down and says, "I want more bubbles" when enjoying time outside with activity.<br>• Child starts to imitate adult social behaviors using words such as "please" and "thank you." | • Mirror back gestures and expand upon what the child might be feeling. For example, "I can tell that you do not want to come inside right now. After we eat, we can go back outside."<br>• Give the child the desired strategy to get what they want. For example, say to the child, "If you want more cheese, say, more cheese please." Then when the child does say "more cheese please," reinforce the child by saying, "You asked for more cheese. That was a good way to let me know you wanted more."<br>• Acknowledge feelings of both children, then model strategies to share. For example, "You're angry and frustrated because you both want to play with the same toy!"<br>• Teach the child new words for complex feelings such as embarrassed, proud, satisfied, and confused. Show them pictures or photos of people with different expressions, and ask him/her what feelings he/she thinks the person might have.<br>• Model proper words and phrases, such as please, thank you, I'm sorry, it's okay, we'll work it out, how can I help, etc.<br>• Respect and reinforce rituals and routines that help the child work through common emotions during the day. (Snack after nap, story before bedtime, etc.) |

Listed above are *sample* behaviors of children and *sample* strategies for adults, they are not a definitive list or an exhaustive inventory. They start from an early developmental level and continue through older ages to the completion of kindergarten.

## A. Emotional Development (continued)

**PERFORMANCE STANDARD:** A.EL.1 EXPRESSES A WIDE RANGE OF EMOTIONS (CONTINUED)

| Developmental Continuum | Sample Behaviors of Children | Sample Strategies for Adults |
|---|---|---|
| Uses verbal and nonverbal language to express emotions in appropriate situations such as distress, contentment, surprise, disgust, jealousy, and confusion. | • Child finds an adult and asks, "Will you help me?" when he/she is feeling frustrated with a task.<br>• Child wants to please friends, can be bossy toward others, and tries to handle situations that he/she has seen modeled by adults, in the media, and elsewhere.<br>• Child starts to become upset and then uses a strategy that an adult has taught him/her to handle his/her feelings. | • The comfort level of the child starts to increase when talking with and accepting guidance and directions from familiar adults.<br>• When a child tells you he/she is feeling upset or angry, calmly and positively reinforce them for recognizing his/her feelings and dealing with them in an appropriate manner.<br>• Read books to the child that show how emotions are expressed in a variety of situations.<br>• Provide the child with a variety of opportunities to express his/her feelings through music, movement, art, nature, and other creative endeavors.<br>• Explain that all emotions are okay, but there are socially acceptable ways to express those emotions. |
| Demonstrates awareness of own emotions and exhibits self-control. | • Child waits to take his/her turn.<br>• Child walks away from a situation when he/she is angry and returns later more self-composed.<br>• Child agrees to the demands or desires of another child.<br>• When frustrated or upset, the child finds a quiet place to play or engages in a calming activity.<br>• Child keeps himself/herself occupied when waiting for food to be served. | • Give the child recognition and reinforcement for being able to manage his/her emotions.<br>• Give the child plenty of time to resolve conflicts independently before stepping in to assist even though his/her solution may not be ideal.<br>• Support the child's decisions whenever possible as long as he/she is safe from harm. |

Listed above are *sample* behaviors of children and *sample* strategies for adults, they are not a definitive list or an exhaustive inventory. They start from an early developmental level and continue through older ages to the completion of kindergarten.

## A. Emotional Development (continued)

**PERFORMANCE STANDARD:** A.EL.2 UNDERSTANDS AND RESPONDS TO OTHERS' EMOTIONS

| Developmental Continuum | Sample Behaviors of Children | Sample Strategies for Adults |
|---|---|---|
| Responds to positive emotional interactions with coos and smiles, and shows distress to negative interactions. | • Child reaches out, smiles, and laughs in order to gain attention.<br>• Child may show distress by waving arms and kicking restlessly.<br>• May cry or grimace when child hears other infants cry.<br>• Child babbles or coos and pauses to wait for a response from an adult. | • A child uses adults for social referencing. This means that a child relies on adults to interpret the world around them, such as how to react in an unfamiliar situation or to unfamiliar people.<br>• Adults' moods, gestures, and facial expressions may impact how a child reacts when perceiving whether he/she is safe or threatened. Synaptic connections are starting to form in the infant brain that set positive or negative patterns in motion. Thus, more positive interactions/experiences in infancy and early childhood strengthen "positive" pathways, while more negative interactions/experiences strengthen "negative" pathways.<br>• Adult depression can affect the emotional security of infants with whom they interact. |
| Observes and imitates emotional interactions of others. | • Child imitates various actions that he/she has seen, such as patting a doll on the back after seeing an adult burp an infant.<br>• Child repeats inappropriate word that he/she has heard adults use, without understanding the meaning.<br>• Child wants rituals to be carried out in the same way every day.<br>• Child watches facial expressions and gestures of others around them and imitates what he/she sees and hears. | • The actions and words of adults set the examples that children will follow. Model kindness, respect, and compassion in your thoughts, words, and actions.<br>• When the child uses an inappropriate word, he/she may only be repeating what he/she heard. Give him/her a better word to use by your example.<br>• Develop short, manageable transitions and rituals that provide consistency and comfort. |
| Associates words and gestures with a variety of emotions expressed by others. | • Child observes friend crying and says, "He's sad because he wants his dad."<br>• Child expresses feelings in symbolic play. May play out roles in dramatic play situations, e.g., child plays doctor in the dramatic play area and talks about fears, previous times he/she was hurt, and how he/she has been comforted in the past.<br>• Child expresses feelings, needs, and opinions in difficult situations or conflicts such as saying, "No, that's mine" or putting up a hand to signal "STOP." | • Through conversation and stories, point out how someone may have felt in a particular situation.<br>• Use music and movement activities to act out feelings.<br>• Use role play with puppets to teach the child how to talk to others during various situations.<br>• Model the framework, "I feel... when..." and encourage child to use these words with each other and with adults. |
| Demonstrates empathy by recognizing the feelings of another person and responding appropriately. | • Child comforts a friend who has been hurt such as getting a band aid for a friend with a scrape on her knee.<br>• Child wants equality in treatment, but starts to understand that someone with greater need should get special consideration.<br>• Child shows progress in developing friendships with peers by sharing food, toys, and interests.<br>• Child starts to show awareness of the world around him/her and that others may have unique challenges that he/she deals with daily, e.g., child says, "Bonnie needs to wear glasses because she needs them to see, so we need to be careful not to bump them." | • Assist the child in recognizing and understanding how others might be feeling by pointing out facial expressions, voice tone, body language, or words.<br>• Model how to show empathy by responding appropriately to others' feelings.<br>• Teach the child to care for others by caring for pets, participating in community projects to help protect the environment, or to help others in need.<br>• Make get well and thank you cards for family, friends, and people in the community.<br>• Visit nursing homes and assisted care facilities to have the child interact with and show compassion for others who have unique needs and challenges. |

Listed above are *sample* behaviors of children and *sample* strategies for adults, they are not a definitive list or an exhaustive inventory. They start from an early developmental level and continue through older ages to the completion of kindergarten.

## A. Emotional Development (continued)

**PERFORMANCE STANDARD:** A.EL.2 Understands and responds to others' emotions (continued)

| Developmental Continuum | Sample Behaviors of Children | Sample Strategies for Adults |
|---|---|---|
| Interprets others' behavior and emotions and responds appropriately. | • Child retreats when another child raises his/her hand as if to hit or stop them.<br>• Child says "It's not nice to hit" when he/she observes another child hitting.<br>• Child observes another child's approach to problem solving and uses the same strategy. | • Tell the child when you notice his/her appropriate response to another child's emotion.<br>• Use stories and puppets to repeat successful and appropriate strategies that the child has demonstrated. |

Listed above are *sample* behaviors of children and *sample* strategies for adults, they are not a definitive list or an exhaustive inventory. They start from an early developmental level and continue through older ages to the completion of kindergarten.

## B. Self-concept

**PERFORMANCE STANDARD:** B.EL.1 DEVELOPS POSITIVE SELF-ESTEEM

| Developmental Continuum | Sample Behaviors of Children | Sample Strategies for Adults |
|---|---|---|
| Begins to recognize own abilities; is aware of self and own preferences. | • Child cries in particular ways to get his/her needs met.<br>• Child moves toward and gets a favorite toy, then smiles.<br>• Child is able to hear what others say and though he/she cannot speak for awhile, integrates other's comments into his/her self-concept.<br>• Child protests when he/she is given water rather than the juice he/she prefers.<br>• Child smiles and claps hands when he/she successfully climbs up stairs. | • Learn to read the child's cues/cries and respond appropriately to meet the child's needs.<br>• Place favorite toys just a little bit out of reach of the child and talk to him/her excitedly, noting his/her accomplishment in getting the toy.<br>• Speak gently and kindly to the child emphasizing that he/she is a valued and loved individual.<br>• Acknowledge that the child knew the difference between water and juice and that he/she will have juice sometimes and water other times.<br>• Clap with the child and say, "You climbed up those stairs all by yourself, you must be so proud." |
| Demonstrates increasing self-direction, resists adult control, and shows independence. | • Child attempts self-directed behavior, e.g., "I can do it myself!"<br>• Child shows initiative by trying new skills that are out of his/her usual comfort zone, e.g., climbing on playground equipment not tried before.<br>• Child repeatedly tries to open a container and does not ask for help although he/she may be frustrated. | • Foster the child's growing independence and self-direction by letting him/her do things according to his/her own ability, e.g., giving him/her time to dress and wash himself/herself. Ignore imperfections and recognize achievements.<br>• Reinforce the child's attempts at new skills, even if he/she does not succeed. For example, "You tried climbing the big ladder—Wow!"<br>• Help the child with tasks that he/she cannot do, saying something like, "You tried to open it but the cover was on too tight. When your fingers get stronger you will be able to open it." |
| Shows positive self-image. Knows and states independent thoughts. | • Child repeats an action or performs a new skill purposefully to attract attention.<br>• Child says, "I think we should play outside today." | • Reinforce the child's independence when he/she accomplishes a new skill or task. Cheer and clap!<br>• Affirm the child's sense of self by positively acknowledging and reinforcing his or her statements, such as saying, "That's a good idea." |
| Exhibits positive self-concept and confidence in his/her abilities. | • Child becomes more comfortable with his/her body and surroundings when he/she is successful at trying new things, which in turn helps to develop competence and confidence through repetition. (This is why young children love to dump things out of containers so often or read the same book over and over again!)<br>• After painting a picture, child wants adult to write a story about it and insists that the picture be put on the refrigerator. | • Be patient when the child tries novel and familiar things over and over. He/she is learning how to manipulate his/her environment and his/her body and to feel successful at tasks and situations.<br>• Admire and comment on the process that the child used to make a painting. Use words such as, "Tell me about your painting." Recognize that the process not the product is important for young children.<br>• Avoid judgmental comments and recognize individual differences. |
| Displays pride in his/her accomplishments. | • Child takes pride in telling about self, e.g., likes and dislikes, accomplishments, body image, etc.<br>• Child proudly dresses himself/herself and admires his/her reflection in the mirror. | • Share in the child's pride by repeating what he/she says such as, "I can see you really like to use the color red."<br>• Overlook shortcomings and comment on the child's positive self-initiative, saying something like, "You chose your own outfit and got dressed all by yourself." |

Listed above are *sample* behaviors of children and *sample* strategies for adults, they are not a definitive list or an exhaustive inventory. They start from an early developmental level and continue through older ages to the completion of kindergarten.

## B. Self-concept (continued)

**PERFORMANCE STANDARD:** B.EL. 2 DEMONSTRATES SELF-AWARENESS

| Developmental Continuum | Sample Behaviors of Children | Sample Strategies for Adults |
|---|---|---|
| Displays personal preferences and individual temperament. | • Child turns head away when no longer hungry.<br>• Child stiffens or pushes away when being held in an uncomfortable position.<br>• Child notices and explores his/her own hands, eventually becoming aware that his/her hands are attached and he/she is in control of making them do things. | • Observe the child's likes and dislikes. Affirm and accept his/her response.<br>• Experiment with different positions when holding the child.<br>• Comment on what the child is doing, "You used your hand to push the mobile. Look how it is swaying." |
| Becomes aware of ones self as an individual while still connected to others. | • Child no longer believes he/she is physically a part of his/her closest adult and becomes more independent, venturing away from the watchful eye of that closest adult.<br>• Child pays attention to his/her own reflection in a mirror and wants to see others in the mirror too.<br>• Child shows interest in touching others' faces and bodies with curiosity.<br>• Child can sometimes appear anxious as he/she is developing an understanding of his/her likes, dislikes, and things that frighten him/her.<br>• Child may not always want to do what everyone else is doing (e.g., at meal time the child wants to play rather than eat.) | • Provide safe, unbreakable mirrors at the child's level for the child to explore his/herself. Show child images of him/herself in a mirror or pictures and state child's name, e.g., "Look, here is David. He has black hair and mommy has brown hair."<br>• Offer two choices when possible, and be prepared for the child to refuse or protest all choices because he/she is developing awareness of his/her own opinions and preferences.<br>• Acknowledge the child's individual idea even when it is not acceptable, e.g., "I know you would like to play right now but we are eating. It is time for you to sit at the table. When we are done you can go play again." |
| Shows awareness of being part of a family and a larger community. | • Child names self and family members, pets, and friends.<br>• Child wonders if his/her teacher lives at the early care and education facility.<br>• When child sees another child at the local library, he/she says, "We go to the same library." | • Look at and talk about photos of family members, friends, pets, etc.<br>• Talk about how family, friends, and other important people in the child's life often live in one place and work in another.<br>• When taking the child to places in the community, talk about how other people he/she knows may go to the same places. |
| Demonstrates awareness of self as a unique individual. | • Child identifies own gender and names likes and dislikes. For example, "You can't play with us, you're a girl!"<br>• Child refers to himself/herself by characteristics such as "smart," "fast," or "strong."<br>• Child notices that other people have different skin, hair, or eye color. | • Read books and have conversations about individual strengths and differences. Acknowledge gender difference without bias.<br>• Use active listening with the child, repeating what he/she says and expanding upon his/her comments, e.g., "You see yourself as strong because you could pick up the large red ball and throw it more than six feet."<br>• Respond to the child's comments about differences with a matter-of-fact approach, e.g., "You noticed that Jamal has curly hair. You have straight hair. You are different from each other and that is okay." |

Listed above are *sample* behaviors of children and *sample* strategies for adults, they are not a definitive list or an exhaustive inventory. They start from an early developmental level and continue through older ages to the completion of kindergarten.

## B. Self-concept (continued)

**PERFORMANCE STANDARD:** B.EL. 2 DEMONSTRATES SELF-AWARENESS (CONTINUED)

| Developmental Continuum | Sample Behaviors of Children | Sample Strategies for Adults |
|---|---|---|
| Identifies self as a member of a specific culture, group, or demographic that fits into a larger world picture. | • Child knows full name and is aware of unique family traditions and routines.<br>• Child talks about whether he/she lives in a large city, small town, or rural area.<br>• Child shows eagerness to learn about other ways to experience the world through dance, music, food, and conversation.<br>• Child starts to learn that humans rely on plants, animals, and each other for food, clothing, medicines, and other needs.<br>• Child shows curiosity about other geographic locations, oceans, rivers, lakes, clouds, stars, etc. | • Encourage the child to tell stories about his/her family traditions.<br>• Model respect for diverse family types and customs.<br>• Read books that describe all types of families, living styles, traditions, and situations.<br>• Visit museums, festivals, stores, and restaurants to help the child become aware of the diversity in the world around them.<br>• Explore the life cycle of plants and animals to help the child understand the interdependence between humans and the natural world.<br>• Show the child world globes, maps, travel books, and science information. Talk about how people travel to different places and how they experience things that are different from where we live. |

Listed above are *sample* behaviors of children and *sample* strategies for adults, they are not a definitive list or an exhaustive inventory. They start from an early developmental level and continue through older ages to the completion of kindergarten.

## C. Social Competence

**PERFORMANCE STANDARD:** C.EL.1 DEMONSTRATES ATTACHMENT, TRUST, AND AUTONOMY

| Developmental Continuum | Sample Behaviors of Children | Sample Strategies for Adults |
|---|---|---|
| Becomes calm when needs are met. | • Child cries to express need for attention and becomes calm when adult holds and comforts him/her.<br>• Child may need additional comforting by being swaddled in a blanket and held by an adult.<br>• After physical needs are met, the child responds with coos and smiles to adults who interact with them.<br>• Child asks and looks for his/her blanket or stuffed animal when it is misplaced and hugs it closely when found. | • A trusting relationship between child and adult is formed when the adult consistently responds to the child's needs with sensitivity, love, and care, e.g., pick up and cuddle when distressed; feed when hungry; change diapers when needed.<br>• Gently wrap the child in a blanket and hold him/her close to you when he/she becomes insecure or afraid.<br>• A soft and calm human voice is very comforting to children. Sing lullabies and songs or hum songs if you are not comfortable singing. |
| Shows anxiety upon separation from primary caregiver and/or familiar adults. | • Child cries when parent(s) leave.<br>• Child resists, rejects, or cries in protest when someone other than a familiar adult tries to hold, play with, or even looks at him/her.<br>• Child becomes fearful of previously accepted things and situations. | • Establish a routine for times when the child must separate from his/her parents and/or caregiver (such as giving hugs, kisses, and waving good-bye).<br>• Introduce the child to new people gradually in the security of the parent(s) arms.<br>• Express the child's fear in simple words and reassure him/her, e.g., "That loud sound scared you, but it won't hurt you." |
| Shows signs of security and trust when separated from familiar adults. | • Child says "bye-bye" and waves when adult leaves, then happily joins play with others.<br>• Child insists that certain routines for transitions happen in a set order when familiar adult is not present and another adult is with him/her.<br>• Child may frequently ask where his/her "mommy, daddy, auntie, grandma or grandpa" are during the day. | • Acknowledge the child's feelings and divert his/her attention to engaging activities, e.g., look at interesting things in the room, sing a song, read a book, etc.<br>• Develop regular routines for the child so that he/she can know what to expect. Write them down for adults who may not know the routine.<br>• Make sure that the child has regular caregivers who are consistent in providing the routines that he/she needs to feel safe and secure.<br>• Reassure the child that his/her "mommy, daddy, or most important adult" is "at work, school, etc." and will be back to get him/her after nap, snack, dinner, etc. |
| Transitions into unfamiliar settings with assistance of familiar adults. | • Child insists on following familiar adult everywhere.<br>• Child plays a short distance away from adult, explores his/her environment, but occasionally looks back for reassurance.<br>• Child may ask a lot of questions in order to feel safe and secure.<br>• Child may want to talk to favorite adult about what he/she did in the unfamiliar experience in order to process it. | • Let the child play where he/she can be within eye contact. Give the child time to adjust gradually to new surroundings and activities.<br>• Smile and nod to let the child know you are paying attention, saying something like, "I see you are playing with the blocks."<br>• Give the child a warning signal several minutes before a change in activity, e.g., "You can play with the truck one more minute and then we will read books." |

Listed above are *sample* behaviors of children and *sample* strategies for adults, they are not a definitive list or an exhaustive inventory. They start from an early developmental level and continue through older ages to the completion of kindergarten.

## C. Social Competence (continued)

**PERFORMANCE STANDARD:** C.EL.1 Demonstrates attachment, trust, and autonomy (continued)

| Developmental Continuum | Sample Behaviors of Children | Sample Strategies for Adults |
|---|---|---|
| Acts independently in unfamiliar settings with unfamiliar adults. | • Child takes cues from others in the situation by watching, listening, and imitating.<br>• Child accepts direction from adult in charge.<br>• Child may question why something has to be done a certain way if he/she has not done it that way in the past.<br>• Child transitions into new situations with confidence.<br>• Child is often eager to take something home to help tell his/her family about a new situation. | • Talk with child in advance of new situations, e.g., going to swimming lessons for the first time, so he/she knows what to expect. Visit or role-play the new situation beforehand.<br>• Be cognizant that each child is an individual and will react to new situations and people in a variety of ways depending upon his/her past experience, learning style, culture, and biology.<br>• Structure new situations with the child so that he/she understands what will happen and what behavior is expected.<br>• Reinforce the success that the child had with a new situation by providing positive comments about what happened. |

Listed above are *sample* behaviors of children and *sample* strategies for adults, they are not a definitive list or an exhaustive inventory. They start from an early developmental level and continue through older ages to the completion of kindergarten.

## C. Social Competence (continued)

**PERFORMANCE STANDARD:** C.EL. 2 Engages in social interaction and plays with others

| Developmental Continuum | Sample Behaviors of Children | Sample Strategies for Adults |
|---|---|---|
| Shows interest in being with others. | • Child is attracted by other children playing nearby and smiles at them.<br>• Child smiles and coos when an older child makes a face at him/her.<br>• Child crawls toward other children to investigate what they are doing. | • Hold or place the child where he/she is able to see other children playing.<br>• Encourage older children to play with the younger child, while adults supervise.<br>• A very young child may explore another child as though the other child is a "toy." Allow him/her to interact, making sure his/her investigations do not cause pain or fear. |
| Begins to engage in short play interactions with others. | • Child hands toys to others in an effort to engage them in play for short periods of time.<br>• Child claps hands to initiate game of *pat-a-cake*.<br>• Child peeks around objects to initiate a game of *peek-a-boo*.<br>• Child participates in songs and finger-plays as part of regular routines and transitions. | • Support the child's engagement in play by sitting on the floor with him/her, joining in the play, and following his/her lead.<br>• Reinforce positive play interactions to set the pattern for successful behavior and reduce challenging behavior.<br>• Engage the child's participation in daily routines and transitions by planning fun activities. |
| Participates in parallel play with others for longer periods of time. | • Child works side-by-side with another child, each putting pieces in his/her own puzzle.<br>• In the sandbox, child plays beside another child but is engaged in his/her own activity.<br>• Child engages in dress-up and imitates the behavior of parents, caregivers, or others but does not attempt to coordinate with other children playing there as well. | • Provide a variety of toys with duplicates of favorites so the child can play next to other children without disputes.<br>• Provide a clear boundary for the child's play space by putting toys on blankets, trays, or placemats.<br>• Provide props for the child to pretend with including vests, shoes, hats, suitcases, pretend food, dolls, etc.<br>• Allow the child to repeat actions he/she enjoys rather than forcing him/her to engage in play initiated by adults or other children. |
| Participates in cooperative play with others. | • Child participates in a group game such as *duck-duck-goose* or *hide and seek*.<br>• Child may have difficulty transitioning into a group activity.<br>• Child identifies a favorite friend and wants to play with that friend frequently.<br>• Child wants to be recognized for being a good friend and helping others. | • Provide opportunities for the child to interact with others in ways that encourages him/her to take turns, exchange toys, and/or assist another.<br>• Provide clear directions as to what will happen next and facilitate cooperative play interactions.<br>• Help a shy child use the skills and words he/she needs to develop friendships.<br>• When the child plays with others successfully say something like, "You are sharing the trucks today and being good friends." |
| Demonstrates respect for others. | • Child returns a toy to another child who has misplaced it.<br>• Child listens when someone else is speaking.<br>• Child acknowledges and accepts differences in others. | • Compliment the child when he/she shows respect. Tell him/her how proud you are and how good it makes the other person feel.<br>• Notice when the child is listening to another person speak and acknowledge him/her before he/she becomes impatient.<br>• Provide frequent opportunities to recognize and celebrate differences. |

Listed above are *sample* behaviors of children and *sample* strategies for adults, they are not a definitive list or an exhaustive inventory. They start from an early developmental level and continue through older ages to the completion of kindergarten.

## C. Social Competence (continued)

**PERFORMANCE STANDARD:** C.EL. 3 DEMONSTRATES UNDERSTANDING OF RULES AND SOCIAL EXPECTATIONS

| Developmental Continuum | Sample Behaviors of Children | Sample Strategies for Adults |
|---|---|---|
| Tests adults' reactions to his or her behavior and understands what "no" means. | • Child puts inappropriate objects in mouth but understands to stop when told "no."<br>• Child plays games with food to see how adults will react.<br>• Child wiggles when adult tries to put a clean diaper on him/her. | • Respond to the child in a calm but firm voice and redirect him/her to an object that is more appropriate to put in his/her mouth such as a teething ring.<br>• Offer a variety of foods at regular intervals. Allow the child to choose what he/she will eat.<br>• Understand that the child is feeling the difference between having the diaper on and off. Tell the child that when the diaper is on, he/she can go play. |
| Demonstrates understanding of simple rules related primarily to personal health and safety. | • Child attempts to touch electric outlet or houseplant but looks to adult for reaction before following through. Leaves the item alone when adult shakes head "no."<br>• Child rides in car seat with straps secured without resisting.<br>• Child imitates behavior of adults, such as washing hands before eating or wiping off table after meals.<br>• Child holds adult's hand when in the store. | • Provide a safe environment (e.g., covers on electric outlets). Use simple words to teach rules, e.g., "Stop - Hot!" Understand that the child is exploring his/her environment and not trying to make anyone annoyed or angry.<br>• Model good personal health and safety behaviors while talking about why those rules are important.<br>• Let the child know when something is unsafe or unacceptable in a calm but firm manner.<br>• The child may need frequent reminders of simple rules because his/her memory is developing and his/her need for exploration is high. |
| Remembers and follows simple group rules and displays appropriate social behavior. | • Child demonstrates awareness of everyday routines such as hanging up coat or washing hands before meals.<br>• Child complies with transitions between activities more readily if they are done in a fun and engaging way.<br>• Child is able to transition from activity to activity if an adult gives him/her gentle reminders of what will happen next throughout the day.<br>• Child is not able to wait for long periods of time or stand in lines. | • Provide consistent routines as much as possible so the child will remember the sequence of events and what is expected when.<br>• Use simple, one-to-two step directions to help the child learn appropriate behavior. For example, "When you go inside, hang up your coat and wash your hands."<br>• Design schedules to minimize the amount of time the child needs to spend waiting without something to do.<br>• Use songs, a singing voice, or props to get the child's attention and direct him/her to the next activity.<br>• Make a pictorial schedule of what happens during the day so that the child can see a visual cue to help him/her move to the next activity. |
| Displays competence at engaging in appropriate social behavior. | • Child waits for his/her turn to come up on the list so he/she can use the computer.<br>• Child uses the words "excuse me" to interject into another person's conversation.<br>• Child wants to make a card for a classmate that has been sick.<br>• Child will tell another child that they cannot participate in *duck-duck-goose* unless they follow the rules.<br>• Child asks for adult assistance when having difficulty in a social situation.<br>• Child needs help and reassurance when dealing with disappointments in social situations. | • Acknowledge and reinforce the child's social competence with encouraging words such as, "You were very polite and used good manners at the doctor's office today."<br>• Respond promptly and consistently to the child's inappropriate behavior to help him/her learn what is appropriate and inappropriate.<br>• Include the child in developing simple rules for home and school, such as "show respect," "help others," and "follow directions." |

Listed above are *sample* behaviors of children and *sample* strategies for adults, they are not a definitive list or an exhaustive inventory. They start from an early developmental level and continue through older ages to the completion of kindergarten.

## C. Social Competence (continued)

**PERFORMANCE STANDARD:** C.EL. 4 ENGAGES IN SOCIAL PROBLEM-SOLVING BEHAVIOR AND LEARNS TO RESOLVE CONFLICT

| Developmental Continuum | Sample Behaviors of Children | Sample Strategies for Adults |
|---|---|---|
| Shows awareness of tension and stressful situations. | • Child reacts when adults argue or raise their voices.<br>• Child looks away from a situation that over-stimulates him/her.<br>• Child finds comfort in a favorite toy or blanket and is able to get himself/herself to sleep.<br>• Child indicates hunger or pain with different cries.<br>• Child continues to cry when adult cannot figure out what he/she needs right away. | • Be aware that the child is sensitive to tension and stress in others. Help him/her to feel safe and secure when others around them may be upset.<br>• Check the child often and talk about how he/she restored his/her comfort or how you helped.<br>• Reinforce the child's ability to comfort himself/herself by providing his/her favorite toy or blanket when he/she is upset.<br>• Respond promptly to the child's cues and cries to set the expectation that his/her needs will be met.<br>• Continue to try to figure out what the child needs if he/she continues to cry. |
| Imitates how others solve problems. | • Child holds tissue to own nose after seeing adult sneeze and wipe his/her nose.<br>• Child blows on cereal after seeing another blow on theirs to cool it before eating.<br>• Child may hide or act out when experiencing conflict among important adults in his/her life.<br>• Child uses napkin to attempt to wipe up spill after watching an adult do the same.<br>• Child pats another person on the back when they are upset. | • Be aware that the child will watch how you solve problems and deal with difficult situations in your life. He/she will start to imitate at a very early age.<br>• Work on your own strategies as an adult to calmly and rationally solve problems and conflicts.<br>• Talk with the child about how you are solving the situation in a calm way and tell him/her that it is okay to make mistakes sometimes.<br>• Read stories together that involve characters who solve problems in positive ways. |
| Experiments with trial-and-error approaches to solve simple problems and conflicts. | • Child uses fingers to eat cooked noodles, after trying unsuccessfully to use spoon.<br>• Child uses spoon then reaches for shovel when trying to fill large bucket with sand.<br>• Child may find another item to offer to another child "to trade" (such as when another child won't let him/her have the shiny purse in the dramatic play area, he/she may offer the other child a shiny necklace).<br>• When one adult won't let the child have a treat he/she wants, the child may go to another adult to try to get the treat. | • Allow the child time to solve his/her problems rather than stepping in right away to solve the problem for the child.<br>• Reinforce the child's strategy by saying something like, "You realized that the spoon was very small and that you could put more sand in the bucket quickly by using the shovel."<br>• Communicate frequently with other caregivers in the child's life to ensure that there is consistency.<br>• Give the child replacement skills and words for situations where the child is trying out inappropriate ways to solve problems. Say something such as, "When you are frustrated that you cannot have a turn on the computer, you can tell Ben, 'I want to have a turn on the computer when you are done,' and then while you are waiting for your turn, you could go look at a book or build with blocks." |

Listed above are *sample* behaviors of children and *sample* strategies for adults, they are not a definitive list or an exhaustive inventory. They start from an early developmental level and continue through older ages to the completion of kindergarten.

## C. Social Competence (continued)

**PERFORMANCE STANDARD:** C.EL. 4 Engages in social problem solving behavior and learns to resolve conflict (continued)

| Developmental Continuum | Sample Behaviors of Children | Sample Strategies for Adults |
|---|---|---|
| Seeks adult assistance to resolve conflicts. | • Child seeks assistance from adult when hurt or upset and reports what happened, e.g., "She pushed me down."<br>• Child demonstrates extreme emotional shifts and contradictory responses when making decisions because he/she is learning about his/her preferences in a world with many choices.<br>• Child starts to suggest solutions to solve a problem although the solution may be self-centered.<br>• Child may "tattle" when other children behave inappropriately. | • Respond by asking, "What happened?" and "How do you feel about that?" The child may be comforted simply by having someone listen to his/her feelings. If the child is not comforted, explore appropriate solutions.<br>• Keep choices simple and limited such as asking, "Do you want to wear your red or blue shirt?"<br>• Teach the child problem solving steps that include the following:<br>  1. What is my problem?<br>  2. What are some solutions?<br>  3. What would happen next?<br>• Try one solution. If it does not work, try another solution. Help the child to understand that there is more than one possible solution. |
| Asserts needs and desires appropriately in conflict situations. | • Child approaches playmate calmly saying, "I want my turn on the tricycle."<br>• Child accepts compromises when suggested by a peer or adult.<br>• Child starts to defend the rights of another child to have a turn.<br>• Child shares a portion of his/her play dough when another child joins the activity. | • Role-play appropriate problem solving techniques. Then allow the child to resolve conflicts independently as long as he/she does so without hurting others.<br>• Create scenarios in which a potential conflict/problem-solving situation occurs. (Such as four children want to sit at the table but there are only three chairs. How can they solve the problem so that everyone can sit at the table?)<br>• Model compromises that result in positive solutions with other adults when the child is present. |
| Uses a variety of strategies to resolve conflict. | • Child notices that there is only one cookie left and suggests, "Let's break it in half so we can both have some."<br>• Child starts to recognize that peers have preferences and will let his/her friend have the desired game piece while playing a board game.<br>• Child avoids a conflict by walking away.<br>• Child enters into more elaborate discussions and interactions to meet his/her needs while respecting the needs and rights of others. | • Reinforce the child's efforts to find solutions to problems using encouraging words such as, "You worked that problem out together."<br>• In daily interactions with the child, recognize that he/she has preferences and point out that each individual has the right to make choices.<br>• Accept avoidance as a conflict resolution strategy at times. If this happens often, it may be an indication of insecurity or fear.<br>• Consider having a "peace table" or "family meeting" that is designed to promote thoughtful discussions on how to maintain harmony in relationships and solve situations when there may be conflict. |

Listed above are *sample* behaviors of children and *sample* strategies for adults, they are not a definitive list or an exhaustive inventory. They start from an early developmental level and continue through older ages to the completion of kindergarten.

# Wisconsin Model Early Learning Standards
## Section Three

| DEVELOPMENTAL DOMAIN | Page |
|---|---|
| III. LANGUAGE DEVELOPMENT AND COMMUNICATION | 42 |
|     A. LISTENING AND UNDERSTANDING | 44 |
|     B. SPEAKING AND COMMUNICATING | 47 |
|     C. EARLY LITERACY | 54 |

# III. LANGUAGE DEVELOPMENT AND COMMUNICATION

This domain refers to children's developing the ability to understand and convey meaning through language. Language development is reflected in children's progress toward acquiring skills in the areas of listening and understanding, speaking and communicating, and early literacy. Language development occurs in the context of relationships, encompasses all forms of communication, both verbal and nonverbal, and moves children along the continuum of early literacy.

## Rationale

During the first years of life, language has an essential impact on the rapid development of a child's brain. Children increase their language and communication skills by expressing their ideas and feelings, and by listening and understanding others while engaging in meaningful experiences with adults and peers. Children learn to communicate in a variety of ways, such as using symbols; combining their oral language, pictures, print, and play into a coherent mixed medium, and creating and communicating meaning through both non-verbal and verbal language.

Early experiences define children's assumptions and expectations about becoming literate as they learn that reading and writing are valuable tools. Long before they can exhibit reading and writing production skills, children acquire basic understandings of concepts about literacy and its functions. Regular and active interactions with print, in books and in the environment, allow children to consolidate this information into patterns, essential for later development in reading and writing. Children whose home language is not English may demonstrate literacy skills in their primary language before they do so in English.

---

### A. LISTENING AND UNDERSTANDING

*Developmental Expectation*

*Children in Wisconsin will convey and interpret meaning through listening and understanding.*

**Performance Standard**

During the early childhood period, children in Wisconsin will show evidence of developmentally appropriate abilities in the following areas:

A.EL.1 Derives meaning through listening to communications of others and sounds in the environment.

A.EL. 2 Listens and responds to communications with others.

A.EL. 3 Follows directions of increasing complexity.

**Program Standard**

Early care and education programs in Wisconsin will provide the environment, context, and opportunities for children to develop their abilities to listen and understand.

# III. LANGUAGE DEVELOPMENT AND COMMUNICATION (continued)

## B. SPEAKING AND COMMUNICATING

**Developmental Expectation**

*Children in Wisconsin will convey and interpret meaning through speaking and other forms of communicating.*

**Performance Standard**

During the early childhood period, children in Wisconsin will show evidence of developmentally appropriate abilities in the following areas:

B. EL. 1   Uses gestures and movements *(non-verbal)* to communicate.

B. EL. 2a   Uses vocalizations and spoken language to communicate. Language Form *(Syntax: rule system for combining words, phrases, and sentences, includes parts of speech, word order, and sentence structure)*

B. EL. 2b   Uses vocalizations and spoken language to communicate. Language Content *(Semantics: rule system for establishing meaning of words, individually and in combination)*

B. EL. 2c   Uses vocalizations and spoken language to communicate. Language Function *(Pragmatics: rules governing the use of language in context)*

**Program Standard**

Early care and education programs in Wisconsin will provide the environment, context, and opportunities for children to develop their abilities to communicate and speak.

## C. EARLY LITERACY

**Developmental Expectation**

*Children in Wisconsin will have the literacy skills and concepts needed to become successful readers and writers.*

**Performance Standard**

During the early childhood period, children in Wisconsin will show evidence of developmentally appropriate abilities in the following areas:

C. EL. 1   Develops ability to detect, manipulate, or analyze the auditory parts of spoken language.

C. EL. 2   Understands concept that the alphabet represents the sounds of spoken language and the letters of written language.

C. EL. 3   Shows appreciation of books and understands how print works.

C. EL. 4   Uses writing to represent thoughts or ideas.

**Program Standard**

Early care and education programs in Wisconsin will provide the environment, context, and opportunities for children to develop literacy concepts and skills.

---

## Important Reminders

The Wisconsin Model Early Learning Standards recognize that children are individuals who develop at individual rates. While they develop in generally similar stages and sequences, greatly diverse patterns of behavior and learning emerge as a result of the interaction of several factors, including genetic predisposition and physical characteristics, socio-economic status, and the values, beliefs, and cultural and political practices of their families and communities. The Wisconsin Model Early Learning Standards reflect expectations for a typically developing child; adapting and individualizing learning experiences accommodates optimal development for all children.

The Wisconsin Model Early Learning Standards developmental continuum and sample behaviors ARE NOT intended to be used as age markers, a prescriptive listing of development with every first item in a continuum starting at birth, nor as a comprehensive or exhaustive set of sample behaviors of children and sample strategies for adults.

## A. Listening and Understanding

**PERFORMANCE STANDARD:** A.EL. 1 Derives meaning through listening to communications of others and sounds in the environment

| Developmental Continuum | Sample Behaviors of Children | Sample Strategies for Adults |
|---|---|---|
| Turns toward source of sound. | • Child looks toward adults or children as they talk.<br>• Child looks toward source of sound such as a book dropping.<br>• Child startles and cries at loud sound or angry voice. | • Talk and sing to the child frequently when holding, diapering, and while in the same room.<br>• Provide multiple sources of sounds and visuals for the child, e.g., crib mobiles, soothing musical toys or CDs, rattles, etc.<br>• Provide ongoing opportunities for hearing screening. This is especially important if the adult is concerned about the child's lack of response to nearby sounds. |
| Attends to same situation or object as another person. | • Child reaches out to an object when wanting an adult to look at or get an object, e.g., bottle, toy, or blanket.<br>• Child turns and smiles when someone says a favorite word or phrase such as "Silly Billy." | • Respond to the child's non-verbal gesture by giving the child the object he/she is requesting or lifting the child up when he/she pulls on the clothing of the caregiver.<br>• Push ball back and forth between adult and child.<br>• Respond to the child's vocalizations or smiles by "mimicking" the behavior of the child. |
| Enjoys short stories, rhymes, finger plays, songs, and music. | • Child enjoys listening to songs such as *Wheels on the Bus* (story, actions, music).<br>• Child laughs when adult says, "This little piggy goes to market."<br>• Child enjoys hearing the same story over and over again. | • To encourage the child's interest in language sounds and words, say nursery rhymes and sing repetitive songs to the child.<br>• Use the same word repeatedly for objects, people, or animals. The child needs to hear the word spoken many times every day so he/she can learn the meaning of the word.<br>• When talking with the child, use language appropriate to the child's level of understanding, get down at the child's level when talking to him/her and maintain eye contact. |
| Shows understanding of concept words and sequence of events. | • Child understands time concepts, such as "When we get home from our walk, we'll have a snack," or "After cleanup we can read the book."<br>• Child demonstrates understanding of a few preposition words such as, "Put your shoes under the bed," or "Please put your chair next to mine."<br>• Child follows all the steps in feeding the hamster (going to the cupboard to get the food, putting it in a dish, and then delivering it to the cage).<br>• Child understands concepts of before and after, above, below, bottom, behind, in front of. | • Use language that talks about time, e.g., "When we go to grandma's, you can play," or "After your nap, you can have a snack."<br>• Show and talk to the child about how to feed the hamster, kitty, or dog saying, "First you get the food from the cupboard, then you put one scoop of food in the dish, then you put the scoop and the food back in the cupboard."<br>• Use concept words such as before, after, above, below, bottom, behind, and in front of when talking with the child. |
| Demonstrates understanding and listening skills by attending and responding appropriately. | • Child listens and attends to someone tell or read a story, such as *The Three Little Pigs*, and is able to retell the story accurately in his/her own words.<br>• Child listens and attends to someone tell or read stories representing real life situations, and is able to retell the story. | • Comment on the child's listening and interaction with the story (real or pretend); give encouragement.<br>• Use meal times and other daily routines as an opportunity for conversation between adult and child.<br>• Be intentional about providing time and opportunities (inside and outside) for the child to have individual conversations with adults and other children. |

Listed above are *sample* behaviors of children and *sample* strategies for adults, they are not a definitive list or an exhaustive inventory. They start from an early developmental level and continue through older ages to the completion of kindergarten.

## A. Listening and Understanding (continued)

**PERFORMANCE STANDARD:** A.EL. 2 Listens and responds to communication with others

| Developmental Continuum | Sample Behaviors of Children | Sample Strategies for Adults |
|---|---|---|
| Responds to voices and intonation of familiar adults and children. | • Child coos or gurgles when someone speaks to him/her.<br>• Child smiles, kicks, and turns head when someone comes near the crib.<br>• Child startles when he/she hears harsh sound or voice.<br>• Child calms to soothing music. | • Talk and sing to the child often throughout the day.<br>• Provide soothing music to relax or calm the child.<br>• Communicate with the child using voice tones, words, and facial expressions. |
| Participates in turn-taking, alternating listening and responding. | • Someone makes a sound or series of sounds and the child repeats it.<br>• Child hears an "excited clap" while playing and claps back in response.<br>• Child repeats laugh when someone else laughs. | • Play "turn-taking" simple games with the child, e.g., *peek-a-boo* with small blanket, clapping when child does something special, repeating same sounds made by the child.<br>• Nuzzle the child's tummy with adult's face; play *pat-a-cake* with hands or feet, or do gentle bouncing games on lap. |
| Responds appropriately when asked to identify familiar objects/ person/body parts (nouns) or when asked to run, walk, jump (action words, verbs). | • When asked, "Where is Sam?" the child looks for brother.<br>• Child points to body parts when asked, "Where is your head?" (feet, eyes, ears, nose, mouth, tummy).<br>• When someone says, "The doll wants to sleep," the child puts the doll in the crib.<br>• Child will jump like a bunny when asked, "Jump like a bunny." | • Repeat and emphasize the names of people and animals, e.g., "Here comes Snuggles. Snuggles wants to play. Feel his fur." Or, "That's your friend Mary eating her snack."<br>• Play games such as Head, Shoulders, Knees, and Toes. Substitute other body parts. Talk about the child's body parts during bath-time, dressing and mealtime, e.g., "You have milk on your face; let's wipe your face (or chin)."<br>• Name the body parts of the doll, e.g., put Band-Aid on the "back" of the doll.<br>• Introduce and name new objects/materials in the child's environment.<br>• Make a book with pictures showing familiar objects, people, and actions.<br>• When reading a book, describe pictures, point to the correct picture, and give simple explanation, "This boy is sleeping.... see his eyes are closed and he's lying on a bed." |
| Responds to increasingly complex language structures, including comments, requests, and questions. | • Adult says, "Daddy is going outside to wash the car. Do you want to help?" Child says, "Me too."<br>• Adults says, "Yes, you can go to Tommy's house, but remember you need to come home before lunch time." Child says, "I'll be home."<br>• When playing with dolls of all sizes, adult says, "Let's put all the little dolls inside the little play house and all the big dolls on the big chairs." The child gets all the small plastic/wood dolls and places them inside the play house and places the big dolls on the chairs. | • Talk to and carry-on a conversation with the child about whatever he/she is doing at the time, e.g., playing, eating, taking a walk, riding in the car.<br>• Provide "wait time" for the child to respond. Some children take longer than others to respond. Wait for the child to respond before starting another statement.<br>• Provide time to play with the child. While playing use increasingly more complex language that helps the child expand on his/her previous knowledge.<br>• When having a conversation with the child, name and describe objects, people, animals, and plants that are unknown to the child. |
| Responds and extends conversations much like adults and can sustain a topic through multiple turns. | • The adult asks the child which animal is his/her favorite animal. Child responds, "The kangaroo, because she carries her baby in her pouch." The adult says, "Where do you suppose kangaroos live?" The child says, "I do not know. How can we find out?" The adult gets the world globe and shows the child where kangaroos live. The conversation continues with the adult and child looking at books to learn more about kangaroos. | • Talk about a variety of topics with the child and model ways to use language to ask questions, give answers, make statements, and share ideas.<br>• Play, "I wonder what would happen if.....?"<br>• Have fun with language and engage the child in ongoing conversations through pretend play, thinking and talking about fantasy, or playing with words. |

Listed above are *sample* behaviors of children and *sample* strategies for adults, they are not a definitive list or an exhaustive inventory. They start from an early developmental level and continue through older ages to the completion of kindergarten.

## A. Listening and Understanding (continued)

**PERFORMANCE STANDARD:** A.EL. 3 FOLLOWS DIRECTIONS OF INCREASING COMPLEXITY

| Developmental Continuum | Sample Behaviors of Children | Sample Strategies for Adults |
|---|---|---|
| Responds to simple requests. | • Child waves bye-bye when asked to "Wave bye-bye."<br>• Child gives an adult the cup when asked to, "Give me the cup."<br>• Child responds to someone saying "No" by taking hand away from potted plant. | • Maintain eye contact with the child as the adult models the behavior. Say to the child "Wave bye-bye" or hold hand out as adult says, "Please give me the cup."<br>• Reinforce child when he/she follows or attempts to follow a direction.<br>• Use gestures to help the child understand requests. |
| Understands and carries out a one step direction. | • Child responds to directions such as, "Wash hands for lunch."<br>• Child responds to directions such as, "Please close the door." | • Provide simple directions that are related to activities that the child is engaged with at the time.<br>• Provide simple directions related to familiar routine daily activities.<br>• Make requests that are clear, e.g., "Get your coat," rather than "Get it." |
| Understands and carries out two-step direction. | • Child follows simple directions such as, "Get your hat and coat and come to the door."<br>• When adult asks the child to, "Put your toys away and come sit with me so we can read a story." The child puts his/her toys away and comes to sit next to the adult. | • Provide clear instruction that helps the child move from simple directions to a more complex sequence of directions.<br>• The order of adult requests matters, e.g., "You can go outside after you clean your room."<br>• Give the child time to follow through, or repeat the request a second time. If still no response, walk the child through the action: "Now, we'll walk you over to the sink and put your hands in the water and wash your hands." |
| Follows a series of three or more multi-step directions. | • Child follows directions given by an adult such as, "Take this book and put it on the shelf and then come to the table."<br>• Child remembers instructions given earlier in the day such as, "After we eat lunch today, remember to call grandma and ask her when she will come over this afternoon."<br>• Child recalls, without reminders, the five steps necessary to put together his/her play house. | • Ask the child to tell in sequence the routine things he/she does such as dressing, going to bed, getting up, etc.<br>• Read a book such as *Three Billy Goats Gruff,* and ask the child to retell the sequence of events.<br>• Play games that involve following directions in sequence, e.g., *Simon Says*.<br>• Use multiple photos of the child's daily routines and have the child put select pictures in order of "What will happen today?" |

Listed above are *sample* behaviors of children and *sample* strategies for adults, they are not a definitive list or an exhaustive inventory. They start from an early developmental level and continue through older ages to the completion of kindergarten.

## B. Speaking and Communicating

**PERFORMANCE STANDARD:** B.EL.1 Uses gestures and movements *(non-verbal)* to communicate

| Developmental Continuum | Sample Behaviors of Children | Sample Strategies for Adults |
|---|---|---|
| Uses gestures and movements to get attention, request objects, protest, or to draw attention to an object in the environment. | • Child puts arms up to be picked up.<br>• When playing outside, the child points to a flower and smiles at someone.<br>• Child points to the cereal box when wanting more Cheerios.<br>• Child pushes own milk bottle away when not hungry.<br>• Child shakes head "no" when asked to finish food he/she does not want to eat.<br>• When someone is wiping off the child's face, makes a face, puts hands over face, and turns away. | • As the child begins to use the "up" gesture, say, "You want me to pick you up?"<br>• Express your delight each time the child tries to get attention or requests an object. Use language to identify the attention the child is seeking, or the object the child is pointing to, e.g., "Nancy, you are pointing to the doll," or "Bill, you want more Cheerios."<br>• Give the child choices and expect him/her to protest at times, e.g., when not hungry or does not want a hat put on his/her head. |
| Uses gestures for greetings and conversational rituals. | • Child waves bye-bye when someone leaves.<br>• Child runs to the door and smiles when familiar adult comes to the door. | • Show the child the ritual of saying "good bye." Wave and say "Bye-bye" each time the adult leaves family and friends. Help the child move his/her arm up and down as the adult says "Bye-bye."<br>• Smile and express emotion when the adult greets family and friends. |
| Uses movement or behavior to initiate interaction with a person, animal, or object. | • Child knocks over sister's blocks and looks up to her for a reaction.<br>• Child offers a doll to friend.<br>• Child looks at the cat and throws a toy for the cat to play with. | • Use small objects, figures of people and animals, dolls, and other play materials to show and talk to the child about how to interact appropriately.<br>• Model appropriate interactions with family members, friends, and family pets. |
| Uses non-verbal communication much like adults. | • Child uses facial expressions of emotions, e.g., sad, happy, angry, distressed, anxious, frustrated, etc.<br>• Child uses body movements, e.g., waving goodbye, motion for "come here," walking away when not wanting to be involved, running toward someone when excited to see them, etc. | • Through actions, continue to show the child appropriate ways to act (greetings, requesting, answering) when interacting with family members, friends, and family pets.<br>• Name the child's emotions, "You look sad." Or, "Are you angry? You sound as if you are angry?" |

Listed above are *sample* behaviors of children and *sample* strategies for adults, they are not a definitive list or an exhaustive inventory. They start from an early developmental level and continue through older ages to the completion of kindergarten.

## B. Speaking and Communicating (continued)

**PERFORMANCE STANDARD:** B.EL. 2a USES VOCALIZATIONS AND SPOKEN LANGUAGE TO COMMUNICATE

**Language Form** *(Syntax: rule system for combining words phrases and sentences, includes parts of speech, word order, and sentence structure)*

| Developmental Continuum | Sample Behaviors of Children | Sample Strategies for Adults |
|---|---|---|
| Uses cries, coos, and other noises to communicate. | • Child cries differently when hungry, wet, tired, or angry.<br>• Child begins to make cooing sounds (vowels and sounds such as "aah" and "eeh").<br>• Child varies pitch, length, and volume of cooing sounds.<br>• Child vocalizes to get someone's attention.<br>• Less crying as cooing increases. | • Listen for different crying patterns and try to respond to the cause of the child's distress.<br>• Respond promptly to the child's crying so that the child knows his/her communication is being understood.<br>• Show the child that the adult is interested in his/her cooing by smiling and repeating the sounds.<br>• Play vocal games with vowel sounds and smiling facial expressions, e.g., "ahh," "oo," or "eee." Initiate a sound and wait for a response by the child. |
| Makes vowel and consonant sound combinations and engages in vocal play (babbles). | • Child makes consonant sounds of "b, m, p, d, and t," and combines them with vowel sounds.<br>• When playing, child says, "Ba ba ba."<br>• Child makes a variety of sounds using tongue and lips such as "clicking" the tongue or blowing air.<br>• Child imitates a vowel/consonant sound made by caregiver. | • Respond with delight and smile when the child babbles. Imitate the sounds of the child.<br>• Encourage the child to repeat sounds by playfully saying the babble sounds the adult heard the child say, e.g., "Ba ba ba," "Ma ma."<br>• The child's first consonant sounds are "b, m, p, d, and t."<br>• During quiet times such as feeding, dressing, bathing, or playing, maintain eye contact with the child and initiate babbling sounds. Wait with a look of anticipation for any kind of vocal response. |
| Uses one word. | • Child says, "Up" when wanting to be picked up.<br>• Child says, "Open" when wanting to get Cheerios out of a container.<br>• Child says family dog name such as "Duke."<br>• Child says "No" when not wanting to take a nap.<br>• Child names family members in the room or photograph.<br>• When asked, "Who is that?" the child can say "David" when looking at him in a photograph. | • When the child uses one word, such as "Up," encourage language development by expanding on the word by saying, "You want me to pick you up." Or, elaborating on the word by saying, "You want me to pick you up so you can see the black doggie?"<br>• Use the names of the objects the child plays with and name the people who are in contact with the child.<br>• Provide the child with exposure to a "rich vocabulary." Children who hear more words will learn more words. |
| Uses two to three word phrases and sentences. | • Child can name body parts, animals, objects, people, and things in the environment.<br>• Child says, "Kitty down," when the kitty jumps down from the chair or the child wants the kitty to jump down from the chair.<br>• Child asks, "What's that?" while pointing to something.<br>• Child says, "Push Karen" when wanting to be pushed.<br>• Child says, "Me want juice" when wanting more juice. | • Respond to everyday activities and talk about the child's actions, thoughts, and ideas.<br>• Provide positive attention when the child uses words to communicate, e.g., smile or laugh, hug or pat, clap, imitate the action or sound and call others' attention to the child's action or words.<br>• Emphasize words the child knows and talk in short sentences, e.g., child says "Kitty go down," and you say "Yes, the kitty is jumping down."<br>• Use simple sentences. Emphasize key words. Model three or four word phrases in a question which can be answered with the same words, e.g., "Kitty's eating her dinner?" |

Listed above are *sample* behaviors of children and *sample* strategies for adults, they are not a definitive list or an exhaustive inventory. They start from an early developmental level and continue through older ages to the completion of kindergarten.

## B. Speaking and Communicating  (continued)

**PERFORMANCE STANDARD:** B.EL. 2a USES VOCALIZATIONS AND SPOKEN LANGUAGE TO COMMUNICATE (CONTINUED)
**Language Form** *(Syntax: rule system for combining words, phrases, and sentences, includes parts of speech, word order, and sentence structure)*

| Developmental Continuum | Sample Behaviors of Children | Sample Strategies for Adults |
|---|---|---|
| Uses:<br>*Plurals* (cats);<br>*Pronouns* (I, he, they);<br>*Past tense* (walked). | *Plurals*<br>• Child tells friend "I have cars and trucks."<br>• Child tells someone, "I want grapes."<br>*Pronouns*<br>• When looking at a picture in a book, the child says, "I see two boys."<br>• Child says, "My shoe," when someone says, "Is that your shoe?"<br>• Child says, "I want water."<br>• Child says, "You come," when wanting someone to come.<br>*Past tense*<br>• Child says, "We runned all the way home."<br>• When asked, "Where's Daddy?" child says, "Daddy went to work."<br>• When the balloon breaks, the child says, "Balloon popped." | *Plurals*<br>• Model correct plural usage, e.g., if child says "My foots are cold," say, "Your feet are cold; let's get some socks."<br>*Pronouns*<br>• Model correct pronoun usage, e.g., if the child says "Me want car," adult says, "I want to play with the car, too."<br>• Use pronouns to describe meaningful activities or actions, e.g., "You look sleepy," "I am making dinner."<br>*Past tense*<br>• Use past tense vocabulary to describe actions that have already happened, e.g., "You stopped your car at the stop sign," "We walked to the park and played on the swings and slide."<br>• Model correct past tense usage, e.g., if the child says, "We goed to the park," adult says, "Yes, you went to the park with Billy." |
| Uses multi-word sentences (parts of speech, word order, and sentence structure) much like that of an adult. | • After hearing his/her favorite story, the child says, "That was a great story. I really liked the part about the boy going on a trip to see his grandmother. It was exciting to hear about how he helped her plant the garden with corn, potatoes, and tomatoes. I think I would like to plant a garden."<br>• After returning from the zoo, the child tells the whole story of what happened, e.g., describing all the animals, telling about experiences feeding the birds, and riding on the merry-go-round. | • Plan many daily opportunities and a variety of experiences for the child to use and expand language.<br>• Talk about a variety of topics and illustrate ways to use language to ask questions, give answers, make statements, share ideas or use pretend, fantasy, or word play.<br>• Encourage conversations with the child by asking the child open-ended questions such as, "Tell me about your toy?" "What did you see at the park today?" "Tell me more about what you and Sally did at the park?" |

Listed above are *sample* behaviors of children and *sample* strategies for adults, they are not a definitive list or an exhaustive inventory. They start from an early developmental level and continue through older ages to the completion of kindergarten.

## B. Speaking and Communicating (continued)

**PERFORMANCE STANDARD:** B.EL. 2b Uses vocalizations and spoken language to communicate
**Language Content** *(Semantics: rule system for establishing meaning of words, individually and in combination)*

| Developmental Continuum | Sample Behaviors of Children | Sample Strategies for Adults |
|---|---|---|
| Uses a word to represent a particular person or object. | • Child says "Bankie" to refer to his/her blanket.<br>• Child calls his/her mother and father, "Momee" and "Dadee."<br>• Child calls his/her bottle a "Baba" and expects that an adult will get his/her bottle. | • A particular word represents a specific object, e.g., "bankie" is always the child's blanket.<br>• When talking with the child, consistently use the same word for people, animals, and objects, e.g., mommy, daddy, kitty, doggy, ball, etc. |
| Uses words for protests and greetings. | • Child pushes adult's hand away and says "No" when he/she does not want to be touched or picked-up.<br>• Child says "No" when he/she does not want a particular kind of food or an object.<br>• Child waves and says "Bye-bye" when leaving.<br>• The child commands another to cease undesired actions, e.g., resists another's action and rejects an offered object. | • Honor the child's efforts to show his/her independence by saying "No." By getting a response from an adult when he/she says "No," the child is learning that he/she can control his/her environment.<br>• The child begins to communicate using conversation rituals that will be used the rest of his/her life, e.g., "Bye-bye." Wave and say "Bye-bye" when the child says "Bye-bye." |
| Uses words to represent various objects. | • Child calls all four-legged animals "doggie."<br>• At different parts of the day, the child points to a doll chair, lounge chair, baby seat, highchair, or other objects to sit in and calls them "chair."<br>• Child calls all toys that have wheels "cars." | • One word can represent several types (kinds) of the same object.<br>• When the child over-generalizes, e.g., uses one name for multiple objects, say the "real" name of the object, person, or animal. If child calls the truck a "car" say, "That is your truck." If the child calls the kitty a "doggie" say, "This is a kitty." |
| Uses a word to relate to itself or something else. | • When the child's glass is empty, the child says, "More" meaning "I want more milk."<br>• When the child's container of food is empty, the child says, "All gone."<br>• Child says, "Down" when he/she wants to get out of the chair.<br>• Child says, "Mine," when he/she wants his/her favorite toy.<br>• The child uses words to mark existence, nonexistence, disappearance, and recurrence. | • When the child says "More," expand and extend the child's language by saying, "You want more milk."<br>• Respond to the child's language by lowering the child down when he/she says "Down," and giving the child his/her favorite toy when the child says, "Mine" and points to a favorite toy. |
| Uses a category of words that shows awareness of common aspects among objects. | • Child says, "Where are my toys for the sand box?" when he/she wants to play with a specific kind of toy.<br>• Child says, "Water, milk, and juice are all something to drink."<br>• Child says, "These are all flowers," as he/she points to flowers that are different colors and shapes. | • The child demonstrates awareness that there are common aspects among objects.<br>• When playing with the child, put objects together based on common aspects, e.g., toys, shoes, balls, say, "These are all toys (cars, blocks, dolls)." |

Listed above are *sample* behaviors of children and *sample* strategies for adults, they are not a definitive list or an exhaustive inventory. They start from an early developmental level and continue through older ages to the completion of kindergarten.

## B. Speaking and Communicating (continued)

**PERFORMANCE STANDARD:** B.EL. 2b USES VOCALIZATIONS AND SPOKEN LANGUAGE TO COMMUNICATE (CONTINUED)
**Language Content** *(Semantics: rule system for establishing meaning of words, individually and in combination)*

| Developmental Continuum | Sample Behaviors of Children | Sample Strategies for Adults |
|---|---|---|
| Asks many questions with "why" to obtain information. | • Child asks, "Where's my shoe?"<br>• Child asks a friend, "Where do you live?"<br>• Child asks, "When will daddy come home?"<br>• When playing with an object or toy child asks, "What's inside?"<br>• Child asks many "why" questions about things in his/her environment, stories being read, actions of people or animals, etc.<br>• As the teacher is reading *Curious George*, the child asks, "Why is George so naughty?" | • The child learns to ask questions by hearing others ask questions.<br>• Ask the child "what, where, when, and why" questions.<br>• Ask questions which require more than a yes or no response.<br>• Respond to all of the child's attempts at questions so that he/she knows that his/her questions are important and will be answered. |
| Comments on as well as produces and comprehends words. | • Child says, "Balls are all round. Some are big and some are little."<br>• Child says, "Ball starts with a /B/."<br>• Child says, "Hats are different sizes and shapes." | • The child has the ability to think about language and comment on it as well as produce and comprehend it.<br>• If the child has an interest in a specific topic or word, talk about it, read about it, and help the child learn more about his interest topic or word.<br>• When a child comments on a word, encourage further discussion by saying, "Tell me more about____," or ask the child questions about the word. |

Listed above are *sample* behaviors of children and *sample* strategies for adults, they are not a definitive list or an exhaustive inventory. They start from an early developmental level and continue through older ages to the completion of kindergarten.

## B. Speaking and Communicating (continued)

**PERFORMANCE STANDARD:** B. EL. 2c Uses vocalizations and spoken language to communicate (continued)
Language Function *(Pragmatics: rules governing the use of language in context)*

| Developmental Continuum | Sample Behaviors of Children | Sample Strategies for Adults |
|---|---|---|
| Seeks attention through vocalizations or actions. | • Child tugs on adult's clothing to let adult know that he/she wants the adult to look at him/her.<br>• Child says "Daddy" when he/she wants daddy to help.<br>• The child wants a person to pay attention to him/her or an aspect of the environment. | • Respond to the child's actions (non-verbal) and vocalizations (verbal) to get the adult's attention. |
| Directs attention to an object. | • Child points to an object that he/she wants and says "Mine."<br>• Child puts adult's hand on jar or box while looking at the adult. Child wants adult to open the jar or box and get him/her what is inside.<br>• Child looks at adult, points to shoes and says, "On" when he/she wants his/her shoes on.<br>• Child points to a cracker and with intonation of a question, says "Uh?" Child wants a cracker.<br>• Child's intent is to act on his/her environment, e.g., child directs attention outside of him/herself.<br>• Child requests or directs another to carry out an action. | • Expand and extend the child's language, e.g., child says, "On," adult says, "You want your shoes on," or child says "Uh?" and adult says "Do you want a cracker?"<br>• Respond to the child's non-verbal requests by saying, "You want me to open the box and get you a cracker?" |
| Engages in short dialogue of a few turns. | • Child says, "That's a big dog." Adult says, "Yes, that is a big dog." Child says, "Will he bite?" Adult says, "No, he will not bite you, he is in his dog pen."<br>• Adult says, "I am going to the store." Child says, "Can I go too?" Adult says, "Yes, and after we go to the store we can stop at the park so that you can play." Child says, "Can Tommy go too?"<br>• Child says, "What is this? (pointing to a large nut on the ground). Adult says, "That's a walnut from this tree."<br>• Child can introduce a topic and provide some descriptive detail.<br>• Child learns that asking questions is one way to keep the attention of adults. | • Maintain a conversational dialogue with the child by maintaining eye contact when speaking, taking turns sharing information, asking and answering questions. |
| Determines how much information a listener needs based on an awareness of listener's role and understanding. | • When a person asks a question such as, "Where do you live?", the child determines whether to tell the person the directions to their home or to tell them their house number.<br>• While the child is engaged in a dialogue with another person, the child stops talking if the other person is not listening.<br>• Child says, "Do you want to hear the story about the big fish I caught?" If the person says, "Yes," and is a fisherman, the child will tell a very detailed story. If the person says, "Yes," and is not interested, the child tells a very short story about the kind and size of the fish.<br>• The child becomes more aware of the social aspects of talking back-and-forth with an adult or a child. | • Model good listening skills for the child by always listening and being interested in the child's communication. |
| Modifies language when talking to younger child. | • Child talks in "baby" language when talking to his/her infant sister or brother, e.g., says goo-goo, ga-ga to the baby.<br>• Child talks in one and two word sentences when talking to a toddler, e.g., "Want milk?"<br>• Child talks in three- and four-word sentences when talking to a child who is one or two years younger, e.g., "Play with me." | • Encourage conversation by involving both the younger and the older child in conversation at the same time.<br>• Offer positive feedback when the older child talks to the younger child, "You are helping Nora to learn more words." |

## B. Speaking and Communicating (continued)

**PERFORMANCE STANDARD:** B. EL. 2c USES VOCALIZATIONS AND SPOKEN LANGUAGE TO COMMUNICATE (CONTINUED)
**Language Function** *(Pragmatics: rules governing the use of language in context)*

| Developmental Continuum | Sample Behaviors of Children | Sample Strategies for Adults |
|---|---|---|
| Initiates conversation, responds to conversations, and stays on topic for multiple exchanges. | • Child asks adult if he/she could make cookies. Adult and child talk about what they will need to bake cookies. After the adult and child prepare what they will need, child says, "Can you help me measure the stuff?" Adult says, "Yes, I can help you measure the ingredients and will show you which measuring spoon and cup to use." Child says, "These cups and spoons have numbers on them." The adult tells the child about the numbers and together they continue their conversation and baking experience for the next 10 minutes. | • Listen to the child, respond, and follow his/her lead in the chosen activity and discussion.<br>• Provide opportunities for the child to engage in turn taking and dialogue in conversation, e.g., during routines such as meals and snacks, and allowing time during the day for the child to talk about events and activities of interest to them. |
| Uses language to effectively express feelings and thoughts, describe experiences and observations, interact with others, and communicate effectively in group activities and discussions. | • During a group discussion on fire safety, the child listens to others and waits his/her turn to express thoughts such as, "We had a fire at our house, and my mom said we all had to get out of the house at once!"<br>• When finding a butterfly, while playing in the backyard with three other friends, the child and the friends take turns talking about the butterfly.<br>• Child says, "I was mad when Ellie took my blocks. I told her to give them back."<br>• After returning from a trip to the zoo, child describes the animals and tells what he/she did such as feeding the monkeys and buying ice cream at the ice cream cart.<br>• Child asks a friend, "Would you like to play with the blocks with me? We could build a big castle together and pretend that we are the kings."<br>• The child uses compound and complex sentences, grammatically correct sentences, and speech that is understandable. | • Talk about a variety of topics and illustrate ways to use language to ask questions, give answers, make statements, and to share ideas.<br>• Encourage conversations with the child by asking the child open-ended questions such as "Can you tell me about your toy?" "What did you see at the park today?"<br>• Engage in pretend play and fantasy play with the child. |

Listed above are *sample* behaviors of children and *sample* strategies for adults, they are not a definitive list or an exhaustive inventory. They start from an early developmental level and continue through older ages to the completion of kindergarten.

## C. Early Literacy

**PERFORMANCE STANDARD:** C.EL.1 DEVELOPS ABILITY TO DETECT, MANIPULATE, OR ANALYZE THE AUDITORY PARTS OF SPOKEN LANGUAGE (*This includes the ability to segment oral language into words, syllables, or phonemes independent of meaning.*)

| Developmental Continuum | Sample Behaviors of Children | Sample Strategies for Adults |
|---|---|---|
| Enjoys and responds to frequently said sounds, words, and rhymes. | • Child moves arms and legs when he/she hears a familiar, happy, sing-song voice.<br>• Child responds by turning and smiling when he/she hears his/her name.<br>• Child enjoys short action play, e.g., "This little piggy went to market…" when adult wiggles toes or "Patty-cake, patty-cake baker's man…"<br>• Child smiles and giggles when hearing rhyming words, e.g., funny bunny, Claire bear, rub-a-dub, etc.<br>• Child laughs, smiles, and enjoys repeated words, e.g., "The wheels on the bus go round and round, round and round, round and round," etc. | • Talk to the child, sing to the child, make up sounds, play children's music, and say rhymes to the child.<br>• Talk with the child when diapering, dressing, eating, and playing. |
| Imitates sounds. | • Child imitates cooing and babbling sounds made by adults.<br>• Child produces sounds found in their home language.<br>• Child imitates "Pa-pa" and "Ma-ma."<br>• Child makes sounds and imitates the tones and rhythms that adults use when talking. | • Make a variety of sounds with the child, playing a game back and forth encouraging the child's participation as he/she tries to imitate sounds and the adult imitates the child's sounds.<br>• Imitate the sounds that objects make: A train goes "choo-choo."<br>• Imitate the sounds that animals make: A cow says "moo." |
| Repeats words in rhymes and actions. | • Child says, "Piggy" when the adult says, "This little piggy went to market…"<br>• While picking up the child, the child says, "Up, up" when adult says, "Up, up." | • Make sounds and ask the child to make them back to you like an echo.<br>• Use the child's name and do silly rhymes and songs, changing the initial consonant.<br>• Laugh and enjoy the child's imitation or attempts to repeat a favorite song, chant, or rhyme. |
| Requests and joins in saying favorite rhymes and songs that repeat sounds and words. | • Child says, "Let's say *Jack and Jill*," or "Let's say *Baa, Baa, Black Sheep*."<br>• Child says, "Let's sing *Wheels on the Bus*."<br>• Child joins adult in singing, *Itsy, Bitsy Spider*. | • Sing and chant with the child often. The child loves rhythm, melody (even off-key), and the magic of music.<br>• Say finger plays and favorite nursery rhymes with the child while playing with him/her or working around the house while the child is playing nearby. |
| Recognizes and matches sounds and rhymes in familiar words. | • Child plays their own rhyming game matching pairs of rhyming words saying, "Down-town," "Sadie-lady." | • Use child's name and do silly rhymes, finger plays, and songs, changing the initial consonant, such as "Sammy, Pammy, Tammy."<br>• Use silly names and change the ending of the word such as Willy, Willoby, Wallaby, Woo.<br>• Invite the child to make up silly names.<br>• When reading a rhyming book to a child, emphasize the rhymes, e.g., *Sheep in a Jeep* by Nancy Shaw.<br>• Read a picture book that features alliteration, e.g., *Alligators All Around* by Maurice Sendak. |

# C. Early Literacy (continued)

**PERFORMANCE STANDARD:** C.EL.1 DEVELOPS ABILITY TO DETECT, MANIPULATE, OR ANALYZE THE AUDITORY PARTS OF SPOKEN LANGUAGE (*This includes the ability to segment oral language into words, syllables, or phonemes independent of meaning.*) (continued)

| Developmental Continuum | Sample Behaviors of Children | Sample Strategies for Adults |
|---|---|---|
| Recognizes sounds that match and words that begin or end with the same sounds. | • Child says, "Sally and Susie start the same. They both start with /s/."<br>• Child makes up words that start with different letter sounds, "I could call you different names, Mom, Tom, Pom, Som, Dom."<br>• Child says, "Tammy and toy start alike. They both start with /t/."<br>• Child says, "Tom and Mom have the same sound at the end." | • Ask the child, "What other words start with the /t/ sound like Tommy?"<br>• Sing songs like *Head, Shoulders, Knees, and Toes* and substitute the first sounds of words: Bed, Boulders, Bees, and Boes.<br>• Play matching games encouraging the child to match or sort pictures that have the same beginning or ending sounds, e.g., ball and bear, cat and bat, to build awareness of alliteration and rhyming.<br>• Play a game by saying an animal name like "pig" and ask the child, "Does Mattie or Patty start like pig?" Continue by using other animal names along with one matching and one non-matching beginning sound.<br>• Play "I Spy" ("I spy with my little eye something in the car that starts with…").<br>• Ask, "Which animal name ends with the sound /g/? Is it dog or cat?"<br>• "I hear a /s/ at the end of bus. That is the same sound at the start of sun. Did you know that bus and sun share a sound? Can you think of a word that shares a sound with your name?" |
| Recognizes and produces rhyming words. | • Child is asked, "Tell me a word that rhymes with 'Pam'." The child says, "Sam."<br>• Child provides a rhyming word when listening to the poem. Adult says, "I have a dog whose name is Lilly, she has a doggie friend named…" and the child injects the last word "Billy."<br>• Child says, "Ricky rhymes with picky."<br>• Child says, "Humpty, Dumpty, Bumpty, Thumpty, Gumpty." | • Have fun with the child by having one person say a word like "cake" and the other person gives a word that rhymes with it, "rake."<br>• Together with the child, enjoy chants, songs, and finger plays involving rhyming and sound substitutions. Make up poems and jingles with rhyming words.<br>• Read poetry and rhyming books to the child on a regular basis.<br>• Sing songs such as, "Oh a hunting we will go, a hunting we will go, we'll catch a snake and put him in a _____ and then we'll let him go." Let the child fill in the rhyming word, e.g., cake, lake, etc. Continue with other names of animals or other objects. Enjoy and giggle about the funny rhymes that the child makes. |

Listed above are *sample* behaviors of children and *sample* strategies for adults, they are not a definitive list or an exhaustive inventory. They start from an early developmental level and continue through older ages to the completion of kindergarten.

## C. Early Literacy  (continued)

**PERFORMANCE STANDARD:** C.EL.1 Develops ability to detect, manipulate, or analyze the auditory parts of spoken language (*This includes the ability to segment oral language into words, syllables, or phonemes independent of meaning.*) (continued)

| Developmental Continuum | Sample Behaviors of Children | Sample Strategies for Adults |
|---|---|---|
| Discriminates separate syllables in spoken words and begins to blend and segment syllables. | • Child can clap syllables in his/her name and other names, e.g., Tam-my (two claps); Bill (one clap); Me-lis-sa (three claps).<br>• Child can tell the number of syllables in a word, "My name has two parts, Bob-by" (while clapping for each part). | • Play games such as, "Can You Guess My Word?" to blend and segment compound words, such as "pop" – "corn," "cup" – "cake," and "butter" – "fly."<br>• Play games with words by clapping the number of syllables in the child's name, favorite toys, other objects, animals, and plants. "How many claps are in your name Tammy?"<br>• Ask the child, "How many parts does _____ (word) have?" If child cannot tell you the number, have him/her clap the syllables, e.g., bum-ble-bee (three claps). |
| Recognizes single sounds and combinations of sounds. | • Child changes initial consonant in rhyming words (onset-rime), e.g., the child says, "Dad and sad have the same middle and last sound."<br>• Child can recognize sounds such as /th/, /ch/, and /sh/ (digraphs). Child says, "Ship starts like shoe and show."<br>• Child can recognize combinations of two consonant sounds (blends) such as /st/ in stop and /st/ in still. While playing "Simons Says," child says, "Stop and stand still. Hey, those words start with /st/." | • Ask the child to guess the word you are trying to say. Begin with easy presentation of stretched-out words such as "mmmaaaannn," then move to onset-rime.<br>• Say each of the following sounds separately and ask the child to blend the sounds together to say the word: /ch/ /e/ /z/ cheese, or /p/ /e/ /ch/ peach.<br>• Play the game, "Cross the Bridge." Say to the child, "I am the lion that guards the bridge; you may not cross the bridge until you tell me what animal you are." The child says, "Tiger." "What is the first sound in tiger?" the lion asks. The child says "/t/." "You may cross the bridge," says the lion. Also, use words with blends such as in "crane" or digraphs as in "sheep."<br>• Play the game, "I Am Hungry. What Can I Eat?" Someone models, saying, "I am hungry for a gr-ape" and the child says, "Grape."<br>• Ask the child to say the sounds separately when someone gives them a word such as "duck." Child says the sounds /d/u/k/. "Let's build the word duck with these unifix cubes (/d/ /u/ /ck/). How many cubes did I need?" |

Listed above are *sample* behaviors of children and *sample* strategies for adults, they are not a definitive list or an exhaustive inventory. They start from an early developmental level and continue through older ages to the completion of kindergarten.

## C. Early Literacy *(continued)*

**PERFORMANCE STANDARD: C.EL.2** UNDERSTANDS CONCEPT THAT THE ALPHABET REPRESENTS THE SOUNDS OF SPOKEN LANGUAGE AND THE LETTERS OF WRITTEN LANGUAGE *(This includes utilizing this concept as an emerging reading strategy.)*

| Developmental Continuum | Sample Behaviors of Children | Sample Strategies for Adults |
|---|---|---|
| Explores, repeats, imitates alphabet related songs and games. | • When adult sings the alphabet song, the child imitates and repeats the alphabet song.<br>• Child sings the ABC song by him/herself singing, "ABCD (other letters may be out of order and run together, such as LMNO sounds like "el-i-minno")... now I know my ABCs."<br>• Child puts a three piece inlaid puzzle together with A, B, and C. | • Sing the alphabet song to the child.<br>• Play videos, CDs, or tapes of favorite children's alphabet songs and games.<br>• Provide the child with simple alphabet puzzles and other simple alphabet manipulative games.<br>• Echo read ABC books with the child; you read a letter and the child repeats the letter.<br>• Purchase or borrow from the library, well-written alphabet books that clearly illustrate the sounds of the letters with pictures of objects. |
| Recognizes the difference between letters and other symbols. | • Child writes A, B, c, t, then says, "See my letters?"<br>• When looking at a mix of magnetic letters and numbers, the child picks up the 'A' and says "This letter is in my name (Alex)." "This number is '4' – I'm four."<br>• While playing with the magnetic alphabet, numbers, and shapes, the child can sort letters and numbers. The child says, "These are all letters. These are all numbers."<br>• Child is able to find and identify some letters and numbers in books, signs, and labels.<br>• Child knows the first letter in his/her name and points to the letter on signs and words in a book and says, "My letter." | • When the child mixes letters and numbers, point out to the child, "These are called letters. These are called numbers." Talk about the letter names and sounds, and the names of the numbers.<br>• Mix magnetic alphabet letters, shapes, and numbers in one bucket and play a game of sorting the alphabet letters, numbers, and shapes.<br>• Play games of looking for letters and numbers during all the experiences the child has during a day. Play, "I'm looking for the letter 'C' can you find a 'C'?" Or, "I am looking for a letter that starts like your name. Can you find two letters that start like your name?" Play the same type of game looking for numbers.<br>• Look for signs that have both numbers and letters. Ask the child to name all the letters he/she knows and all the numbers he/she knows. |
| Recognizes letters and their sounds in familiar words, especially in own name. | • When looking at a book, the child says, "This word (bike) starts like my name. 'B' is in my name, Becky."<br>• Looking at a stop sign, the child says, "Stop starts with the same letter as my name (Susie)."<br>• Child says, "Look, I used the alphabet stamp letters to make my name J-i-m-m-y." | • Alphabet letters in isolation do not have meaning to the child. When the child is shown that letters grouped together represent his/her name or objects they know, the alphabet takes on new meaning. Start with familiar words, talking about the letter names and sounds.<br>• Say and point to letters in books, on puzzles or toys, on the child's clothing.<br>• Surround the child with print so the whole alphabet is presented in the child's environment.<br>• At bath time or during water play, print letters using foam soap.<br>• Provide magnetic letters for child. Place letters on the refrigerator, a magnetic board, or a cookie sheet and play games saying the sounds of the letters.<br>• Point out alphabet letters on signs in the community, labels, and written names on lists and cards.<br>• Echo read ABC books with the child. Adult reads a letter and the child reads the letter too. Adult says sound and child repeats.<br>• Encourage the child to find letters in books that are the same as the letters in the child's name. Adult says sound of that letter.<br>• Provide books, puzzles, alphabet stamp letters, and stickers so that the child can play with alphabet letters in different ways.<br>• Celebrate with the child when he/she reads a new letter. For example, at breakfast time the child says, "That's an 'M.' It says /m/," pointing to the milk carton. |

Listed above are *sample* behaviors of children and *sample* strategies for adults, they are not a definitive list or an exhaustive inventory. They start from an early developmental level and continue through older ages to the completion of kindergarten.

## C. Early Literacy *(continued)*

**PERFORMANCE STANDARD:** C.EL.2 UNDERSTANDS CONCEPT THAT THE ALPHABET REPRESENTS THE SOUNDS OF SPOKEN LANGUAGE AND THE LETTERS OF WRITTEN LANGUAGE *(This includes utilizing this concept as an emerging reading strategy.) (continued)*

| Developmental Continuum | Sample Behaviors of Children | Sample Strategies for Adults |
|---|---|---|
| Makes some letter/sound connections and identifies some beginning sounds. | • Child sees the letter D on a block, points and says, "'D' is for Daddy."<br>• Child's name is Matt. Matt says to his friend, Michael, "'M' starts your name, too."<br>• Child says, "Banana starts with /b/."<br>• Child whose name is Cory says, "My name starts like cat; both words start with a /k/ sound."<br>• Child puts magnetic letters on the board, saying each letter sound as the magnetic letters are placed in a row: "/s/, /k/, /t/, /b/, /j/, /m/." | • Using the magnetic letters, make simple words on the magnetic board, refrigerator, or cookie sheet that start with the same letter as the child's name. Say, "Mom and mop start like Mike." Overemphasize the /m/ by holding out the sound and saying it loudly.<br>• Play games with letters and the sounds they make like alphabet bingo.<br>• "Let's find all the words that start with the same letter and sound as your name." Change the game to find words that end with the same letter and sound as the child's name. Play the game anywhere and anytime, e.g., while traveling in the car and reading signs, or at the grocery store noticing labels on food items.<br>• When reading a favorite story, stop and point to the next word and say, "Tell me the word that comes next. Look at the first letter. What sound does that letter make?"<br>• When looking at a picture book with objects, people, and animals, point to the word under the picture and ask the child, "What do you think this word says?" |
| Uses a combination of letter sounds, familiar environmental print, and picture cues to recognize a printed word. | • Child recognizes some environmental print, or popular words and signs, e.g., "Stop": /s/, /t/, /o/, /p/.<br>• Child can recognize his/her own name.<br>• Child points to book cover and says "Moon" for *Goodnight Moon* by Margaret Wise Brown.<br>• When looking at the picture book, the child looks at the picture of the bird in the tree and says, "Bird."<br>• Child sees the toy store and asks, "Does that say 'toy'? Does it start with /t/?" | • Point out signs or pictures in the child's environment and ask the child, "What do you think this word (unfamiliar word) says on (or under) the sign or picture? What sound does it start with?"<br>• Label objects with pictures and words both inside and outside the house.<br>• Label child's clothing, drawings, and special toys with his/her name.<br>• Label drawings or paintings with a title. Say "Tell me what to write about your picture." Point to the first letter and ask, "What sound does it makes?"<br>• When writing a story with a child, draw a picture as they say a difficult word such as "igloo" or "airplane." Then write the word under the picture to connect script with meaning. |
| Recognizes that most speech sounds (both consonants and vowels) are represented by single letter symbols. | • Child can match single letter symbols with the vowel sounds they represent, e.g., /u/ is for the "u" in "up."<br>• As the child puts letters on the magnetic board, the child says, "I know these letter sounds" as he/she says each sound for the letters: "/b/, /t/, /s/, /m/, /d/, and /k/."<br>• When the child sees the vowels, "a,e,i,o,u," the child can say their short sounds correctly. For example, the child may say, "'A' says /a/ like in apple. 'E' says /e/ like in elephant. 'I' says /i/ like in igloo. 'O' says /o/ like in the word octopus. 'U' says /u/ like in umbrella."<br>• Child can match all single letter symbols with the consonant sounds they represent. | • As the adult is reading or speaking, say and repeat the sound that corresponds to the letter. Letter/sound correspondence is a basic tool for figuring out new words.<br>• When you read the word "cat," count, clap, or tap the sounds in words, e.g., /k/a/t/, or /t/e/n/. Helping the child recognize initial phonemes and how that sound corresponds to letters in words is crucial to segmenting and blending sounds.<br>• Ask the child to select two words that begin with the same sound from a list, e.g., cat, cup, dog with an appropriate response of cat and cup.<br>• While waiting at the dentist office, ask the child to point to a letter in a book. The adult names the letter and says: "'M' makes the sound of /m/." Next, the child points to a letter, names the letter, and says the sound the letter makes.<br>• Begin to model spelling simple, common CVC (consonant, vowel, consonant) words, such as "cat," "dog," "mom," and "dad." |

## C. Early Literacy  (continued)

**PERFORMANCE STANDARD:** C.EL.2 UNDERSTANDS CONCEPT THAT THE ALPHABET REPRESENTS THE SOUNDS OF SPOKEN LANGUAGE AND THE LETTERS OF WRITTEN LANGUAGE *(This includes utilizing this concept as an emerging reading strategy.) (continued)*

| Developmental Continuum | Sample Behaviors of Children | Sample Strategies for Adults |
|---|---|---|
| Experiences success in reading by sounding out words (decoding). | • Child can decode the first and sometimes the last letter of the word such as the word "mean." The child would know the "m" and "n" However, the child may not know what "ea" sounds like.<br>• Child says, "I know 'f' makes the sound of /f/ and 'i' sounds like /i/ and the end of the word sounds like /sh/. This word is fish. I know what a fish is."<br>• Child begins to understand that if words sound alike, they should look alike, e.g., pot, hot, and lot look alike. Uses this information to decode words.<br>• Child can break words into "chunks" and then "blend," them back into words, e.g., s/ing, b/ed. Child says, "My big b/ed 'bed'." | • When reading with the child and the child comes to a word he/she doesn't know, help him/her sound out the letters of the word, pointing to each letter starting from the left, e.g., f/l/a/g/ or b/e/s/t/. Then ask the child to blend the sounds together to discover the word. Offer encouragement for all attempts.<br>• Play "Going Fishing" with the child using a fish pole to fish for three- and four-letter words on word cards (four to five letter words that are both familiar and unfamiliar). Assist the child in sounding out the words he/she does not know.<br>• The child sees and reads word families like pit, hit, sit, kit, and sat, hat, bat, and mat. Through practice he/she will learn that the sound of some words is the same at the end and that sometimes it is just the beginning of the word that's different. The child can use this understanding to sort words.<br>• Play word games with the child using word tiles and asking "What sound does this 'p' make?" After making the /p/ sound, add the /o/ sound and letter, say it, then add the 't' and say the sound /t/. Blend the sounds together and say the word 'pot.' |
| Recognizes and names all letters of the alphabet (upper and lowercase) in familiar and unfamiliar words. | • Uses alphabet stamps and names the letters: "C, D, A."<br>• Child says, "This is a 'big A' and this is a 'little a'."<br>• Child says, "My name starts with a capital 'A' and has a small 'a' next to it. My name looks like this." Child points to his name Aaron.<br>• Child says, "I know all my letters." | • Playing together with the child, make familiar and unfamiliar words using magnetic letters. Ask the child to name the words and letters, e.g., m-o-m, s-i-s, d-a-d, m-a-d, t-o-p, b-u-g.<br>• Play alphabet bingo games.<br>• Provide an alphabet chart for the child with both lower and upper case letters.<br>• Point out upper and lower case letters while reading a book or looking at signs and labels.<br>• When writing a story, let the child take turns "spying" for different letters and circling them in his/her favorite color. |
| Reads familiar decodable and some irregular words in books, signs, and labels. | • Child begins to read a book alone or with an adult, and reads some of the words he/she knows and has learned from past experiences of reading a variety of books with the adult.<br>• Child can read signs of favorite places to eat or shop, and familiar signs such as "Stop" or "Men" (on a bathroom door).<br>• Child can read words that he/she sees frequently such as his/her own name, other children's names, 'mom,' 'dad,' or 'I love you.'<br>• Child recognizes high frequency words and reads them when seen in the environment, in a list, or in stories. The child may read another child's story, "I like dogs, cats, and fish."<br>• Child consistently recognizes the words 'I,' 'me,' 'mom,' 'dad,' 'no,' and 'yes' when written in a book, on signs, and on labels. | • The child recognizes about 50 high-frequency words as he/she encounters the words in reading (some children will read more, other children will read less). Simple high-frequency words are recognized by "sight." For example, when the child encounters the words, they do not need to sound the words out. Some high frequency words are not easily decodable, such as 'the,' 'they,' and 'was.' Other words may not yet be easily decoded by the child.<br>• When the child asks "What is this word," tell the child the word. Or say, "Let's sound it out together. My turn first and then we can do it together." Help your child look for the word again or write the word for him/her on a piece of paper. Encourage the child to read and find the new word. "Jimmy learned a new word; it is 'dog'." Have the child draw a picture of the new word.<br>• Provide positive feedback to the child when he/she reads signs, labels (environmental print), and tries to read unfamiliar words in a book – say, "You are learning to read." |

## C. Early Literacy *(continued)*

**PERFORMANCE STANDARD:** C.EL.3 SHOWS APPRECIATION OF BOOKS AND UNDERSTANDS HOW PRINT WORKS

| Developmental Continuum | Sample Behaviors of Children | Sample Strategies for Adults |
|---|---|---|
| Explores and enjoys books. | • Child looks at pages in the book as adult reads.<br>• Child turns pages of a book to look at pictures.<br>• Child recognizes favorite book by its covers.<br>• Child brings book to the adult indicating that he/she wants the adult to read the book.<br>• Child picks up and explores books. | • The child recognizes faces and voices of those who are familiar to him/her and will begin to connect books with what he/she loves most, the voice and the closeness. Hold the child and use a happy, sing-song voice using inflection while reading.<br>• Provide "board books" (thick cardboard pages) or pliable plastic books that have colorful pictures and some words that relate to the pictures, e.g., pictures of animals with words telling what the animal says.<br>• Some very young children have a "favorite book" and will show their excitement with smiles and sounds when the book is read. |
| Points to and names pictures in a book when asked. | • Child points to the appropriate picture in the book when adult asks, "Put your finger on the kitty."<br>• When the adult points to a picture of a dog in a book and asks, "What's this?" The child says, "Doggie."<br>• Child points to pictures in a book and makes sounds or smiles. | • Provide the child with a variety of books. Model holding and using books properly.<br>• When reading stories, actively involve the child by asking him/her to point to a picture and ask, "What's this?" Talk about the picture.<br>• Provide touch or pop-up books like *Spot Goes to School* that require physical interaction, e.g., lifting up the table cloth or pulling a string. The child learns to attend carefully to pictures with anticipation to interact with the story in the book. |
| Looks at picture books and asks questions or makes comments. | • After the adult has completed reading the print on the page, the child reaches and turns the page.<br>• While pointing to a picture, child asks, "What's this?"<br>• When looking at a picture book, the child names animals. | • Invite the child to hold the book and/or turn pages as the adult reads.<br>• When the adult reads, point to the print so the child knows when it is time to turn the page.<br>• Ask the child open-ended questions, such as, "Why do you think this happened?"<br>• Allow the child to choose his/her favorite book to read in the afternoon or for bedtime. |
| Understands that print in the book carries the message. | • Child notices that the print rather than just the picture has meaning, e.g., begins to understand that the adult is reading the word under the picture on the page.<br>• Child points to some words as the adult reads the story.<br>• Adult says, "Point to the picture," and the child points to the picture of butterflies. Pointing to print, the adult asks, "What is this?" "That tells the story," says the child. The adult asks, "How did you know that?" "It has letters," says the child.<br>• When the adult asks the child, "Where do I start to read," the child points to where the print begins. | • When books are first read to the child, he/she does not always understand that the print holds the message, not the pictures. By pointing to the print as the adult reads the book, the child comes to realize that words can be put together to tell the story and hold the message.<br>• When the adult reads, point to the print so the child knows when it is time to turn the page.<br>• When writing names or things on lists, invitations, etc., explain to the child what you are writing.<br>• Help your child make his/her own book. The child can choose pictures for the book and then tell the adult the words to write under the picture, or the child can draw pictures and the adult can write the story for the child's picture. |

Listed above are *sample* behaviors of children and *sample* strategies for adults, they are not a definitive list or an exhaustive inventory. They start from an early developmental level and continue through older ages to the completion of kindergarten.

## C. Early Literacy *(continued)*

**PERFORMANCE STANDARD:** C.EL.3 Shows appreciation of books and understands how print works (continued)

| Developmental Continuum | Sample Behaviors of Children | Sample Strategies for Adults |
|---|---|---|
| Views one page at a time from the front to the back of the book and knows that the book has a title, author, and illustrator. | • Child turns the pages one page at a time and "reads" (pretend or real) the book to an adult, friend, or younger sibling.<br>• Child says, "This is my favorite book; Dr. Seuss is the author. The title is *Horton Hatches the Egg*."<br>• Child asks, "Who drew the pictures in this book?" | • Talk about the noticeable features of pictures and tell the child that the pictures are created by illustrators. Tell the child that words and stories in a book are written by authors.<br>• Ask the child, "What do you think the author is trying to tell us in this part of the story?"<br>• Ask the child, "What is the title of your favorite book?" |
| Chooses reading activities and responds with interest and enjoyment. | • Child asks adult to read him/her a story in a book.<br>• Child chooses a book to read that has some words in it that he/she knows and browses.<br>• Child "reads" the story in his/her own words.<br>• After visiting the library, the child asks, "Can I take this book home to read?"<br>• After going to the library, child wants to "play library."<br>• Child shows a favorite page in the book and tells about the character.<br>• Child wants to read (pretend or real) his/her favorite book to an adult or another child. | • Comment on the child's interest in reading, assuring the child that he/she will learn to read as he/she grows. It is this interest and joy that takes the child from enjoying books to wanting to continue to read alone.<br>• Take the child to the library to choose some books to take home. Choose books that match the child's interest. Attend "Story Time" at the library with the child.<br>• Read adult books while the child is looking at or reading his/her own books.<br>• Encourage the child to retell a story including details and connections between the story events or drawings. |
| Recognizes some familiar environmental print. | • Child sees popular words and signs, e.g., "Stop."<br>• Child looks at the shape and color of the stop sign (red, octagon sign) to "read" the associated word, "Stop."<br>• Child begins to recognize his/her own name.<br>• The child uses strategies such as looking at symbols, shapes, and colors to determine words. | • Point out signs in the environment and tell what they say.<br>• Praise attention to print.<br>• Label child's clothing, drawings, and special toys with his/her name.<br>• Label drawings or paintings with a title. Say, "Tell me what to write about your picture." |

## C. Early Literacy  (continued)

**PERFORMANCE STANDARD:** C.EL.3 SHOWS APPRECIATION OF BOOKS AND UNDERSTANDS HOW PRINT WORKS (CONTINUED)

| Developmental Continuum | Sample Behaviors of Children | Sample Strategies for Adults |
|---|---|---|
| Handles books correctly, and shows increasing skills in print directionality. | • Child holds the book properly.<br>• Child reads (pretend or real) the book going from front to back, left to right, and top to bottom.<br>• Child reads (pretend or real) a list of classmates' names from top to bottom. | • Use book terms, e.g., title, author, illustrator, front cover, back cover, spine, etc.<br>• Say, "Let's start reading at the top of the page and read to the bottom of the page" or, "We start reading on this side (left) and move to this side (right)."<br>• When eating out and receiving a menu, point to and read the food choices to the child.<br>• Show the child lists of names; move a finger down the list and say "Let's see if we can find your (or your mother, father, brother, or sister's) name."<br>• When making lists for the grocery store, model reading the list to the child by pointing at the words from top to bottom.<br>• When reading stories, ask the child, "Where does the story begin?" Assist the child by pointing to where you will start reading words. Show him/her by pointing to the words and saying, "You start to read here" (moving his/her finger left to right). Eventually the child will know that he/she needs to do a return sweep when starting to read the next line of print.<br>• Model pointing to words to help children attend to print as well as pictures.<br>• Ask child to point to the words as adult reads the story. |
| Understands the difference between letters, words, and sentences. | • Child asks, "What is this word?"<br>• Child says, "This is a long sentence. I am going to count the words in this sentence."<br>• Child says, "I know all the letters on this page." | • Ask child to point to the first word in the sentence and then the last word in the sentence.<br>• When reading a book with the child, count the number of words in a sentence and the number of letters in a word.<br>• Use the words 'letter,' 'word,' and 'sentence' as you read books or see letters, words, or sentences in everyday print.<br>• "Here's your letter, Lauren (pointing to letter 'L'). This is the letter 'L'." |
| Understands that books have characters, sequence of events, and story plots. | • Child acts out the story of *The Three Bears* by telling about each of the character's actions and what happened in the beginning, middle, and end of the story.<br>• When listening to a reading of *Three Billy Goats Gruff*, the reader says, "The little goat crossed the bridge to the other side," the child says, "You forgot to say trip-trap-trip-trap."<br>• When someone asks the child, "Why did the monkeys throw down their hats?" after reading *Caps for Sale* by Esphyr Slobodkina, the child gives the reason. | • Help the child set up the table with three sizes of bowls. Set up three sizes of chairs and beds. Assist the child with "play acting" the story of *The Three Bears* by taking a character part in the story.<br>• Read stories that have repetition of words or actions and a sequence of events. Encourage the child to tell the story by saying, "What happened in the beginning of the story? What happened next? And what happened at the end of the story?"<br>• If the child becomes upset when the adult leaves out part of the story as the adult reads, assure him/her that you didn't mean to skip it and reinforce him/her for accurately remembering what comes next in the story, "You remembered what came next in the story."<br>• When reading a book such as *Caps for Sale*, talk to the child about the reason why the monkeys would throw their hats down. |

## C. Early Literacy (continued)

**PERFORMANCE STANDARD:** C.EL. 4 Uses writing to represent thoughts or ideas

| Developmental Continuum | Sample Behaviors of Children | Sample Strategies for Adults |
|---|---|---|
| Begins to use writing tools to make marks. | • Child picks up crayon or marker and holds it in his/her fist and makes marks on paper or plastic.<br>• Child makes marks with a crayon or writing tool in a book. | • Provide a variety of opportunities and tools for writing, e.g., shaving cream, chalk, paint, markers, colored pencils, paper, sheets of plastic.<br>• Provide crayons (short, fat), pencils (child size), markers (washable), and paper so that the child can make marks. To ensure safety, an adult needs to be present when very young children are using writing tools. |
| Scribbles and creates unconventional shapes. | • Child covers the paper with lines and zigzags and says, "Look."<br>• Child randomly makes one kind of mark, then fills another part of the paper with another kind of scribbling, or shapes, etc., and points to one area and says, "Kitty" then points to another area and says, "Doggie."<br>• Child makes lots of circle-type marks and shows an adult his/her writing and says, "See, I write this."<br>• Child scribbles on paper and says, "This is my name." | • When the child writes or draws making random symbols, ask, "What does that say?"<br>• Write and draw with the child, talking about what the adult and the child are drawing and writing.<br>• Continue to smile and encourage the child for writing words or messages.<br>• When outside, allow the child to write with chalk on the sidewalk, at the beach, or in the sand.<br>• Encourage the child's attempts at writing by saying, "You're a writer." |
| Writes lists, thank you notes, names, and labels objects in play. | • In the dramatic play center, the child pretends to use a telephone book to find the phone number of a friend, and then writes a first name and some numerals on a note pad.<br>• Child makes signs/labels for things in the house or in a play center, e.g., hospital, store, house, post office.<br>• When playing marching music, the child makes a pretend stop sign and holds it up to tell everyone when to STOP.<br>• Child makes a list of things he/she wants to do. | • The child comes to know different types of writing (stories, signs, letters, and lists) with different purposes. The child comes to understand the "power" of written words when he/she writes a sign that says "Do Not Touch" on a block structure that has been created.<br>• Provide a variety of paper materials and writing tools in the play area. |
| Labels pictures using scribbles or letter-like forms to represent words or ideas. | • After the child writes the letter "B" and wiggly lines, the child says, "This says 'books'."<br>• Child makes marks, including wiggly lines and some letters mixed together, and places it under a picture of his/her mother and "pretends" to read the writing, saying, "This says, 'I love you'."<br>• Child uses a letter that looks like "M" and other marks to label Mom's picture, a letter that looks like "D" and marks for Dad's picture, and writes several letters in his/her name under his/her picture.<br>• Child hears someone is sick and draws a picture with a sad face. (Drawings represent a spoken message.) | • Provide the child with larger, shorter crayons (or break longer crayons in half and remove the paper), and large pencils to use when drawing or writing. Larger writing instruments are easier for children to use and manipulate.<br>• Accept any and all ways the child uses writing instruments. The child may hold the instrument by his/her fist or use thumb and fingers when he/she begins to learn to write.<br>• Show how adults label things at home. Help the child draw or write labels for things in his/her environment such as door, table, toys, etc.<br>• Have a special writing place to make and display the child's writing.<br>• Model writing for the child, e.g., grocery list, to-do list, thank-you cards, and invite the child to write similar lists and cards. Provide encouragement to the child for early scribbles, shapes, and attempts at letters. |

Listed above are *sample* behaviors of children and *sample* strategies for adults, they are not a definitive list or an exhaustive inventory. They start from an early developmental level and continue through older ages to the completion of kindergarten.

## C. Early Literacy  (continued)

**PERFORMANCE STANDARD:** C.EL. 4 Uses writing to represent thoughts or ideas (continued)

| Developmental Continuum | Sample Behaviors of Children | Sample Strategies for Adults |
|---|---|---|
| Writes recognizable letters and begins to write name and a few words. | • Child makes letters when working at his "Writing Place." <br> • Child writes letters in his/her own name. <br> • Child spontaneously writes letters of the alphabet he/she knows on the white board and says "See all my letters?" <br> • Child writes his/her name on art work. <br> • Child writes "Mom" and "Dad." | • Provide the child with tracing letters, paper, and large pencil, crayons, or markers (washable). <br> • Model for the child how to make letter formations and say, "Start at the top and pull down, then start in the middle, come down around 'b'; now, you try it." <br> • The child usually starts writing the letters in their name. If the child is interested in writing alphabet letters, ask, "What letter do you want to write?" <br> • Using a finger, draw letters on the child's back (this is fun using soap in the tub while taking a bath). <br> • Assist the child to write letters using rope (on the floor) or use string on the table. |
| Uses knowledge of sounds and letters to write some words and phrases (inventive and conventional spelling). | • After going for a walk, the child gets a piece of paper and says, "I'm going to write a story about our walk." The child writes, "Today is Monday. I wlkd (walked) to the prk (park)." <br> • Child writes, "I ms you." <br> • Child sounds out the correct consonant sounds, matching them to the correct letter as he/she reads aloud and writes, putting each letter in the correct sequence with only a few words misspelled, e.g., "I lke appl pie." <br> • After drawing a picture of a computer in his/her journal, the child uses invented spelling to write "I LK CMPTRS." <br> • Child writes sounds he/she hears in familiar words like mom, dad, and Tom. The child writes, "Mom, Dad, Tom" and "I love you." | • Set-up a writing center with many types of writing tools and papers. Include name cards, word lists, picture dictionaries, and alphabet posters for copying. <br> • Make ABC books (both upper and lower case) that have pages with letters written on them. Allow the child to draw a picture that starts with the letter and write a word that starts with the letter (first letter correct; other parts of the word may be spelled phonetically and that's O.K.). <br> • When the child writes you a message, e.g., "Can I go," read it and answer it as soon as possible. Save messages and ask the child to read it back to you again. <br> • When cooking, ask the child to make a list of what he/she needs to get ready to make a favorite snack recipe. <br> • When looking at pictures in books, magazines, or at the child's artwork, ask the child to tell you about the picture or artwork and write a story about it. |

# Wisconsin Model Early Learning Standards
## Section Four

| DEVELOPMENTAL DOMAIN | Page |
|---|---|
| IV. APPROACHES TO LEARNING | 66 |
|     A. CURIOSITY, ENGAGEMENT, AND PERSISTENCE | 68 |
|     B. CREATIVITY AND IMAGINATION | 71 |
|     C. DIVERSITY IN LEARNING | 73 |

# IV. APPROACHES TO LEARNING

This domain, the one most subject to individual variation, recognizes that children approach learning in different ways and emphasizes the development of positive attitudes and dispositions to acquire information. It honors that children learn within the context of their family and culture. It is inclusive of a child's curiosity about the world and the importance that imagination and invention play in openness to new tasks and challenges. It stresses the importance of nurturing initiative, task persistence and attentiveness in learning while encouraging reflection and interpretation. It addresses the important aspect of how we learn as well as what we learn.

**Rationale**

The acquisition of knowledge, skills, and capacities is an insufficient criterion of developmental success. Children must be inclined to marshal such skills and capacities. The way young children approach learning is influenced by their sociocultural environment as well as by individual temperament and gender. All children can and do acquire knowledge. Their ability to integrate information and to demonstrate what they know varies based on all other areas of development along with their individual biology, history, and culture. Children's approaches to learning are often determined by their openness to and curiosity about new tasks and challenges, task persistence, and attentiveness, reflection and interpretation of experiences, imagination and invention, and individual temperament. Approaches to learning encompass attitudes, habits, and learning styles. Young children benefit most from meaningful hands-on experiences and nurturing interactions where the intrinsic joy of learning is emphasized and valued.

## A. CURIOSITY, ENGAGEMENT, AND PERSISTENCE

*Developmental Expectation*

*Children in Wisconsin will use curiosity, engagement and persistence to extend their learning.*

**Performance Standard**

During the early childhood period, children in Wisconsin will show evidence of developmentally appropriate abilities in the following areas:

A.EL. 1   Displays curiosity, risk-taking, and willingness to engage in new experiences.

A.EL. 2   Engages in meaningful learning through attempting, repeating, experimenting, refining, and elaborating on experiences and activities.

A.EL. 3   Exhibits persistence and flexibility.

**Program Standard**

Early care and education programs in Wisconsin will provide the environment, context, and diverse opportunities for children to extend their learning through curiosity, engagement, and persistence.

# IV. APPROACHES TO LEARNING (continued)

## B. CREATIVITY AND IMAGINATION

*Developmental Expectation*

*Children in Wisconsin will use invention, imagination, and play to extend their learning.*

**Performance Standard**

During the early childhood period, children in Wisconsin will show evidence of developmentally appropriate abilities in the following areas:

B. EL. 1 Engages in imaginative play and inventive thinking through interactions with people, materials, and the environment.

B. EL. 2 Expresses self creatively through music, movement, and art.

**Program Standard**

Early care and education programs in Wisconsin will provide the environment, context, and diverse opportunities for children to expand their creativity and imagination.

## C. DIVERSITY IN LEARNING

*Developmental Expectation*

*Children in Wisconsin will engage in diverse approaches to learning that reflect social and cultural contexts such as biology, family history, culture, and individual learning styles.*

**Performance Standard**

During the early childhood period, children in Wisconsin will show evidence of developmentally appropriate abilities in the following areas:

C. EL. 1 Experiences a variety of routines, practices, and languages.

C. EL. 2 Learns within the context of his/her family and culture.

C. EL. 3 Uses various styles of learning including verbal/linguistic, bodily/kinesthetic, visual/spatial, interpersonal, and intrapersonal.

**Program Standard**

Early care and education programs in Wisconsin will provide the environment, context, and opportunities for children to extend their learning through partnerships with parents to honor diversity and individual learning styles.

### Important Reminders

The Wisconsin Model Early Learning Standards recognize that children are individuals who develop at individual rates. While they develop in generally similar stages and sequences, greatly diverse patterns of behavior and learning emerge as a result of the interaction of several factors, including genetic predisposition and physical characteristics, socio-economic status, and the values, beliefs, and cultural and political practices of their families and communities. The Wisconsin Model Early Learning Standards reflect expectations for a typically developing child; adapting and individualizing learning experiences accommodates optimal development for all children.

The Wisconsin Model Early Learning Standards developmental continuum and sample behaviors ARE NOT intended to be used as age markers, a prescriptive listing of development with every first item in a continuum starting at birth, nor as a comprehensive or exhaustive set of sample behaviors of children and sample strategies for adults.

## A. Curiosity, Engagement, and Persistence

**PERFORMANCE STANDARD**: A.EL.1 Displays curiosity, risk-taking, and willingness to engage in new experiences

| Developmental Continuum | Sample Behaviors of Children | Sample Strategies for Adults |
|---|---|---|
| Exhibits brief interest in people and things in their surroundings. | • Child reaches toward objects that captures his/her attention.<br>• Child picks up and explores interesting objects but soon drops them and goes on to something else.<br>• Child notices other children at play.<br>• Child watches a ball as it rolls away, but loses interest when it rolls out of view. | • Include objects and experiences that stimulate the child's senses such as walks outdoors, colorful mobiles, and a variety of music. Notice what captures the interest of the child.<br>• Provide opportunities for child to interact with safe toys as long as he/she is interested. Accept their short attention span.<br>• Provide opportunities for child to play near other children.<br>• Encourage child to look for objects that have gone out of site by asking "Where did the ball go?" |
| Shows growing eagerness and delight in self, others, and in surroundings. | • Child delights in building with simple blocks or puzzles.<br>• Child laughs and giggles when trying to catch water draining from a funnel.<br>• Child asks many questions about new experiences they encounter. | • Provide opportunities to experiment with new materials and activities without fear of making mistakes.<br>• Provide safe toys and natural objects such as sand and water for child to manipulate and explore.<br>• Encourage the child's natural inclination to ask questions and to wonder. Help him/her refine questions and think of ways he/she might gain answers. |
| Attends for longer periods of time and shows preference for some activities. | • Child sits to listen to short stories being read and requests them often.<br>• Child selects favorite toy from a shelf or storage area and plays with it for 15 minutes or more.<br>• Child shows growing capacity to concentrate on a task despite distractions or interruptions.<br>• Child asks for a favorite toy that he/she cannot find. | • Gradually lengthen time child is expected to remain engaged in activities or experiences. For example, read longer stories to expand their attention span.<br>• Rotate toys and books to provide a fresh variety but keep those that the child seems most interested in for longer periods of time.<br>• Store toys, books, and playthings in a way that the child can easily find items he/she prefers, such as on a shelf or book display. Display books so the child can see the covers easily. |
| Is curious about and willing to try new and unfamiliar experiences and activities within their environment. | • Child tries to climb on outdoor play equipment that he/she has not tried before.<br>• Child digs in the dirt to find bugs and worms.<br>• Child watches other children at the table eating a food he/she has not eaten, and then tastes it for the first time.<br>• Child uses woodworking tools he/she has not used before (with supervision). | • Provide play equipment that safely challenges the child. Encourage him/her to expand skills and abilities and still experience success.<br>• Enable the child to explore safely in nature even if you are not comfortable with natural objects or animals yourself. Learn new things together.<br>• Introduce new foods several times. The child may not eat it the first time, but may be willing to try it at a later time.<br>• Offer encouragement that is meaningful and specific to what the child has done, e.g., "You learned how to use a hammer today." |

Listed above are *sample* behaviors of children and *sample* strategies for adults, they are not a definitive list or an exhaustive inventory. They start from an early developmental level and continue through older ages to the completion of kindergarten.

## A. Curiosity, Engagement, and Persistence (continued)

**PERFORMANCE STANDARD:** A.EL. 2 ENGAGES IN MEANINGFUL LEARNING THROUGH ATTEMPTING, REPEATING, EXPERIMENTING, REFINING AND ELABORATING ON EXPERIENCES AND ACTIVITIES

| Developmental Continuum | Sample Behaviors of Children | Sample Strategies for Adults |
|---|---|---|
| Attempts a new skill when encouraged and supported by a safe and secure environment. | • Child reaches for a toy when adult holds it out to him/her.<br>• Child tries to pull self into a standing position when adult holds his/her hands.<br>• Child rolls from back to stomach.<br>• Child takes first steps without holding onto supportive objects.<br>• Child tries to put on own clothes with help from adult. | • Encourage the child to try new skills within the safety of your watchful care.<br>• Offer toys and objects to the child allowing him/her to reach and grasp them in order to strengthen eye-hand coordination.<br>• Hold the child's hands and allow him/her to pull themselves up to standing position in order to strengthen arm and leg muscles.<br>• When child is learning to walk, make sure there is enough space in the room so that he/she does not bump into things. If the child falls, do not alarm him/her, but encourage the child to try again.<br>• When dressing the child, allow him/her to help as much as possible. |
| Attempts a new skill in a variety of environments. | • Child balances and walks on a variety of surfaces, such as grass, sand, ramps, steps, and play structures.<br>• Child puts on own hat when it is time to leave.<br>• Child explores opening doors, cabinets, and drawers.<br>• Child wants to go down the slide repeatedly, and may want to climb up the slide instead of using the steps. | • Allow the child to explore many environments, encouraging exploration while keeping a watchful eye.<br>• Although it may seem time-consuming, allow the child to "do it him or herself" before offering to help<br>• If a child starts to engage in an undesirable or unsafe behavior, gently redirect them to an acceptable activity.<br>• Talk about what the child is doing to enhance his/her learning. |
| Repeats an action many times to gain confidence and skill. | • Child puts the same puzzle together repeatedly.<br>• Child asks for the same story to be read over and over again.<br>• Child continues to do somersaults, even though the child may fall over sideways and bump into things. | • When the child completes a task, ask if he/she would like to do it again? This encourages the child to keep practicing.<br>• Be patient with repeated requests for the same story. The child is becoming familiar with the words and sequence of events and may soon be able to "Read it him/herself" from memory.<br>• Support the child's desire to practice a skill he/she is trying to perfect. |
| Experiments and practices to expand skill level. | • Child begins to do a somersault in a kneeling position and then expands to beginning the somersault from a standing position.<br>• Child paints with a paint brush and then asks adult, "Can I use this sponge to paint a picture?"<br>• After learning how to introduce himself, e.g., "My name is Bill." The child introduces his sister to another friend saying, "This is my sister, her name is Anna." | • Provide materials and equipment so that the child can experiment with new approaches to accomplish a task that the child has learned previously.<br>• Encourage the child to practice and expand a skill by asking about his/her ideas to complete the task.<br>• Praise child for trying something new.<br>• Talk to child while you are trying new ways of cooking, doing activities, or engaging in other routines. Share stories with child about experiences you had trying something new. |
| Refines skills that have been successfully accomplished. | • Child uses new tools to build a sand castle.<br>• Child uses a variety of strategies to get the basketball into the hoop.<br>• Child draws pictures of himself/herself with more attention to detail.<br>• Child builds a block structure with more intricate design. | • Model exploration and use of a variety of familiar and new learning materials and activities.<br>• Encourage child to try new approaches to solving problems. Invite the child to think of multiple solutions. Talk about how it is okay to make mistakes and then keep trying.<br>• Acknowledge child's efforts to expand on previous skills, "Wow, I see you have added earrings, glasses, and eyelashes to your drawing!"<br>• Reinforce child's efforts by taking photographs of his/her and his/her projects and displaying them for the child to comment on and admire. |

Listed above are *sample* behaviors of children and *sample* strategies for adults, they are not a definitive list or an exhaustive inventory. They start from an early developmental level and continue through older ages to the completion of kindergarten.

## A. Curiosity, Engagement, and Persistence *(continued)*

**PERFORMANCE STANDARD:** A.EL. 3 EXHIBITS PERSISTENCE AND FLEXIBILITY

| Developmental Continuum | Sample Behaviors of Children | Sample Strategies for Adults |
|---|---|---|
| Attends to sights and sounds and persists with (continues in) activity only when supported by adult interaction. | • Child continues to play with a ball when the adult rolls it back and forth to him laughing and talking about the ball.<br>• Child concentrates on stacking blocks if the adult helps rebuild the stack when it gets knocked over. | • Encourage child's attention and persistence at tasks by interacting and talking with the child about what he/she is doing.<br>• Respond to child's request for help promptly without being intrusive.<br>• When a child quits or gives up too easily, gently encourage his/her saying "Try one more time." |
| Focuses on activity but may be easily distracted. | • Child continues to roll and retrieve a ball for several minutes with adult nearby until the ball rolls under a shelf and the child cannot find it. The child then abandons the ball and looks for another toy.<br>• Child stacks blocks and knocks them down with adult nearby. After knocking the stack down and briefly trying to restack the blocks, may become frustrated.<br>• Child starts to pick up toys that he/she was playing with but gets re-engaged and starts to play with them again. | • Acknowledge the child's persistence and help him/her to maintain attention with comments such as "Wow! Look how tall you can stack those blocks! Let's try again."<br>• Make frequent comments about the child's efforts such as "You're almost finished. You worked very hard at stacking those blocks."<br>• Understand that in order for the child to learn, he/she will knock down block structures, drop things to watch them fall, and experiment with how things work. Use these opportunities as teachable moments instead of sources of conflict. |
| Persists with activity independently until goal is reached. | • Child continues to roll a ball attempting to knock down cones until all cones are down, and then sets them up and tries again.<br>• Child builds a block structure and rebuilds it after another child accidentally knocks it over.<br>• Child asks if he/she can keep his/her picture and continue to work on it later. | • Provide places and times where child can play or work without interruption.<br>• Reinforce child's persistence by acknowledging his/her behavior such as taking photos of the child's block structure, and posting it so the child can see it often.<br>• Provide a safe place for child to store projects that he/she has not finished and wants to keep working on. |
| Sets and develops goals and follows through on plans making adjustments as necessary, despite distractions and mishaps. | • Child engages in a game of "bowling" with another child; setting up pins and rolling the ball to knock them down.<br>• Child is able to put unfinished work away temporarily and come back to complete it later.<br>• Child has an idea, may ask an adult to help him/her think it through and then carries out the project, adjusting for availability of materials, space or time (block structure, art project, garden planting, simple cooking project). | • Encourage goal setting by asking the child what he/she plans to do.<br>• If the child changes plans, acknowledge the change with comments such as "I see you decided to try something different."<br>• Review with the child what he/she has done during the day, and ask the child to think about what he/she would like to do the next day. |

Listed above are *sample* behaviors of children and *sample* strategies for adults, they are not a definitive list or an exhaustive inventory. They start from an early developmental level and continue through older ages to the completion of kindergarten.

## B. Creativity and Imagination

**PERFORMANCE STANDARD:** B. EL. 1 Engages in imaginative play and inventive thinking through interactions with people, materials, and the environment

| Developmental Continuum | Sample Behaviors of Children | Sample Strategies for Adults |
|---|---|---|
| Watches and imitates the actions of others. | • Child imitates facial expression of adults.<br>• Child smiles when adult smiles at them.<br>• Child imitates giggling when another child giggles.<br>• Child engages adult by playing peek-a-boo. May imitate adult covering eyes or holding up a blanket. | • Smile, talk, and laugh with young children often—even the youngest baby. Even if not talking directly to the child, talk about the task or activity you are engaged in at the moment. This will enhance the child's language and thinking skills.<br>• Hide your face behind your hands or an object such as a book to play peek-a-boo with the child. A small stuffed animal—such as a bunny—can also play peek-a-boo and might capture the child's attention.<br>• Talk to the child with a fun hand puppet. Use a "silly" voice for the puppet. |
| Uses objects in pretend play as they are used in real life, and gradually begins to substitute one object for another in pretend play. | • Child pretends to cook by stirring a spoon in a pan.<br>• Child rolls a round object across the floor to see if it will roll like a ball.<br>• Child holds the toy telephone receiver up to his/her ear with one hand and pokes at the number buttons with the other hand. | • Give young children real and pretend toys that are part of everyday life such as pots and pans, spoons, bowls, or old phones. (Note: Do NOT allow children to play with old cell phones or hand held phones containing batteries for safety reasons.)<br>• Place unbreakable mirrors low on the wall near the child's play area. Make silly faces or pretend animal noises together in front of the mirror.<br>• Select toys and materials that could be used in a variety of ways (sometimes referred to as "open-ended" toys) in which the child's imagination will be engaged. For example: cardboard boxes, drawing/painting materials, and old dress-up clothes. Complex toys (that are often expensive) usually are not as engaging to the child as the box they came in! |
| Recreates and acts out real-life and fantasy experiences in pretend play. | • Child puts a bib on the doll as he/she feeds it from a dish, takes the bib off, and then puts the doll to bed.<br>• Child acts out a visit to the doctor by giving a "shot" to the stuffed animals and then comforting them after the shot.<br>• Child explores being a mommy or daddy as he/she feeds the doll and puts it to bed.<br>• Child makes play dough "cookies" on a plate and offers them to adults or friends to "eat." | • Read books with child and act out some of things that happened in the book such as pretending to be an animal or character (e.g., huff and puff like the wolf in *The Three Little Pigs*).<br>• Have a box of real clothes for the child to "pretend" with.<br>• Play house, cook "pretend" dinner, have a tea party, etc. along with child. Engage the child's imaginative thinking and have fun together.<br>• Take child (even young children) to events such as community children's theatre performances, story hour at the library or local coffee shop, high school theatre or musical performances, etc. |
| Engages in elaborate and sustained imaginative play and can distinguish between real-life and fantasy. | • Child dresses in make-believe clothes and acts out the part dressed for such as mommy/daddy, singer on a stage, firefighter, etc.<br>• Child "plays school" by pretending to read a book to others or does "homework" next to siblings doing real homework.<br>• Child creates and tells made-up and/or silly stories.<br>• Child plans and acts out a tea party with stuffed animals and talks about how the animals cannot really drink the tea because they are not alive. | • Brainstorm ideas, such as "What would happen if…" "What else do you need to know?"<br>• Give space and time for children to explore their interests in depth. If a child has a superior knowledge of outer space, encourage him/her to represent his learning by constructing a spaceship out of cardboard boxes with many realistic details involving windows, gears, and dials.<br>• Expose child to lots of new and different places and experiences such as the fire station, hospitals, airports, a Native American Pow Wow, museums, theatrical performances, etc. |

Listed above are *sample* behaviors of children and *sample* strategies for adults, they are not a definitive list or an exhaustive inventory. They start from an early developmental level and continue through older ages to the completion of kindergarten.

## B. Creativity and Imagination (continued)

**PERFORMANCE STANDARD:** B. EL. 2 EXPRESSES SELF CREATIVELY THROUGH MUSIC, MOVEMENT, AND ART

| Developmental Continuum | Sample Behaviors of Children | Sample Strategies for Adults |
|---|---|---|
| Attends to or responds to movement, music, and visual stimuli. | • Child shows expression of joy when gazing at familiar picture.<br>• Child is comforted by the slow rhythm of a lullaby or may be excited by music with a lively beat.<br>• Child sways to music along with adult.<br>• Child shakes the rattle harder and harder, delighting in the louder noise. | • Play soothing lullaby music at nap time or bedtime for child to listen to when going to sleep.<br>• Play a variety of music (classical, jazz, rock, etc.) for child to listen to in the everyday environment. Sing and dance together with the child—helping him/her to sway or feel the beat of the music.<br>• Provide pictures at the child's eye level for him/her to see. Pictures can be placed next to the diaper changing area or next to a high chair or on the wall next to the child's play area. |
| Shows a preference towards certain types of movement, music, and visual stimuli. | • Child attempts hand movements to finger plays and simple songs.<br>• Child claps their hands to start a game of pat-a-cake.<br>• Child prefers books with bright colors of people, animals, and familiar objects.<br>• Child becomes calm and listens intently to a favorite tune.<br>• Child recognizes a favorite tune on the radio or stereo and dances along. | • Sing simple songs and finger play with the child helping him/her to follow along by gently moving their hands along with yours.<br>• Provide simple noisemakers or instruments and "make music" together by tapping to a beat. Encourage child to make a louder or softer noise to help him/her discriminate between sounds. Note—rice or macaroni in a plastic bottle that is securely sealed makes a simple noisemaker.<br>• Provide books with bright colors, faces of people, animals, and familiar objects in the child's world. Read books together every day.<br>• Give the child old silky scarves to dance with to music. Dance along with the child.<br>• Provide simple drawing materials such as large crayons or markers and encourage experimenting with these materials. (Non-toxic and washable materials are recommended.) |
| Explores the process of using a variety of artistic materials, music, and movement. | • Child uses crayons, paintbrushes, markers, chalk, etc., to mix colors and draw simple pictures.<br>• Child explores a variety of materials such as glue, colored rice, macaroni, glitter, cotton balls, etc., to create pictures.<br>• Child follows a rhythm and beat in music with a simple musical instrument such as a shaker, drum, or triangle.<br>• Child participates in musical games such as the *Hokey Pokey*. | • Provide a larger variety of drawing materials for child to experiment with. Add things such as colored pencils, chalk, or watercolor paints. Provide a variety of materials to draw or paint on such as large freezer wrap paper, old paper bags, old magazines or catalogs, sidewalks, etc.<br>• Help child learn to use glue and provide lots of various materials for the child to "create." Items found in nature (acorns, feathers, leaves, sand, etc.) are particularly appealing to young children to use for creative projects.<br>• Play and sing simple songs and finger plays together (*Itsy Bitsy Spider*, nursery rhymes, or a favorite song on the radio). This is especially fun and helpful during long car rides.<br>• If child is in a school or childcare setting, make a recording of favorite songs to sing and dance to at home. |
| Expresses self (ideas, feelings, and thoughts) through a variety of artistic media, music, and movement. | • Child tries new ideas with play dough, such as using toothpicks as candles for a birthday cake.<br>• Child expresses through movement and dancing what is felt and heard in various musical tempos and styles.<br>• Child progresses in abilities to create drawings, paintings, models, and other art creations that are more detailed, creative, or realistic.<br>• Child participates in musical performances with others that include singing, dancing, or the use of simple instruments. | • Have a variety of art materials available all the time for the child to "create" with. Let child experiment with the materials in any way he/she likes to. Encourage creative expression. (Remember to have a smock or old shirt for the child to help with those "messy" projects.)<br>• Talk to the child about his/her creations. Ask questions such as, "Tell me about your pictures," or "Tell me what's happening in this picture."<br>• Take child to musical performances (ballet or musicals as well as children's performances) so that he/she is exposed to a variety of musical forms. Comment about how the music makes you feel so that the child begins to associate different feelings with different types of music.<br>• Take child to art museums, and use the names of famous artists and talk about their style or how they created their work. Having similar materials available for the child to experiment with can extend this. (An example is providing watercolors after studying Georgia O'Keeffe artwork.) |

Listed above are *sample* behaviors of children and *sample* strategies for adults, they are not a definitive list or an exhaustive inventory. They start from an early developmental level and continue through older ages to the completion of kindergarten.

## C. Diversity in Learning

**PERFORMANCE STANDARD:** C. EL.1 Experiences a variety of routines, practices, and languages

| Developmental Continuum | Sample Behaviors of Children | Sample Strategies for Adults |
|---|---|---|
| Depends on adults to communicate about their routines, cultural preferences, and learning styles. | • Child may be fussy when a routine they have come to expect does not happen in all settings.<br>• Child may become confused when caretakers have different practices in child rearing and varying expectations for child.<br>• Child imitates and repeats the language most commonly heard in their family. (This may be a specific dialect or a blend of languages.)<br>• Child may begin to learn to use simple sign language for "more," "stop" and "sleep." | • Learn about child development so that unrealistic expectations are not placed on the child.<br>• The caregivers of the child need to communicate frequently about routines, and understand the importance of consistency for the child.<br>• Take time to understand various perspectives on child rearing and how these practices may influence how a child is raised.<br>• Use simple sign language for child to signal common activities, and help children who do not speak the primary language.<br>• Explore a variety of ways to communicate between caregivers. |
| Starts to notice differences in routines, practices, and languages. | • Child will become fussy if he/she does not have favorite blanket when it is naptime.<br>• Child will not play in the sandbox because he/she is afraid to get clothes dirty.<br>• Child may eat certain foods with fingers instead of using a utensil.<br>• Child notices that someone is using a cane and wants to touch it.<br>• Child hears someone using another language and tries to imitate it. | • Acknowledge the importance of routines for the child, and honor their need for consistency and comfort.<br>• Take time to understand the reasons for the action of a child and whether it might be the result of their biology or culture.<br>• Be open to various ways of doing things based on biology, culture, or family history.<br>• Help child understand differences by commenting, "we are all different, some of us need canes to walk, some can't walk and need wheelchairs, and some can walk by themselves."<br>• Incorporate opportunities for the child to experience other languages through music, stories, and interactions with persons from various cultures. |
| Asks questions of adults about the differences between various routines, practices, and languages in a variety of settings. | • Child wants to know why they need to take a nap when a friend does not.<br>• Child asks why his/her hair is not braided like other children.<br>• Child tries a new food and wants to know where and how the food is grown.<br>• Child asks why someone needs to wear a hearing aid.<br>• Child asks what a word means in another language. | • Talk to the child about how we are all different: some people need more sleep than others or some need hearing aids to hear. Engage the child to talk about how he/she is special and unique.<br>• Read books about a variety of cultures, geographical locations, and differences.<br>• Honor the language of the child and access resources to enhance learning in his/her primary language as well as other languages. |

Listed above are *sample* behaviors of children and *sample* strategies for adults, they are not a definitive list or an exhaustive inventory. They start from an early developmental level and continue through older ages to the completion of kindergarten.

## C. Diversity in Learning (continued)

**PERFORMANCE STANDARD:** C.EL. 2 Learns within the context of his/her family and culture

| Developmental Continuum | Sample Behaviors of Children | Sample Strategies for Adults |
|---|---|---|
| Reflects their family, culture, and community when engaged in play and learning. | • Child plays with items that are familiar and similar to toys he/she is exposed to in their most common setting.<br>• Child may imitate the mannerisms and behaviors of his/her family members.<br>• Child has certain expectations of adults based upon his/her primary relationships. | • Recognize that a child learns from nurturing interactions with adults with or without materials.<br>• Allow child to display individuality, while teaching him/her about socially appropriate behaviors.<br>• Parents, grandparents, caregivers, and all adults in the lives of the child will benefit from learning about child development and appropriate expectations. |
| Starts to notice that other children and families do things differently. | • Child wants to use chopsticks to eat rice when they see a friend doing so.<br>• Child asks questions while listening to a story about hats from different cultures.<br>• Child wants to know why someone is wearing clothes that are different than what he/she wears. | • Encourage child to try new experiences, and then ask them how it felt to try something different.<br>• Answer the child's questions in a matter-of-fact way, indicating that the world is full of interesting ways to do things.<br>• Read a variety of books about the child's culture as well as other topics that interest them. |
| Understands and accepts diversity in other children and families. | • Child requests song of a particular style or ethnic culture.<br>• Child requests a food prepared the way another family prepares it.<br>• Child talks positively about diverse experiences.<br>• Child seeks recognition for his/her individuality and uniqueness. | • Keep a variety of music available to respond to child's requests.<br>• Share recipes for favorite foods, and try different foods with the child.<br>• Model acceptance and tolerance for diversity in your words and actions.<br>• Reinforce the child for positive comments and experiences when engaged in diverse learning opportunities. |

Listed above are *sample* behaviors of children and *sample* strategies for adults, they are not a definitive list or an exhaustive inventory. They start from an early developmental level and continue through older ages to the completion of kindergarten.

## C. Diversity in Learning (continued)

**PERFORMANCE STANDARD:** C.EL. 3 USES VARIOUS STYLES OF LEARNING SUCH AS VISUAL/SPATIAL, VERBAL/LINGUISTIC, BODILY/KINESTHETIC, INTERPERSONAL, AND INTRAPERSONAL.

| Developmental Continuum | Sample Behaviors of Children | Sample Strategies for Adults |
|---|---|---|
| Tends to have a preferred learning style. | • Child watches how a task is performed before attempting the task himself/herself (visual/spatial).<br>• Child listens for clues to understand how to proceed (verbal/linguistic).<br>• Child learns best when he/she is able to move about (bodily/kinesthetic).<br>• Child prefers to learn new skills when by himself/herself (intrapersonal).<br>• Child learns new skills more quickly when interacting with others (interpersonal). | • Visually demonstrate the appropriate way to use toys and games.<br>• Use language and stories to describe how an activity is done.<br>• Allow child to move around when exploring a new activity.<br>• Permit child to explore new materials independently.<br>• Introduce some activities in small group settings with one or two other children present. |
| Explores other learning styles when introduced by an adult or peer. | • Child follows another child's example of how to dance which is not his/her usual preference.<br>• Child who usually plays alone joins in a small group activity when invited by another child or adult.<br>• Child tries to tie his/her shoe in a different way after watching another child. | • When introducing a new skill or material, use a variety of approaches.<br>• Be aware of your learning style and how that might influence how you interact with a child.<br>• Invite a child who usually learns best independently to join a small group. Start by involving only one other child, then later expand the size of the group when the child is comfortable. |
| Uses a variety of learning styles to meet their needs or achieve their goals. | • Child who does not usually engage in physical activities, joins a new game of tag when invited by a friend.<br>• Child who usually prefers verbal directions, uses a picture diagram to complete a task.<br>• Child who is usually not comfortable handling sticky materials, uses "goop" to complete an art project. | • Provide multiple opportunities to learn using different learning styles.<br>• Encourage child to demonstrate what he/she is learning in a variety of ways.<br>• Encourage child to learn from others, and support his/her efforts to share ideas and different approaches to learning. When looking at how a task can be accomplished, discuss a variety of approaches.<br>• Provide directions in a variety of formats such as verbal, written, diagrams, and modeling. |

Listed above are *sample* behaviors of children and *sample* strategies for adults, they are not a definitive list or an exhaustive inventory. They start from an early developmental level and continue through older ages to the completion of kindergarten.

# Wisconsin Model Early Learning Standards
## Section Five

| DEVELOPMENTAL DOMAIN | Page |
|---|---|
| V. COGNITION AND GENERAL KNOWLEDGE | 78 |
| A. EXPLORATION, DISCOVERY, AND PROBLEM SOLVING | 80 |
| B. MATHEMATICAL THINKING | 85 |
| C. SCIENTIFIC THINKING | 96 |

# V. COGNITION AND GENERAL KNOWLEDGE

This domain recognizes children's search for meaning as the basis for intellectual development. The components focus on children's curiosity about the world and their developing ability to acquire, organize, and use information in increasingly complex ways to satisfy that curiosity. Children are engaged in and appreciate the arts as an organizing framework for expressing ideas and feelings. Primary components include mathematics and logical thinking, scientific thinking, and problem-solving.

## Rationale

Children acquire knowledge by linking prior experiences to new learning situations. As a child applies and extends prior knowledge to new experiences, he or she refines concepts or forms new ones. Cognition is a fluid process by which children use thinking skills to conceptually develop a construct of the world, thus enabling active learning. General knowledge is a product of cognition, which expands and grows through learning and self-expression.

## A. EXPLORATION, DISCOVERY, AND PROBLEM SOLVING

### Developmental Expectation

*Children in Wisconsin will develop their capacity to use cognitive skills as a tool to acquire knowledge and skills. These skills include reasoning, reflection, and interpretation.*

### Performance Standard

During the early childhood period, children in Wisconsin will show evidence of developmentally appropriate abilities in the following areas:

A. EL. 1   Uses multi-sensory abilities to process information.

A. EL. 2   Understands new meanings as memory increases.

A. EL. 3   Applies problem solving skills.

### Program Standard

Early care and education programs in Wisconsin will provide a supportive context and increasingly complex opportunities for children to explore, discover, and solve problems.

## B. MATHEMATICAL THINKING

### Developmental Expectation

*Children in Wisconsin will understand and use early mathematical concepts and logical thinking processes to extend their learning.*

### Performance Standard

During the early childhood period, children in Wisconsin will show evidence of developmentally appropriate abilities in the following areas:

B. EL. 1   Demonstrates an understanding of numbers and counting.

B. EL. 2   Understands number operations and relationships.

B. EL. 3   Explores, recognizes, and describes, shapes and spatial relationships.

B. EL. 4   Uses the attributes of objects for comparison and patterning.

B. EL. 5   Understands the concept of measurement.

B. EL. 6   Collects, describes, and records information using all senses.

### Program Standard

Early care and education programs in Wisconsin will provide a supportive context and increasingly complex opportunities for children to extend their learning though the use of mathematical and logical thinking processes.

# V. COGNITION AND GENERAL KNOWLEDGE (continued)

**C. SCIENTIFIC THINKING**

*Developmental Expectation*

*Children in Wisconsin will understand and use scientific tools and skills to extend their learning.*

**Performance Standard**

During the early childhood period, children in Wisconsin will show evidence of developmentally appropriate abilities in the following areas:

C. EL. 1 Uses observation to gather information.

C. EL. 2 Uses tools to gather information, compare observed objects, and seek answers to questions through active investigation.

C. EL. 3 Hypothesizes and makes predictions.

C. EL. 4 Forms explanations based on trial and error, observations, and explorations.

**Program Standard**

Early care and education programs in Wisconsin will provide the environment, context, and increasingly complex opportunities for children to extend their learning through the use of scientific reasoning.

---

### Important Reminders

The Wisconsin Model Early Learning Standards recognize that children are individuals who develop at individual rates. While they develop in generally similar stages and sequences, greatly diverse patterns of behavior and learning emerge as a result of the interaction of several factors, including genetic predisposition and physical characteristics, socio-economic status, and the values, beliefs, and cultural and political practices of their families and communities. The Wisconsin Model Early Learning Standards reflect expectations for a typically developing child; adapting and individualizing learning experiences accommodates optimal development for all children.

The Wisconsin Model Early Learning Standards developmental continuum and sample behaviors ARE NOT intended to be used as age markers, a prescriptive listing of development with every first item in a continuum starting at birth, nor as a comprehensive or exhaustive set of sample behaviors of children and sample strategies for adults.

## A. Exploration, Discovery, and Problem Solving

**PERFORMANCE STANDARD:** A.EL. 1 USES MULTI-SENSORY ABILITIES TO PROCESS INFORMATION

| Developmental Continuum | Sample Behaviors of Children | Sample Strategies for Adults |
|---|---|---|
| Uses senses to explore the environment. | • Child responds to too much stimulation (touch, sounds, light, and voices) by looking away, crying, yawning, or sleeping.<br>• Child follows objects and people with eyes. May prefer shiny objects and faces, especially eyes and mouth.<br>• Child looks at hands or plays with feet while lying in the crib or on the floor.<br>• Child turns head toward familiar (caregiver or family members) voices.<br>• Child explores objects using hands, mouth, and tongue. | • Talk and sing to the child while holding, changing diapers, bathing, and when working or moving anywhere near the child.<br>• Provide a variety of interesting objects and toys that make noise, e.g., rattle, crinkly material, music box, squeeze toys.<br>• Provide stuffed animals, doll with happy face, and toy with a smiling person face.<br>• Place a safe, interesting mobile on the child's crib. |
| Uses senses to explore and experiment with new materials. | • Child laughs while splashing and playing with water and water toys during bath time.<br>• Child experiments with tastes of new foods and decides likes and dislikes<br>• Child engages in poking, dropping, pushing, pulling, and squeezing objects to see what will happen.<br>• Child explores and experiments with modeling clay, shaving cream, and other materials such as sand, dirt, and water. | • Provide the child with water toys during bath time.<br>• Introduce new foods to determine which foods the child likes and dislikes. A doctor or pediatrician will tell the adult when to introduce certain types of foods.<br>• Provide the child with safe toys and objects that he/ she can chew, push, pull, squeeze, and roll. Provide the child with toys that make sounds when the child pushes on or moves certain parts of the toy.<br>• Provide safe ways for the child to try something new, e.g., painting with fingers, hands, or wooden sticks. Use plastic gloves to work with shaving cream. Use plastic cooking cutters when playing with modeling clay. |
| Uses senses and a variety of strategies to investigate information. | • Child uses cups, spoons, hands, and other tools to dig in dirt, sand, and rice table to find out "What's in here?" and to hide objects.<br>• Child inspects all moving parts of toys such as the wheels, doors, and other small moving parts.<br>• Child smells odor from another room and asks, "Who made popcorn?" | • Fill a large tub with rice and give the child toys, kitchen items, and other small safe items to play with in the "rice tub."<br>• Bring toys and objects to play with in the sand at the beach.<br>• Call attention to and talk with the child about smells outside and inside the house. "What do you smell?"<br>• Help the child to compare and contrast by going on "hunts" around the room for something that looks, sounds, feels, or smells the same. |
| Uses senses to generalize and apply prior learning. | • Child uses a variety of ways to use crayons, markers, scissors, and paper to create "works of art."<br>• Child uses tools to take things apart and attempts to put them back together the same way or invent new structures using the parts.<br>• Child compares smells saying, "That smells good like my mother's perfume." Or "That smells yucky like my grandpa's barnyard."<br>• Child has preferences for sounds and music and asks adult, "Will you play guitar music?" "I don't like loud drum music." | • Provide the child a place to "work" with a variety of materials and let him/her create own art work, take apart real objects (safe objects) such as toaster and clock, and put them back together. Allow the child to create with natural materials, e.g., sand, grass clippings, rocks, water etc. in a safe place outside of the house.<br>• Provide experiences that require the child to use multiple senses, e.g., cooking to experience seeing changes and smelling and tasting the results.<br>• Have child close his/her eyes. Have several different items such as fruits and ask the child, "What does this smell like?" Use two different fruits and say, "Does this one smell like this one?"<br>• Provide child with toys and instruments that make music. Provide variety of musical experiences in which the child can participate by singing, playing, listening, and dancing. Select music from many cultures. |

Listed above are *sample* behaviors of children and *sample* strategies for adults, they are not a definitive list or an exhaustive inventory. They start from an early developmental level and continue through older ages to the completion of kindergarten.

## A. Exploration, Discovery, and Problem Solving (continued)

**PERFORMANCE STANDARD:** A.EL. 2 UNDERSTANDS NEW MEANINGS AS MEMORY INCREASES

| Developmental Continuum | Sample Behaviors of Children | Sample Strategies for Adults |
|---|---|---|
| Observes and imitates sounds and movements. | • Child imitates waving bye-bye and playing peek-a-boo.<br>• Child picks up telephone and places it next to ear and starts to "babble/talk."<br>• Child pushes chair up to computer and pushes at the keys to "work" with adult.<br>• Child points to some body parts when asked, "Show me your head (nose, eyes, tummy, feet)." | • Wave bye-bye to your child as you say "bye-bye" when you or other people are leaving.<br>• Play simple peek-a-boo game by putting a very small blanket over the child's head, pulling it off and saying "Peek-a-boo, Timmy" "Where's Timmy?" Child puts small blanket over his/her own head and waits for adult to say "Peek-a-boo."<br>• Encourage child's play and "babble/talk" as they make-believe with objects such as a phone by saying "Hello Jose, this is mom," etc. |
| Understands that objects and people continue to exist when they are removed from the child's immediate environment. (Object Permanence.) | • Child hides a toy car and later remembers and looks in the same location for the toy car.<br>• When the child sees his/her "blankie" under one bucket and then under another bucket, the child watches and can correctly locate the "blankie" in the second hiding place.<br>• When playing hide and seek with an adult, the child can find the adult in the same hiding place used previously by the adult.<br>• When asked, "Where's your coat?" the child looks for the coat. | • Play a game showing the child an object, and then slowly removing it from the child's view. See if the child will look for the object, and then play the same game by hiding the object himself/herself and then find it again.<br>• As the child watches, hide a favorite object or toy under one bucket and then under another bucket. After watching, the child will correctly locate the object or toy in the last hiding place.<br>• Play hide-and-seek with your child. Watch and observe the child finding you in the same place you hid the last time. |
| Remembers and recalls events. | • After reading a book with an adult, child can tell what happened in the story.<br>• After watching adult make cookies, child wants to roll the cookies and pat them in the pan.<br>• After seeing an adult stack boxes, the child plays independently nesting and/or stacking toys as previously seen done.<br>• Child sings parts of a song, rhyme, or finger play heard earlier said or sung by an adult. | • Adult tells a story and asks the child, "What happened first, and then what happened next?"<br>• Child makes cookies with adult. When another adult comes into the room, child is asked, "Can you tell _____, how we made cookies?"<br>• Provide lots of opportunities for conversation and for children to hear and use language in its many uses and forms, e.g., poems, nursery rhymes, recordings, games, stories. |
| Recognizes functional uses of items in the environment. | • Child pretends to feed the doll with a dish and spoon and covers the doll with a blanket when putting the doll to bed.<br>• Child uses the small shovel found in the garage to dig in the dirt. The child asks for help to put water in a watering can so that he/she can water the plants outside.<br>• When adult says, "It is time to clean the carpet," child goes to the closet to get the vacuum cleaner. | • Using everyday household items, play and pretend with your child.<br>• Name the items you are using, and talk to your child about the items. When appropriate and safe, show your child how to use the item.<br>• Both inside and outside of the house, provide the child with "child size" tools so that they can do the same thing the adult is doing with a larger tool. |

Listed above are *sample* behaviors of children and *sample* strategies for adults, they are not a definitive list or an exhaustive inventory. They start from an early developmental level and continue through older ages to the completion of kindergarten.

## A. Exploration, Discovery, and Problem Solving *(continued)*

**PERFORMANCE STANDARD:** A.EL. 2 UNDERSTANDS NEW MEANINGS AS MEMORY INCREASES (CONTINUED)

| Developmental Continuum | Sample Behaviors of Children | Sample Strategies for Adults |
|---|---|---|
| Practices and applies new information or vocabulary to an activity or interaction (representation and symbolic thinking). | • Child takes on pretend roles such as being the "dad, mom, or teacher" as he/she plays with two other children.<br>• Child uses objects and other materials to "make believe."<br>• Child makes and interprets what he/she creates, e.g., uses blocks to build a building and says, "This is the king's castle. I want to tell you a story about the king." | • Allow large amounts of time for independent child directed activities. Offer a wide range of learning experiences and materials.<br>• Ask child to tell you about his/her very creative drawing. While the child is telling you the story, ask the child if he/she would like you to write the story on his/her paper.<br>• Participate in "make believe and pretend" play with the child and other children. |
| Generates a rule, strategy, or idea from a previous learning experience and applies to a new context. | • Child explains to family members about fire safety learned at school. The child asks, "How do we get out of the house if we have a fire (at home)?"<br>• In the house area the child says, "We all need to be sitting at the table before we can start to eat." (Rule at home)<br>• Child says to little brother at home, "My teacher says we always need to say, 'Thank You' when someone does something nice for you."<br>• Child enjoys playing games that have simple rules such as *Candy Land* and *Go Fish*. | • When child talks about rules at school, have a conversation with the child about why the rule is important for the child and other children.<br>• Provide predictable routines and simple rules for the child during bath time, bed time, dinner time, play time, e.g., sitting at the table to eat a meal, picking up toys when finished playing with them, reading a book before bedtime, etc. The child will learn that "This is the way we do it at our house."<br>• Provide board games such as *Candy Land* and *Color Bingo*. Provide card games such as *Go Fish* and *Old Maid*. Remind child if he/she forgets a part of the game rules. |

Listed above are *sample* behaviors of children and *sample* strategies for adults, they are not a definitive list or an exhaustive inventory. They start from an early developmental level and continue through older ages to the completion of kindergarten.

## A. Exploration, Discovery, and Problem Solving (continued)

**PERFORMANCE STANDARD:** A.EL. 3 APPLIES PROBLEM SOLVING SKILLS

| Developmental Continuum | Sample Behaviors of Children | Sample Strategies for Adults |
|---|---|---|
| Demonstrates awareness of a problem. | • Child indicates hunger or pain with different cries.<br>• Child kicks foot when it becomes stuck in blanket.<br>• Child grunts when toy rolls out of reach. | • Become aware of and sensitive to the various cries of the child. React and respond to the child's cries for hunger or pain.<br>• When the adult can see that the child is struggling, rearrange the environment or material and/or remove the child from the situation or problem.<br>• If the child is unable to get the toy he/she wants, get it for him/her and give it to him/her. |
| Uses an object or part of an object to obtain another object and moves around large objects. | • Child uses a stick to get a ball that rolled under the couch.<br>• Child pulls the cord on the telephone to obtain the telephone.<br>• Child climbs on a stool to get something he/she wants.<br>• Child pushes cart around furniture or obstacles.<br>• Child pushes a chair out of the way to get what he/she needs.<br>• Child will go around a person, chair, or table to get to a desired toy or object. | • Play a game by placing a desired object out of reach but visible to the child. Provide the child with a small safe stool, a stick from a drum set, or other objects that he/she can use to reach other desired objects.<br>• Provide the child with push toys for both inside and outside.<br>• Play games with the child such as putting your body in front of something the child would like to have access to, and watch how the child will try to find a way to get around your body. |
| Asks questions, seeks information, and tests out possibilities. | • Child asks the question, "Will the new rabbit cage be big enough for all the new baby bunnies?"<br>• Child says to adult, "Will this little rock grow into a big rock?" Adult says, "How can we find out if the rock will grow?"<br>• Child shows adult a game and asks, "Do I have enough birthday money to buy this game?" Adult says, "How will we find out?" | • Encourage child to try new things and solve problems creatively. Respond positively to mistakes or errors.<br>• Introduce everyday household materials and toys that can be used in more than one way.<br>• Encourage the child to ask questions and to wonder. Help him/her refine questions and think of ways he/she might get answers.<br>• When the child asks if the cage will be big enough for all the new rabbits, say to the child, "Do you think it will be big enough?" "How can we find out if it is big enough?" "What can we do if the cage is not big enough?"<br>• Use children's books as resources to find the answers to the child's questions, e.g., "Will little rocks grow into big rocks?" |
| Determines and evaluates solutions. | • Given a chair that would fit a doll, child, or an adult, the adult asks, "Could I sit in this doll chair," and the child says, "No, you need to sit in this big chair."<br>• The adult asks the child, "Can we use this water to glue these two pieces of paper together?" The child says, "No, water isn't sticky."<br>• When cleaning up blocks, the child says, "We can't put the blocks in this can, because the blocks are too big." | • Talk to your child about situations, and ask questions that will cause the child to think about the situation, evaluate the situation, try-out some solutions, and tell you what worked and why.<br>• Ask your child questions, e.g., "What do you think, Mary? Should we try using this bag (large) or this bag (small) to put the toys in?"<br>• Ask the child, "What can you try?" when the child asks for help, e.g., the paint jar has dry paint in it so the paint will not work for painting a picture. |

Listed above are *sample* behaviors of children and *sample* strategies for adults, they are not a definitive list or an exhaustive inventory. They start from an early developmental level and continue through older ages to the completion of kindergarten.

## A. Exploration, Discovery, and Problem Solving *(continued)*

**PERFORMANCE STANDARD:** A.EL. 3 APPLIES PROBLEM SOLVING SKILLS (CONTINUED)

| Developmental Continuum | Sample Behaviors of Children | Sample Strategies for Adults |
|---|---|---|
| Makes statements and appropriately answers questions that require reasoning about objects, situations, or people. | • Child says, "She is sad." The adult asks, "How do you know the girl is sad?" The child answers, "She is crying."<br>• Child pushes the train around the track. When the child notices the track is broken, the child says, "Uh-oh, the train is going to fall off the track."<br>• The adult points to the doghouse and asks, "What would happen if I rolled the ball over there?" The child says, "The dog would chase it and chew it up." | • When reading an exciting book to the child, stop and ask, "What do you think will happen next?"<br>• Deliberately interfere with the child's activity, e.g., remove a piece of the track from the train set, and see what the child will do to solve the problem.<br>• Engage child in determining solutions to questions or problems, "It is raining, and we can't go outside. What could we do instead?" |
| Uses multiple strategies to solve problems. | • Child tries to tie shoe by self. After no success, asks another child to help. After no success, asks an adult for assistance.<br>• Child attempts to shovel the snow off the sidewalk. When the child cannot make the shovel pick-up the snow, child uses a box to put the snow in and then realizes that the box is too heavy for him/her to carry off the sidewalk. Child then decides to ask his/her caregiver to use the snow blower to get the snow off the sidewalk. | • Provide materials and activities that are open ended, allowing the child opportunities to experiment and problem-solve to carry them out. Take time with the child after activities to talk about the solutions that the child chooses, how the solutions worked, and how other solutions might have worked.<br>• When the child has tried several strategies and nothing is working, provide the child with strategies, e.g., "It really helps when you look for the very first letter of your name to find the paper that belongs to you." |

Listed above are *sample* behaviors of children and *sample* strategies for adults, they are not a definitive list or an exhaustive inventory. They start from an early developmental level and continue through older ages to the completion of kindergarten.

## B. Mathematical Thinking

**PERFORMANCE STANDARD:** B.EL. 1 Demonstrates understanding of numbers and counting

| Developmental Continuum | Sample Behaviors of Children | Sample Strategies for Adults |
|---|---|---|
| Explores numbers and imitates counting. | • Child plays with magnetic numbers on the refrigerator.<br>• Child points to number "2" when reading a picture book with adult.<br>• Child holds up 3 fingers when asked, "How old are you?"<br>• Sings counting songs and participates in counting finger plays.<br>• The adult counts 1, 2, 3 and the child repeats 1, 2, 3. | • Read children's books together about numbers, counting, and other concepts.<br>• Find as many ways as possible to make counting and numbers a part of everyday activities.<br>• When playing with the child, count people, blocks in a tower, and buttons on a jacket.<br>• Sing number songs, say rhymes and finger plays with numbers such as "1, 2, Buckle My Shoe." |
| Arranges sets of objects in one-to-one correspondence. | • Child sets table so that everyone gets 1 plate and 1 napkin.<br>• Child gives each friend 1 cookie. | • Working together, do one-to-one matching with small colored cubes or stringing beads for a necklace.<br>• Set the table with the child, adult puts the plates on the table, child places napkins and forks.<br>• Tell the child, "Give one cookie to each friend." |
| Can rote count and counts concrete objects to 5 and beyond. | • Child counts 5 blocks in the block center.<br>• Child fills in with the next number (4) when counting beads, "1, 2, 3..."<br>• Child counts correctly while pointing to each object saying, "1, 2, 3, 4, and 5..."<br>• Child counts 1, 2, 3, 4, 5 while going up the steps.<br>• When the child sees 5 brown coins says, "There are 5 pennies." | • Teach and sing counting songs, rhymes, and chants having the child use flannel board pieces or objects to count, e.g., "1-2-3-4-5, I caught a fish alive."<br>• Play games that ask children to clap and count, stomp and count, e.g., "Simon says, "Clap 4 times, stomp 5 times, etc."<br>• Look at counting books together, asking the child, "count how many balloons there are on this page." If there are 5 balloons on the page on the left and 6 puppies on the page on the right ask, "Which page has more?" |
| Recognizes some numerals and associates number concepts with print materials in a meaningful way. | • Child sees a 5 on a calendar and says, "That's a 5."<br>• Child counts number of animals on the page of a picture book.<br>• Child puts 5 flannel apples on the flannel tree that has the number 5 written under it.<br>• When playing with rubber number puzzles, the child puts the correct piece with the number on it with the number of dots on the other puzzle piece. | • Display numerals in order in the environment in meaningful ways, e.g., on a calendar, on a counting line, on sign-in sheets.<br>• Encourage the child to point to the numbers he/she can count.<br>• Ask the child when counting and ordering objects in everyday activities, "Which is first, second, third, etc.?" |
| Names and writes some numerals. | • Child writes "4" and says "I am 4"(years old).<br>• Child makes a 1 through 5 (or 10) number book after visiting an apple orchard, e.g., 1 apple (cut from paper), 2 apple prints, 3 apple seeds glued on, etc. The child writes the number on the page with the representation of that numeral.<br>• Child writes numbers on tags and puts them on items for sale in the pretend "store area." | • Provide the child with different writing materials and number stencils for tracing or number stamps to use for printing.<br>• Make individual number books with stickers, pictures, handprints, or collage materials. Make sets and allow child to write the number to represent "how many on each page." |

Listed above are *sample* behaviors of children and *sample* strategies for adults, they are not a definitive list or an exhaustive inventory. They start from an early developmental level and continue through older ages to the completion of kindergarten.

## B. Mathematical Thinking (continued)

**PERFORMANCE STANDARD:** B.EL. 1 Demonstrates understanding of numbers and counting (continued)

| Developmental Continuum | Sample Behaviors of Children | Sample Strategies for Adults |
|---|---|---|
| Counts with 1 to 1 correspondence up to 20 objects and can tell the number that comes next. | • Child counts using objects such as cards, number cubes, or dominoes that have familiar dot patterns.<br>• When selecting 10 apples from a bag, the child takes out 6 apples and continues counting 7, 8, 9, and 10.<br>• Child can count 3 sets of 5 bundles of sticks up to 15 (5, 10, 15) and then finishes counting the rest of the sticks by ones 16, 17, 18, 19, 20.<br>• Child says, "I am 5, next year I will be 6." "My sister is 9, next year she will be 10." | • Make use of fingers for counting and encourage the child to do so.<br>• The adult points to each object as he/she counts to model that one number corresponds with each object, e.g., counting pennies, crackers, sticks, cups, glasses, plates.<br>• Assist the child to count money. Count money in his/her piggy bank or play money used to play store. Count out change so that the child becomes familiar with the coins and their amounts.<br>• Provide the child with counting sticks and tell the child to put 1 stick on each number on a number line or calendar. When the child has 10 sticks, put a band around the set of 10. Then start counting from 10 by ones until the child has 10 more sticks, and again band them together to show a second set of 10 equaling 20. |
| Names and can write number symbols 1 through 20 and beyond. | • Child can name the numbers on a calendar.<br>• Child points out numbers he/she knows in the: grocery store, shopping in other stores, noticing house numbers, street numbers, or fire numbers.<br>• Child enjoys writing numbers while playing "store." He/she writes the cost of each of the food items and puts the tag on the food or pretends to add the amount of the foods at the cash register. | • Provide number charts or calendars for the child so that he/she can look at the number and copy it.<br>• Point to numbers at the grocery store and say, "See, the bananas cost 27 cents per pound." "The apple costs 35 cents." |
| May rote count to 100 and may count to 100 by 5's and 10's. | • Child tells family member, "I can count to 100, do you want to hear me?"<br>• Child can count by 5's using the numbers chart when 5's are in blue, counts to 100 by saying 5, 10, 15, 20, etc. Child can do the same when counting by 10's when the 10's are in blue on the number chart by saying 10, 20, 30, etc.<br>• Child can count to 100 by 5's and 10's without the use of a number chart. | • Play counting games outdoors. Walk together outside and count as each step is taken. Say, "Let's see if we can count 100 steps?" or "Let's see how many cars (trucks, buses) we can count as we travel in the car."<br>• Say to the child, "Count as far as you can go."<br>• Provide number charts containing 1 through 100. |

Listed above are *sample* behaviors of children and *sample* strategies for adults, they are not a definitive list or an exhaustive inventory. They start from an early developmental level and continue through older ages to the completion of kindergarten.

## B. Mathematical Thinking (continued)

**PERFORMANCE STANDARD:** B.EL.2 UNDERSTANDS NUMBER OPERATIONS AND RELATIONSHIPS

| Developmental Continuum | Sample Behaviors of Children | Sample Strategies for Adults |
|---|---|---|
| Compares concrete quantities to determine which has more, less, or the same. | • At snack-time, the child uses number words saying, "I have the same number of pretzels you do," or "Everyone at snack has 2 crackers and 1 cup of juice," or "I have less juice in my cup, because asked for just a little."<br>• Child says, "I have more modeling clay."<br>• Child equally distributes a set of objects into 2 or more smaller sets, e.g., shares 6 crackers with 3 friends equally. | • When you are playing with the child in the bathtub or working at the water/sand table or cooking, use the words "more, less, same."<br>• Ask child questions about which has more, less, or same. "Is there more milk in this glass or this one?" "Do we have the same number of spoons as bowls?"<br>• Ask comparison questions such as, "Do we have enough chairs for everyone?" |
| Recognizes that a set of objects remains the same amount if physically rearranged. | • Child counts 3 blocks in a vertical line and 3 blocks in a horizontal line and recognizes that each row contains 3 blocks.<br>• Child can group and regroup a given set in the context of daily activities and play, e.g., 5 blocks can be 2 blue and 3 green or 1 blue and 4 green blocks.<br>• Child tells "how many" 3 is when looking at 3 objects in a row, or 3 objects diagonally placed, or 3 object in a vertical row.<br>• 5 raisins are in the child's hand, and 5 raisins are spread on the table. Child knows that there are the same number of raisins in the hand as the raisins spread out on the table. | • When the child understands number order, the child will observe that whether counting a row of 3 cookies from left to right or the 3 cookies are in a different order, the child will know that the amount of cookies is still 3.<br>• Place 5 pennies in a bowl, 5 pennies spread out in a row, and 5 pennies close together on the table. Ask the child, "Point to which one has more pennies?" If the child says there are more pennies in the row say, "Let's count the pennies to find out." |
| Identifies "1 more" and "1 less." | • Child counts 2 groups of blocks and determines if 1 group has 1 more or less than the other group.<br>• Child says, "I need 1 more mitten." | • Play finger games of "Which is more and which is less?" Hold up 4 fingers on 1 hand and 3 fingers on the other. Which hand has "1 more?" Or, which hand has "1 less."<br>• When playing with toys or games ask, "Who needs 1 more car?" or say, "I have 1 less block than you do" or "I need to move 1 more space on the game board." |
| Joins (combines) and separates groups of objects. | • Child combines 2 sets of 3 objects and says, "Now there are 6."<br>• Child discovers that 7 can be made up of 2 green cubes and 5 orange cubes or 3 orange cubes and 4 green cubes.<br>• When shown a picture with 4 cookies and asked, "If your mom said you could share these cookies with a friend, mark how many cookies you could have." The child puts a mark on 2 cookies and says, "I could have only 2."<br>• Solves single digit addition and subtraction problems verbally, e.g., 5+1=6 or 5-4=1. | • Assist the child to put groups together and take groups apart so that he/she begins to understand the concept of addition and subtraction using concrete objects.<br>• Encourage the child to make new arrangements by putting materials together and taking them apart so the arrangement looks different. Use materials such as blocks, paper, boxes, beads, etc.<br>• Place 8 blocks in a group, have the child count them. Say, "If I take 2 of your blocks away, how many will you have left?" Then ask "If I give you 2 more blocks, how many will you have all together?" |

Listed above are *sample* behaviors of children and *sample* strategies for adults, they are not a definitive list or an exhaustive inventory. They start from an early developmental level and continue through older ages to the completion of kindergarten.

## B. Mathematical Thinking *(continued)*

**PERFORMANCE STANDARD:** B.EL. 2 UNDERSTANDS NUMBER OPERATIONS AND RELATIONSHIPS (CONTINUED)

| Developmental Continuum | Sample Behaviors of Children | Sample Strategies for Adults |
|---|---|---|
| Recognizes that there are parts that make up a whole and recognizes "less than" a whole. | • When having a snack the child says, "This is a little piece of the big apple."<br>• Child picks up a puzzle piece and says, "This piece belongs to the cat puzzle."<br>• When asked, "We have 1 small pizza and 2 people to eat it, what can we do?" The child says, "We can cut it in half."<br>• Child says, "I have half a peanut butter cookie and half a sugar cookie," after breaking the 2 whole cookies in half and sharing 2 halves with a friend. | • Give the child 4 crackers and tell him/her to "Share the crackers with a friend so you both have the same amount of crackers." After the child has shared the crackers say, "You divided the crackers, and now you each have 2."<br>• The adult says, "Lisa, can you show us how old your brother is?" Lisa holds up 5 fingers on one hand and 1 on the other hand. Adult says, "Can you think of another way to show 6 with your fingers?"<br>• Provide the child with three-dimensional objects such as balls, toy animals, and people that come apart in pieces and can be put back together as a whole. |
| Estimates and uses words such as more than, less/fewer than, about, near, approximately, and in between. | • Child says, "I don't think there are enough apples for all the kids."<br>• Child says, "I think there are about a hundred ants in this sand pile."<br>• Adult says, "How many children do you think could fit into the wagon?" Child says, "More than 2." Adult says, "Let's find out." | • Ask the child to tell the adult about how many cups of sand it will take to fill the bucket.<br>• Play games of guessing how many red cars you will see as you drive to a friend's house.<br>• Ask the child questions such as, "Do you think we will have enough crackers for snack?"<br>• During snack, sand or water play, and art activities, encourage the child to "test" his/her estimation to see if it is correct. |

Listed above are *sample* behaviors of children and *sample* strategies for adults, they are not a definitive list or an exhaustive inventory. They start from an early developmental level and continue through older ages to the completion of kindergarten.

## B. Mathematical Thinking (continued)

**PERFORMANCE STANDARD**: B.EL. 3 EXPLORES, RECOGNIZES AND DESCRIBES SHAPES AND SPATIAL RELATIONSHIPS

| Developmental Continuum | Sample Behaviors of Children | Sample Strategies for Adults |
|---|---|---|
| Explores shapes and spatial relationships. | • Child puts a small ball in a container.<br>• Child fits some shapes into a ball with corresponding cutout shapes.<br>• Child completes simple puzzles (pieces fit separate spaces).<br>• Child plays inside a cardboard box or a small child's playhouse and brings other objects and materials that fit inside the space. | • Provide simple puzzles and manipulatives that include a variety of shapes and sizes.<br>• Provide simple puzzles with 4 to 6 individual pieces that fit into shapes that match the puzzle pieces.<br>• Provide shape forms and colored rubber bands for the child to explore making shapes and experience spatial relationships.<br>• Provide large boxes (refrigerator, stove boxes), small tents, child playhouse, and other places for the child to explore and play inside. |
| Recognizes basic shapes. | • Child can point to a circle, square, and triangle and put correct shape in matching space.<br>• When shapes are overlapping, the child can find individual shapes of circles, triangles, and squares.<br>• Child makes pictures with magnetic shapes.<br>• Child draws or paints shapes on paper and names the shape. Child says, "This is a heart shape."<br>• Child identifies and names shapes that are unseen enclosed in a "touch box." The child describes the shape by touching and feeling it and then takes it out to sort it.<br>• Child sorts different triangle and square shapes noticing that, "All triangles have 3 sides and corners. Some are tall and thin. Some are short and fat. A rectangle has 4 sides and corners." | • Include a variety of geometric shapes throughout the environment, e.g., shape labels on tables and cubbies, shapes on bulletin boards, and shape mobiles.<br>• When riding in the car play *I spy*, e.g., "Let's spy any squares we see. I spy a square house, square windows, or square signs." Do the same with other shapes like triangles and rectangles.<br>• Play games such as *Memory* and *Shape Bingo*.<br>• Provide materials for the child to make shape pictures using shape forms, drawing shapes, painting shapes.<br>• For snack, give the child shape crackers and peanut butter to hold them together.<br>• Provide pre-cut Styrofoam shapes and let the child construct 2- and 3-dimensional structures. Use the shapes for dipping in paint and printing on paper. |
| Assembles puzzles of at least 15 intersecting pieces (5-10 at age 3; 15 at age 4; 25 at age 5). | • Child can put simple puzzles together where each shape goes into one slot, e.g., house shape, ball shape, progressing to more difficult puzzles with interlocking pieces.<br>• When given a puzzle, the child can independently put together correctly a 5-10 piece puzzle increasing to 15-25 piece puzzles.<br>• While putting the puzzle together, the child chooses a puzzle piece and after placing it chooses another explaining, "This piece will fit with these two other pieces." | • Provide a variety of interesting children's puzzles for the child. Provide puzzles that have a large open area where the puzzle pieces "interlock" to fit into the entire space. Children enjoy puzzles with animals, people, cars, buses, trees, flowers, and other pictures of things they know.<br>• Play games with the child. The adult puts in a piece of the puzzle and then the child puts in a piece of the puzzle. |

Listed above are *sample* behaviors of children and *sample* strategies for adults, they are not a definitive list or an exhaustive inventory. They start from an early developmental level and continue through older ages to the completion of kindergarten.

## B. Mathematical Thinking (continued)

**PERFORMANCE STANDARD:** B.EL. 4 USES THE ATTRIBUTES OF OBJECTS FOR COMPARISON AND PATTERNING

| Developmental Continuum | Sample Behaviors of Children | Sample Strategies for Adults |
|---|---|---|
| Categorizes objects based on physical or functional similarity. | • Child calls both roses and petunias "flowers."<br>• Child identifies adults as "big people."<br>• Child places all "blue blocks" together in one place.<br>• Child puts all the "big buttons" together saying, "they're all round."<br>• Child notices a pattern on another child's shirt saying, "I have checks (squares) on my shirt too."<br>• Child arranges leaves, sticks, and stones in separate piles.<br>• Child recognizes that all the tables in the room are "rectangles."<br>• Child refers to a yellow circle as "the sun" when making a drawing or picture. | • Show the child how to count, group, and order household objects, e.g., plastic spoons and forks, raisins in one bowl, and cheerios in another bowl.<br>• Talk to the child as the adult puts away the dishes after washing them, e.g., the plates go here, the glasses go here, the forks go here, etc.<br>• When walking outside with the child, find sticks, stones, leaves, acorns, pinecones and put them into separate piles or boxes.<br>• Name several objects in the house and say, "Look the table top is a rectangle just like the top of your stool." |
| Matches objects. | • Child matches colors. Matches red bead to a picture of a red bead.<br>• Child decides (when cleaning up) where the wooden block goes on the shelf by matching the shape of the block to the paper shape on the shelf.<br>• Child says "same" when he/she picks up a car that looks like the car in the book the adult is reading to him/her. | • Play games with the child, e.g., *Candy Land, Go Fish, Shape* or *Color Bingo*.<br>• Encourage the child to make-up his/her own matching games, e.g., matching a blue car to a picture of a blue car, one chicken to a picture of a chicken.<br>• Provide pictures of objects on the shelves in the child's room so that he/she can put toys, clothes, and books in the same place as the picture of the object. |
| Sorts and/or describes objects by one or more attributes or characteristics. | • Child can name and discriminate differences in color and shapes by making a necklace with all yellow beads or sorting the squares from the circles.<br>• Child says, "That's a big blue circle and this is a little yellow square."<br>• Child places pennies in one cup and dimes in another cup and says, "These (dimes) are shiny silver and these (pennies) are brown."<br>• Child sorts buttons, beads, or pegs into egg cartons, with each compartment holding a different color or size.<br>• Child sorts six stones into three buckets by color and next sorts them into three buckets according to size. Sorts sticks by size, e.g., long or short<br>• Child sorts clothes and describes why the clothing is in a certain pile, e.g., "These are all my socks and these are dad's socks." | • Play *I spy* with the child saying, "I spy something red," (red door) or "I spy a red ladybug," then let the child choose what color to spy for next.<br>• Play *Color* or *Shape Bingo*.<br>• Ask the child to tell what is the same about each group, as the child sorts the bear counters by color (e.g., red, yellow and blue).<br>• Talk to the child about similarities and differences among objects. Talk about the color, shape, and size differences.<br>• Encourage the child to make up his/her own sorting games for the adult to try.<br>• Play people sorting games, e.g., all boys with tie shoes, or children with brown hair, girls with red clothes. Let the child decide the characteristic to be sorted.<br>• Allow child to sort clothes that come out of the dryer or off the line after being washed and dried. |

Listed above are *sample* behaviors of children and *sample* strategies for adults, they are not a definitive list or an exhaustive inventory. They start from an early developmental level and continue through older ages to the completion of kindergarten.

## B. Mathematical Thinking *(continued)*

**PERFORMANCE STANDARD:** B.EL 4 Uses the attributes of objects for comparison and patterning (continued)

| Developmental Continuum | Sample Behaviors of Children | Sample Strategies for Adults |
|---|---|---|
| Uses positional and comparative words to demonstrate understanding direction and location, e.g., on-top, below, bottom, over, under, above, on, and next to. | • When observing the shell on the science table, the child describes it as "very big" or standing next to a classmate says, "You're taller than me."<br>• When playing games and asked to line up first, middle, or last the child goes to the specified place in line.<br>• Child uses distance words like near/far, in front, behind, beside, e.g., the child walks over to a friend and asks, "Can I sit beside you?"<br>• On a flannel board, the child places flannel pieces in a variety of positions, e.g., the child places a tree behind the sandbox, a flag next to it. | • Use everyday words to indicate space, location, shape, and size of objects, e.g., as the child works and plays, converse back and forth about the locations of objects saying, "You just went *under* the bridge," or ask, "Where will you put the cone shape on your tower?" The child replies, "On top."<br>• Play games like *Simon Says* using positional and directional words, e.g., put your hands between your knees, touch the bottom of your foot, or take two steps forward. |
| Recognizes, duplicates, extends simple patterns and creates original patterns. | • Using a peg board or beads for stringing, the child completes a row of pegs alternating orange and blue pegs and makes a necklace by stringing small beads of different shapes, e.g., ball bead, square bead, ball bead, square bead.<br>• Child finds sticks and leaves outside and wants to make a pattern like the adult who has made a pattern of one stick and one leaf, one stick and one leaf, etc.<br>• Child cuts strips to make a paper chain and makes a pattern of green, blue, red, purple then green, blue, red, purple, etc.<br>• When given shape crackers at snack, the child makes a circle, square, circle, square pattern on the table.<br>• Child echo claps a pattern modeled for him/her, two claps and a stomp and then the child creates his/her own pattern (clap, stomp, clap, and stomp). | • Play with the child, making patterns of shape, size, color using kitchen utensils, toys, items of clothing etc.<br>• Provide the child with pegboards and pegs or string and beads of different colors, sizes, and shapes. Play games with the child by starting a pattern and asking the child to continue the pattern. Tell the child to start the pattern, and then the adult will finish it.<br>• Create pictures of patterns using different shapes, colors, and sizes, and ask the child to duplicate the pattern using real objects or matching pictures. Ask the child to create his/her own pattern.<br>• Provide child with a variety of art materials such as crayons, scissors, chalk, and markers to create patterns inside. Outside, provide large pieces of chalk so that the child can create his/her own patterns for the adult to duplicate on the sidewalk or driveway. |
| Locates which out of 5 objects does not belong in same class or category. | • Child knows that one of the objects is not a food.<br>• Child takes the giraffe out of the bin filled with four farm animals.<br>• When shown a picture of four children and one adult and asked, "Which one is not the same?", the child points to the adult and tells why the adult is not the same as the four children, e.g., the adult is older or the adult is bigger. | • Sing the song, "One of these things is not like the others, one of these things doesn't belong. Can you tell which thing is not like the other by the time we finish our song?"<br>• Give the child picture cards of different foods and include some toy pictures, asking "Which of these go in the same group? Which ones don't belong... and why not?" |

Listed above are *sample* behaviors of children and *sample* strategies for adults, they are not a definitive list or an exhaustive inventory. They start from an early developmental level and continue through older ages to the completion of kindergarten.

## B. Mathematical Thinking *(continued)*

**PERFORMANCE STANDARD:** B.EL. 4 Uses the attributes of objects for comparison and patterning (continued)

| Developmental Continuum | Sample Behaviors of Children | Sample Strategies for Adults |
|---|---|---|
| Matches at least 6 items according to class or category. | • When given models of a person, a toy car, and an apple, the child can match 9 assorted pictures as he/she puts them into categories and says, "All of these are people, all of these are toys, and these are all foods."<br>• Child can match all of his/her clothes by color. | • Play games with pictures and objects, e.g., place a picture of food, leaf, person, animal, flower, insect on the table. Ask the child to find more pictures that match the categories and place them under the picture at the top.<br>• Provide the child with 6 empty containers and groups (categories) of little people, little animals, rocks, sticks, etc., and say to the child, "Put all of the things that are the same in one container." |
| Matches groups having equal numbers of objects up to 10. | • When provided number puzzles, the child matches the number to the set of dots.<br>• Child can match all the cards in a card deck with numbers of dots on them, e.g., all cards with 4 dots.<br>• Child says, "I have 10 pennies so I can buy 10 pieces of candy (candy costs 1 cent per piece).<br>• Child says, "There are enough chairs (5) for each of us (5 children) to have a chair." | • Provide matching games and sorting boxes that show a different number of objects above each slot, and have the child match his/her number cards by putting each card in the slot that has the same number of objects.<br>• Use objects inside and outside to make groups of objects, e.g., utensils, buttons, bottle caps, sticks, and stones. |

Listed above are *sample* behaviors of children and *sample* strategies for adults, they are not a definitive list or an exhaustive inventory. They start from an early developmental level and continue through older ages to the completion of kindergarten.

## B. Mathematical Thinking (continued)

**PERFORMANCE STANDARD:** B. EL. 5 UNDERSTANDS THE CONCEPT OF MEASUREMENT

| Developmental Continuum | Sample Behaviors of Children | Sample Strategies for Adults |
|---|---|---|
| Recognizes objects can be measured by height, length, and weight. | • The child measures the table, a window, and the height of another child, using small connecting cubes.<br>• When making paper chains at the table, the child says, "Mine is longer than yours," as he/she compares with a friend to see if it is longer.<br>• Child says, "Rocks are heavier," when using the balance scale to weigh rocks and blocks, then tries to balance the rocks with more blocks. | • Put an apple on the balance scale, and see how many rocks it takes to balance the apple.<br>• Hang a piece of paper on the wall, have the child stand with his/her back on the paper. Draw a line on the paper to show how tall the child is.<br>• Look for opportunities for the child to make comparisons and measurements during daily activities such as building with blocks, cooking, and walking in the park.<br>• Talk with the child about measurements you are making with tape measures, rulers, and scales. |
| Determines more, less, many, and few. | • Child says, "I put many spoons of sand in this cup," while using a measuring spoon to fill cups at the sand table.<br>• Child asks a friend, "Are there more people that live at your house than at my house?"<br>• Child says, "I have a few gold fish." | • Allow the child to experience cooking in the kitchen with an adult. Talk about measuring quantities while using measuring spoons and cups to measure sugar, flour, salt, oatmeal, rice, etc.<br>• As a child works and plays with toys, use words to talk about the child's play, e.g., which has more, less, many, and few. |
| Compares and orders by size. | • Child says, "Daddy is taller than me."<br>• Child stacks nesting rings by size.<br>• Child says, "My ball is bigger than yours."<br>• Child measures the strings to see who has the longest string or compares play dough snakes to see which one is longer.<br>• Child puts five crayons on the table from shortest to longest. | • As the child works and plays inside and outside, use words to talk with the child, such as heavier, lighter; longer, shorter; largest, smallest; wider, narrower; and thinner/thicker. |
| Categorizes and sequences time intervals and uses language associated with time in everyday situations. | • Child says, "In the morning we get up. At night it gets dark."<br>• Child says, "After lunch we go outside."<br>• Child says, "I watch Mickey Mouse on Saturday." | • Everyday talk to your child about time, e.g., "Good morning, it is time to get up." Or "Billy, it is time for lunch." Or, after reading the book *Good Night Moon*, say, "It is night and it is time for bed."<br>• Point to the calendar and say, "Today is Monday. On Saturday it will be your birthday. Let's count the days until your birthday and put your picture on the day of your birthday." |
| Identifies coins and understands their value. | • Child examines both sides of coins using a magnifying glass.<br>• Child matches and sorts coins by size or denomination.<br>• Child identifies penny and nickel.<br>• Child identifies penny and nickel, recognizing that coins have different values by matching five pennies to one nickel.<br>• Child knows that a nickel is worth more than a penny.<br>• Child uses coins to give change when playing in the play store or play post office.<br>• Child pays for an item at the store by counting his/her money and giving correct amount of change. | • When shopping with the child in a store, show the child the coins and dollars you will be using to pay for an item/s.<br>• Name coins that you are counting out to use in the parking meter. Let the child put coins in the parking meter and talk about how much.<br>• Set up a store or post office and provide the child with play coins or real coins to use in the store or post office. Together build a store or post office, using boxes and other easily accessible objects and materials that are available or are very inexpensive.<br>• With the child, count the money in his/her piggy bank. |

Listed above are *sample* behaviors of children and *sample* strategies for adults, they are not a definitive list or an exhaustive inventory. They start from an early developmental level and continue through older ages to the completion of kindergarten.

## B. Mathematical Thinking (continued)

**PERFORMANCE STANDARD:** B.EL. 5 Understands the concept of measurement (continued)

| Developmental Continuum | Sample Behaviors of Children | Sample Strategies for Adults |
|---|---|---|
| Uses tools to explore measuring (non-standard units). | • Child pretends to measure the length of a road made of blocks with a tape measure.<br>• Child uses cups, bowls, and spoons to measure in the sand table, e.g., tries to see how many cups of sand fit into the bowl.<br>• Child places objects on each side of a balance scale, manipulating objects to alter the balance and using words such as heavy, light, and equal.<br>• Child measures a piece of carpet using blocks and says, "The carpet is 10 blocks long." Or, builds a road with blocks and says, "The road is 7 blocks long."<br>• Child measures using a string or paper strip to compare the length of two objects.<br>• Child uses teddy bears to measure the side of a table and says, "This is 5 teddy bears long."<br>• Child places objects on each side of the balance scale and says, "This side is more." | • Use non-standard measurement tools such as yarn to "measure" around the giant ball. Then introduce and use more standard kinds of measurement tools, e.g., tape measure, yard stick, ruler.<br>• Model using measuring tools as the child works and plays, e.g., "What can we use to tell how tall that is?" Or, "What could we use to tell how much the watermelon weighs?" |
| Categorizes, sequences time intervals in everyday situations, and demonstrates an awareness of time related to a clock. | • Child says, "My birthday is in summer."<br>• Child says, "At nighttime it gets dark." Adult asks, "What time is it then?" And the child responds, "It is midnight."<br>• When looking at the clock, child says, "The big hand is on the 12 and the little hand is on the 5; dad is coming home."<br>• Child says, "When both hands of the clock are on the 12, it will be time for lunch."<br>• Child relates time to his/her daily activities, e.g., the child says, "My mom is picking me up this afternoon."<br>• Child asks, "Is the trip to the apple orchard this week?" Child then looks at the calendar, counts the days to the picture of the apple (put on the calendar to show it is the day of the field trip to the apple orchard) saying, "Is it in 4 days?"<br>• Child says, "My birthday is in May, and I will be 6 years old." | • Initially time is viewed as a sequence of events. Through experiences, routines, schedules, clocks, and calendars, the child begins to use words like day, night, morning, evening, yesterday, week, and month.<br>• Read books and talk about the things that can be done in the different seasons. Have the child tell the adult something he/she likes to do in each season.<br>• Talk with the child about day and night, naming things that can be done in the daytime and things that can be done at night.<br>• Talk about animals that can be seen in the daytime and ones that move around at night.<br>• When the child asks, "What time is it?" adult says, "What could we use to find that out, e.g., clock, watch?"<br>• Adult tells the child that they will play outside at 10 o'clock and points to the clock, explaining to the child he/she will play outside when the big hand points up at the top and the shorter hand points to 10. |
| Explores, compares, and describes length, weight, or volume using standard measures. | • Child says, "I need to get the ruler to measure how tall my building is. Oh, it is 10 inches tall."<br>• Child asks adult to measure how tall he/she is on the "Growth Chart" in his/her room.<br>• Child says, "I wonder if this pumpkin weighs as much as dad's bowling ball? Let's get the scale." The bowling ball weighs 12 pounds and the pumpkin weighs 8 pounds. The adult says, "Which is heavier and weighs more?" The child says, "The bowling ball weighs more."<br>• Child uses measuring cups to measure ingredients for the cake that he/she and an adult are making.<br>• Child guesses (estimates) how many cups of water can fit in his/her tall plastic drink container. | • Provide the child with a 12 inch ruler that is marked in 12 inches, bathroom scales or child sized scale that weighs up to 10 or 20 pounds; and measuring cups (I cup, 1/2 cup and 1/4 cup).<br>• Provide a growth chart for the child, and paste a picture of the child on the chart when the adult measures him/her (at least once per year on his/her birthday). Say to the child, "You are 3 feet tall." As the child gets older, hold your hand on the chart to show the height of the child, and let the child tell how tall he or she is.<br>• Cook and bake with the child. Point to the measurements in the cookbook, and ask the child to measure one cup (or another measure) of liquid or solids.<br>• Ask the child, "How many cups of water do you think could fit into your water bottle?" |

Listed above are *sample* behaviors of children and *sample* strategies for adults, they are not a definitive list or an exhaustive inventory. They start from an early developmental level and continue through older ages to the completion of kindergarten.

## B. Mathematical Thinking (continued)

**PERFORMANCE STANDARD:** B.EL. 6 Collects, describes, and records information using all senses

| Developmental Continuum | Sample Behaviors of Children | Sample Strategies for Adults |
|---|---|---|
| Draws and describes pictures of objects and actions from memory. | • Child draws a picture of a butterfly and describes the butterfly to an adult or friend.<br>• Child paints a picture of a family vacation or field trip. Child describes the picture he/she has drawn. | • Encourage the child to draw pictures of something the child has done or seen. When the child is telling about what he/she has done or seen, say, "I think you could draw a picture about your trip to the zoo. Would you like some paper and crayons, or would you like to paint a picture?" |
| Describes and records information through a variety of means, including discussion, drawings, maps, graphs, and charts. | • Outside the window is a large thermometer. Each day the child marks on a chart if the temperature rises (went up) or falls (goes down).<br>• By the gerbil's cage, there is a chart with different pictures and words of the foods the gerbil can eat (seeds, apple, and carrot). When the child feeds the gerbil, he/she makes a check next to the food given to the gerbil.<br>• After collecting leaves, the child lays the leaves in rows by their shape or color telling why they were put in different groups. On a graph sheet, the child records by coloring in a square for each leaf in the column that represents its color starting at the bottom of the graph, e.g., the first column has 5 squares colored yellow to represent the 5 yellow leaves collected.<br>• Child says, "I made a map of the road to take from my house to my friend Jimmy's house." | • Pose a question of the day. Show the child how to make tally marks under "Yes" or "No" on the question board, e.g., "Do you like to eat peas?" or "Do you like summer better than winter?" or "Do you live on a farm?" or "Have you ever read a book about dinosaurs?"<br>• Assist the child to make graphs and charts to record information about his/her collections of stickers, leaves, rocks, shells, buttons, cars, dolls, etc.<br>• After the child has grouped sets of objects, ask questions, such as, "How did you make your groups?" After the child tells you, say, "Let's make a graph of how many you have in each group to see which group has the most." Help the child make a picture graph of the child's groups (or use the real objects to make the graph).<br>• Assist the child to make maps of the rooms in the house, his/her room, or the outside of the house and yard.<br>• Use maps to show the child where the adult and child will be going in the car. Use a marker to show where the adult and child are now and where the two of you will be going. |
| Begins to apply information collected to similar situations by designing own charts or graphs. | • Child lays sea shells on blank grid and graphs the shells by shape, putting them in different rows. Later, the child lays some long, single strings of yarn on the floor to make a grid and puts photographs of family in one column, photos of friends in another column, and photos of pets in another, talking about the information on the grid. | • Assist the child when they have collections, such as rocks, flowers, to collect data, and show the information using graphs or charts, discussing why we collect data and other ways to show it so it can be shared. |

Listed above are *sample* behaviors of children and *sample* strategies for adults, they are not a definitive list or an exhaustive inventory. They start from an early developmental level and continue through older ages to the completion of kindergarten.

## C. Scientific Thinking

**PERFORMANCE STANDARD:** C.EL. 1 USES OBSERVATION TO GATHER INFORMATION

| Developmental Continuum | Sample Behaviors of Children | Sample Strategies for Adults |
|---|---|---|
| Shows awareness of differences in their environment (smell, touch, sight, sound, and taste). | • Child responds to too much stimulation (touch, sounds, light, and voices) by looking away, crying, yawning, or sleeping.<br>• Child shows awareness of loud and soft noises.<br>• Child responds differently to sound, light, and temperature intensity.<br>• Child responds to familiar voices (caregiver or family members) by turning head toward the sound.<br>• Child responds to being wrapped tightly in a soft, light, receiving blanket and responds to having "no" clothes on during diaper changes. | • Watch and observe how the child responds to sounds, such as a door being shut; to visuals, such as seeing a person walk past him/her; or to touch, such as being touched by an adult.<br>• Watch to see if the child stops what he/she is doing or increases what he/she is doing. The child will let the adult know what he/she likes or dislikes.<br>• Try differences of light intensity in the child's room at night. Does the child like dark, or low or high levels of light in the room when he/she sleeps?<br>• Wrap the child (infant) tightly in a soft, light receiving blanket while being held or while sleeping. Does the child like to be wrapped tightly?<br>• Does the child like having no clothes on during diaper changing. |
| Recognizes and responds to differences in the environment. | • Child shows preference for familiar person as opposed to a stranger.<br>• Child shows preference of certain toys and materials, e.g., soft, fuzzy, rough, shinny, spongy, or hard.<br>• Child shows preference for being "dry" rather than "wet." Indicates by a cry or sounds when "wet." | • Encourage child's interest in discovery and exploration by providing a variety of different materials and toys for the child to hold and manipulate.<br>• Provide a variety of motion experiences for the child, e.g., swing, child sling, front or back carrier, stroller, car seat for ride in car.<br>• Follow the lead of the child's responses to differences in the environment so that you know what he/she prefers. |
| Purposefully seeks information through observation to satisfy curiosity or need for answers. | • Child asks many questions as he/she finds frogs in the pond, worms in the garden, and bugs in the woods.<br>• Child uses magnets to see what "sticks" and "what doesn't stick."<br>• Child asks, "Why is it cold when it snows and hot when it is time to go to beach at the park?"<br>• Child wants to plant his/her own garden when the adult is planting in the garden.<br>• Child asks many questions as he/she watches and helps the adult cook. | • Encourage children to explore, experiment, and share his/her thoughts and ideas about the world. Ask questions that will encourage children to think about what they have seen, heard, and done.<br>• Provide the child with a variety of magnets and materials that "stick" and do not "stick." Answer the child's questions about magnets.<br>• Talk about the weather with the child, using words, such as sunny, cloudy, rainy, hot, and cold. Talk about what the weather is like each day.<br>• Encourage cooking and gardening experiences as an adult and child activity.<br>• Model thinking out loud and talk about ideas and observations with children. Use descriptive words when talking about things, people, trees, animals, insects, etc. |
| Discriminates properties of nature, using a variety of senses (part to whole, living/non-living, weather, etc.). | • Child says, "The rose is the only flower in our garden that smells."<br>• Child draws pictures of all of the animals he/she saw at the zoo and wants an adult to put the name of the animal under each picture.<br>• Child has an insect container/collector and wants to use it to collect different kinds of insects.<br>• Child asks, "Why do trees have pine cones? What are all these prickly pieces on the cone?"<br>• Child uses a bottle to collect water from a shallow pond and asks, "Why is the water so dirty?" | • As a child works and plays, talk with the child about living plants and animals, modeling the use of descriptive words.<br>• If the adult/family has plants and a pet, allow the child to help take care of the plants and pet.<br>• Go on insect hunts and bird-watching walks. Later ask the child to draw pictures or tell what he/she saw so the adult can write it on the drawing made by the child.<br>• Encourage child to experiment with opening acorns, pulling apart pieces of the pine cone, and exploring the inside of seeds. Discuss what he/she has observed.<br>• Explore and talk about land, water, rocks, and other non-living things in the neighborhood and community.<br>• Involve child in planning family outings to interesting places, such as, the zoo, farm, aquarium, orchard, parks, markets, museums, and other family trips. |

Listed above are *sample* behaviors of children and *sample* strategies for adults, they are not a definitive list or an exhaustive inventory. They start from an early developmental level and continue through older ages to the completion of kindergarten.

## C. Scientific Thinking (continued)

**PERFORMANCE STANDARD:** C.EL. 2 USE TOOLS TO GATHER INFORMATION, COMPARE OBSERVED OBJECTS, AND SEEK ANSWERS TO QUESTIONS THROUGH ACTIVE INVESTIGATION

| Developmental Continuum | Sample Behaviors of Children | Sample Strategies for Adults |
|---|---|---|
| Engages in behavior to investigate consequences; notices cause and effect relationships in daily environment. | • Child shakes rattle, stops, and then shakes again.<br>• Child drops plate from high chair and looks down to floor where it hits and repeats action again and again<br>• Child uses an egg beater to whip up bubbles in the bath tub or water table.<br>• Child continues to poke or hit at a toy to keep it in motion or make it repeat actions.<br>• Child turns objects over and over to thoroughly explore (pushing, pulling, dropping, squeezing).<br>• Child looks carefully inspecting, trying, and moving parts of toys, such as wheels, doors, and other moving parts. | • Provide child with a variety of tools that can be used in a variety of ways, e.g., measuring cups, child sized plastic bottles, small plastic plates, and containers.<br>• Provide tools that can be used in the water during bath time, e.g., plastic containers, small plastic eggbeater, and other water toys.<br>• Show the child new ways to use a toy or tool to scoop, push, turn over, and use the side or bottom of a toy or tool. |
| Works toward an objective, may use tools or others in the environment to obtain the object. | • Child walks toward favorite toy, and then starts to crawl to get there faster.<br>• Child hands toy or object to adult to have them make it work or open it up.<br>• Child uses motions or sounds, or asks adult for help to reach bottle or cup. | • Provide an environment for the child to move around safely.<br>• Provide toys and objects that are safe for the child to put in mouth and manipulate.<br>• Respond to the child's request for assistance by giving the child the desired object or showing the child how the toy works. |
| Uses buttons/levers to produce desired responses. | • Child investigates the buttons on the telephone or computer to see how they work.<br>• Child presses on multiple buttons and lifts and pushes on multiple levers on toys to make a variety of sounds; recalls which lever or button was pushed, lifted, pulled to make favorite sounds.<br>• Child lifts and opens doors on toys to see what is inside or to put something inside. | • Provide the child with a variety of safe toys that the child can investigate and explore.<br>• When a toy is new, allow the child to explore the toy to see how it works. Clap, smile, and say "Yea!" when the child gets a reaction from the new toy (positive reinforcement). Watch the child try it again and continue to explore. |
| Uses books to look for information. | • Child sees a ladybug outside and asks an adult, "Can we find a book about ladybugs?"<br>• Child asks, "Why do some bugs have spots?" while looking at pictures of bugs in a book and observing that some of them have spots and some of them do not.<br>• Child asks an adult, "Do we have books to tell how airplanes fly?" | • Provide a wide range of children's books including books about animals, insects, plants, people, water, air, land, and other environmental books.<br>• Read often to and with the child. Ask the child questions such as, "What do you think is going to happen when the girl plants the little seed?" Or, "How do you think airplanes are able to fly?" |
| Uses magnifying glass (hand lens), binoculars, and maps for investigation of the environment. | • Child is working with "Flaom" (rice crispy, crystal-like, sticky substance) and goes to get a magnifying glass to take a closer look at the "Flaom" to see what it is made of.<br>• Child says, "Look at my roads from my house to grandma's house."<br>• Using the binoculars, child says, "Look at this bird, it is red and white and black and has a long beak." | • Provide tools such as a magnifying glass, binoculars, and maps. Encourage children to use the tools to explore objects, plants, seeds, and hands.<br>• Encourage child to draw a map of the neighborhood or a map of his/her house or the way to get to the park or the way to get to a friend's house<br>• Take binoculars along when the child and adult take a walk outside. Play a game of "How many different birds can we see?" Keep a journal of all the different kinds of birds. Remember to bring a reference book of birds along! |

Listed above are *sample* behaviors of children and *sample* strategies for adults, they are not a definitive list or an exhaustive inventory. They start from an early developmental level and continue through older ages to the completion of kindergarten.

## C. Scientific Thinking (continued)

**PERFORMANCE STANDARD:** C.EL. 2 USES TOOLS TO GATHER INFORMATION, COMPARE OBSERVED OBJECTS, AND SEEK ANSWERS TO QUESTION THROUGH ACTIVE INVESTIGATION (CONTINUED)

| Developmental Continuum | Sample Behaviors of Children | Sample Strategies for Adults |
|---|---|---|
| Makes comparisons between objects that have been collected or observed. | • Child examines a shell collection and responds to requests, such as "Find some more pink ones." or "Show me a shell that isn't smooth."<br>• Child floats and sinks various objects at the water table.<br>• Child observes differences among the birds in the yard or at the feeder.<br>• Child tells whether the sounds made by rhythm instruments are the same or different. | • Encourage child to share his/her thoughts and ideas about the world around them.<br>• Ask question that will encourage child to think about what he/she has seen, heard, and done.<br>• Model thinking "out loud" and talk about ideas with child. |

Listed above are *sample* behaviors of children and *sample* strategies for adults, they are not a definitive list or an exhaustive inventory. They start from an early developmental level and continue through older ages to the completion of kindergarten.

## C. Scientific Thinking (continued)

**PERFORMANCE STANDARD:** C.EL 3 HYPOTHESIZES AND MAKES PREDICTIONS

| Developmental Continuum | Sample Behaviors of Children | Sample Strategies for Adults |
|---|---|---|
| Locates object hidden from view. | • Child finds toy that is hidden under blanket after watching someone hide it.<br>• Child retrieves a ball that has rolled behind couch.<br>• Child searches under two boxes to find block. | • Provide time for the child to try to think about "What just happened?" and to think about "What am I going to do?"<br>• Play games of having the child hide and put the object under first one box and then the other. Play the game again, and hide it under a different box the next time. |
| Creates mental images of objects and people not in immediate environments. | • Child looks for a favorite toy in the same place it was yesterday.<br>• Child looks around the room in buckets and under the couch for "nuk" when adult says, "Where's your 'nuk?" Child finds it in the same place where the child left it.<br>• Child asks for favorite toy when it has been left at home.<br>• Child likes to play Peek-A-Boo and Hide-and-Seek. | • Play games of *Hide-and-Seek* and *Peek-a-Boo* with your child.<br>• Ask the child, "Where's your nuk?" or "Where's your coat?"<br>• Provide special places for the child's clothes and toys. Child will learn and remember where to find coat, pajamas, shoes, and special toys.<br>• Show pictures to the child of favorite people like grandma, grandpa, brothers, sisters, caregivers. Make a picture book for the child of favorite people. |
| Asks questions, seeks information, and tests out possibilities. | • Child asks, "Why does the moon look different at night? Sometimes it is big like a ball, and sometimes it looks like a dish."<br>• Child asks adult, "What if we planted a stick in the ground, would it grow to be a tree?" Adult says, "Should we try planting the stick to see if it grows into a tree?"<br>• Child says, "My truck does not float in the bathtub. I tried it out, and it just sits on the bottom of the tub." | • Encourage the child to ask questions and to wonder. Help them refine questions.<br>• When the child asks questions, encourage him/her to test out possibilities to find answers to questions. Test out possibilities with the child.<br>• Use children's books as resources to find the answers to the child's questions, e.g., "What if we planted a stick in the ground, would it grow to be a tree?" |
| Asks simple scientific questions and draws conclusions based on previous experience. | • Child says, "Look at all my leaves (leaves are different kinds, color, shape, size). Did they come from the same tree?"<br>• Child says, "We planted a seed at school, and my teacher said it would grow into a sunflower. Can we plant a seed at home and see what happens?" | • Be available to answer the child's questions and talk more or show the child more about the current interest of the child, e.g., the child wants to know more about the difference in the shapes of leaves.<br>• Help the child find books about different kinds of trees, take a walk to see what the leaves look like from particular kinds of trees, make a book with the child displaying leaves with a real picture of the particular tree. Let the child take the picture of the tree with a camera.<br>• Participate with the child in natural events, e.g., growing seeds, caring for animals, charting the weather.<br>• Conduct some longer-term experiments, such as growing seeds in differing light conditions and keep ongoing records or pictures. |
| Makes plans for testing hypotheses to prove or disprove predictions. | • Child says to a friend, "Should we try to mix the red paint with green paint? Maybe we can make blue."<br>• Child brings a snowball into the house and asks to put it in the freezer to see if it will still be a snowball tomorrow or if it will melt.<br>• Child wants to plant 3 different sized seeds to see if the biggest seed grows into the biggest plant.<br>• Child plants seeds in two flowerpots and puts one in the closet and the other on the windowsill. Child says, "I think the seed in my closet will grow, but it will be a very small plant. The seed in the window will grow to be a big plant." | • Provide opportunities for the child to try new activities and experiences.<br>• Create environments that offer an appropriate amount of stimulation for the child to use a wide variety of equipment and materials.<br>• Help child verbalize his/her reasoning and thinking out loud about how to solve a problem or answer a question.<br>• Write down the child's recommended ways of solving problems as well as his/her solutions to problems. Try them out. |

Listed above are *sample* behaviors of children and *sample* strategies for adults, they are not a definitive list or an exhaustive inventory. They start from an early developmental level and continue through older ages to the completion of kindergarten.

## C. Scientific Thinking (continued)

**PERFORMANCE STANDARD**: C.EL. 4 Forms explanations based on trial and error, observations, and explorations

| Developmental Continuum | Sample Behaviors of Children | Sample Strategies for Adults |
|---|---|---|
| Identifies and investigates the physical qualities of living and nonliving things. | • Child recognizes a cup when it is turned upside down.<br>• Child says "little dog" when seeing the neighbor walk his dog.<br>• Child describes kitty as "soft" when petting the kitty. | • Provide opportunities for children to experiment with new materials and activities without fear of making mistakes. |
| Explores and formulates conclusions based on observation and past experiences. | • Child points out stripes on a caterpillar.<br>• Child notices it gets darker when the sun goes behind a cloud.<br>• Child points out changes in animals or plants in the room. | • Be available and respond to the child when he/she encounters problems while exploring (without being intrusive).<br>• Respond to the child's conversation, expand on his/her language, and use descriptive words while playing with the child. |
| Makes reasonable explanations, using data gathered from observation and experiments. | • Child says, "When I mix the color red and blue, it makes purple."<br>• Child says, "Look, when I shake this jar of water, it makes bubbles."<br>• After spinning around and stopping, the child says, "Spinning makes the room look like it is moving up and down." | • Provide tasks and materials in which the goal is trying different strategies or solutions rather than right or wrong answers.<br>• Model exploration and use of a wide variety of familiar and new learning materials and activities.<br>• Help the child make a "special place" for all his/her experiments and collection boxes. |
| Offers and seeks explanations of questions and experiments, using references such as books and computers. | • Child says, "Look, it's just like the *Hungry Caterpillar* book. My mom and I tried to put a caterpillar in a jar with some leaves and a stick and look what happened."<br>• After trying to take a toaster apart, the child asks adult, "Do you have a book that can help me put this back together?"<br>• Child asks adult to help him/her use the computer to find out how an acorn can grow into a tree. | • Provide a rich array of children's books that relate to animals, insects, people, plants, air, and water.<br>• Join the child in searching through books or doing a search on the computer for an explanation or an answer to their questions or wondering.<br>• Encourage the child's demonstration of flexibility and inventiveness in play and problem solving. |

Listed above are *sample* behaviors of children and *sample* strategies for adults, they are not a definitive list or an exhaustive inventory. They start from an early developmental level and continue through older ages to the completion of kindergarten.

# Wisconsin Model Early Learning Standards
## Interest Areas: Children Learn From Play

| CHILDREN LEARN FROM PLAY | Page |
|---|---|
| SENSORY MATERIALS, ACTIVE PLAY EQUIPMENT, AND CONSTRUCTION MATERIAL | 102 |
| MANIPULATIVE TOYS, DOLL AND DRAMATIC PLAY, BOOK AND RECORDINGS, AND ART MATERIALS | 103 |
| ACTIVITIES AND SPECIFIC SKILLS LEARNED | 104 |

# Interest Areas: Children Learn From Play

*Here are some suggestions for each area. Begin at the youngest age and add items for the age of each child in your group. Remember to change materials regularly to keep areas fresh and interesting. Allow children to play with any item as long as it is safe for his/her age.*

| Sensory Materials | Active Play Equipment | Construction Materials |
|---|---|---|
| (To stimulate the five senses) | (In large, open spaces, and outside) | (In a quiet spot for building) |
| **INFANTS** *(Birth to 12 months)*<br>Sucking toys<br>Rattles<br>Unbreakable mirrors (acrylic)<br>Patterned crib sheets<br>Mobiles<br>Music | **INFANTS** *(Birth to 12 months)*<br>Bounce chairs<br>Mobiles (activated by movement)<br>Things to reach and grab<br>Adults to bounce gently upon (with caution)<br>Bright colored balls | **INFANTS** *(Birth to 12 months)*<br>Nesting toys<br>Large, soft blocks |
| **TODDLERS** *(12 – 24 months)* **add**<br>Music boxes<br>Busy boxes<br>Push toys<br>Large bells, drums<br>Non-toxic play dough and finger paint (with close supervision)<br>Water play with cup & spoon<br>Fruit to taste (cut into small pieces) | **TODDLERS** *(12 – 24 months)* **add**<br>Crawling tunnel<br>Riding toys<br>Cardboard boxes<br>2-3 steps to climb<br>Ramps to walk on<br>Balls<br>Push and pull toys | **TODDLERS** *(12 – 24 months)* **add**<br>Cardboard blocks<br>Cups to stack<br>Toy pounding bench |
| **2 – 3 YEARS add**<br>Sand-play with household objects<br>Scarves for dancing<br>Listening games<br>Texture boards<br>Tasting activities | **2 – 3 YEARS add**<br>Low climber<br>Low slide<br>Wagon<br>Homemade obstacle course<br>Sandbox with toys | **2 – 3 YEARS add**<br>Wood unit blocks<br>Little people figures<br>Animals<br>Cars and trucks<br>Train and tracks<br>Wooden pegs, mallet, and styrofoam |
| **3 YEARS AND UP add**<br>More tools for working with sand, water, and play dough<br>Rhythm instruments<br>Wide variety of music<br>Cooking activities (with close supervision) | **3 YEARS AND UP add**<br>Swings<br>Low balancing beam<br>Low basketball hoop<br>Tricycle/big wheels<br>Jump ropes<br>Easy-to-play games such as "Follow the Leader"<br>Parachute | **3 YEARS AND UP add**<br>More unit block shapes and accessories<br>Props for road, town scenes<br>Woodworking bench and accessories (with careful one-on-one supervision)<br>Construction sets with small pieces (keep away from smaller children) |

From Growing Smart and Healthy Babies. Reprinted by permission of Bright from the Start: Georgia Department of Early Care and Learning.

# Interest Areas: Children Learn From Play

| Manipulative Toys (On a low table) | Doll & Dramatic Play | Book & Recordings (In a soft, cozy spot) | Art Materials (Near water & low tables/chairs) |
|---|---|---|---|
| **INFANTS** *(Birth – 12 months)*<br>Large rings<br>Squeeze toys<br>Textured balls<br>Large measuring spoons | **INFANTS** *(Birth – 12 months)*<br>Soft dolls<br>Peek-a-boo games<br>Songs and finger plays | **INFANTS** *(Birth – 12 months)*<br>Records of voices, sounds, animal sounds, music<br>Sturdy cloth or cardboard books<br>Lap books with large illustrations, picture of faces, large objects, bright shapes<br>Puppets | **INFANTS** *(Birth – 12 months)*<br>Bright socks on hands/feet<br>Textured objects<br>Brightly colored toys<br>Edible finger paint (baby food) |
| **TODDLERS** *(12 – 24 months)* add<br>Puzzles: 2 – 6 pieces with knobs<br>Nesting toys<br>Large pegboards<br>Snap-together toys with big pieces | **TODDLERS** *(12 – 24 months)* add<br>Blankets to wrap dolls<br>Dishes, pans, spoons<br>Broom, sponge<br>Hats<br>Unbreakable mirror (acrylic)<br>Shopping cart<br>Purses<br>Telephones<br>Pretend food | **TODDLERS** *(12 – 24 months)* add<br>Books with simple stories<br>Songs, finger plays<br>Pictures on wall at eye level (laminated)<br>Flannel board and flannel people | **TODDLERS** *(12 – 24 months)* add<br>Frequent opportunities to explore messy edible/nontoxic substance (food, water-based finger painting)<br>Non-toxic markers (on boxes)<br>Chalk (on paper, cardboard, sidewalk)<br>Fat crayons (one color at a time)<br>Large paper to draw on (tape down) |
| **2 – 3 YEARS add**<br>Puzzles: 4 – 6 pieces<br>Big beads to string<br>Stacking toys<br>Scissors and cards to cut up | **2 – 3 YEARS add**<br>Doll bed, carriages<br>Doll clothes<br>Realistic dolls<br>Tables and chairs<br>Toy stove, etc.<br>Dress-up clothes (simple)<br>Puppets | **2 – 3 YEARS add**<br>Books with stories about familiar things<br>Short story records, more songs, finger plays<br>Written and picture labels on objects<br>Flannel board accessories | **2 – 3 YEARS add**<br>Water-based paint with large brushes<br>Scissors and things to cut<br>Play dough<br>2-3 crayons at a time<br>Large paper, different textures, colors<br>Stickers and paper |
| **3 YEARS AND UP add**<br>Puzzles, pegboards<br>Stringing and snap together toys with smaller pieces according to ability level | **3 YEARS AND UP add**<br>Boxes with dress-up clothes and realistic accessories to encourage theme<br>Play "restaurant," "store," "gas station," "office," "airport."<br>Let the children be your GUIDE! | **3 YEARS AND UP add**<br>More and more detailed stories<br>Access to record/tape player with instructions on care and use<br>Written and picture labels on objects such as: name on cup, etc., to help associate written word with objects<br>Child's own words as dictated on artwork and in homemade books to be read back by child/adults<br>More flannel accessories | **3 YEARS AND UP add**<br>Water colors<br>Hole punchers<br>Glue/paste and a variety of things to glue onto paper<br>Magazines to cut up<br>Things to lick and stick<br>Crayons and markers of many colors<br>Natural objects (leaves, pine cones, etc.)<br>Collage materials |

From Growing Smart and Healthy Babies. Reprinted by permission of Bright from the Start: Georgia Department of Early Care and Learning.

# Interest Areas: Children Learn From Play

| Activity | Specific Skills Learned |
|---|---|
| Finding toys or learning materials to work with alone or with others. | **Cognitive:** Makes decisions about interests and abilities.<br>**Self-help:** Find toys by him/herself or sets up environment for play.<br>**Social/Language:** Learns to share, barter, manage conflict, and ask for help.<br>**Emotional:** Learns about acceptance and rejection. Expresses needs. |
| Block play | **Physical:** Learns to balance blocks and line them up (small motor coordination). Matches blocks that look alike.<br>**Cognitive:** May count blocks, sees pattern and design. Learns to build and plan structure.<br>**Social:** Learns to share and cooperate. |
| Dramatic play | **Social:** Plays adult roles. Develops self-image and coordinates with others.<br>**Language:** Learns to express self in another role.<br>**Cognitive:** Decides appropriate dress and appearance for role; uses visual perceptions to assess self, others, and play environment. Learns and remembers behaviors to imitate. Develops abstract thinking abilities.<br>**Self-help:** Dresses self: Sets up play environment and finds props. |
| Setting the table | **Cognitive:** Counts silverware, glasses, and napkins, or places one object by each setting. Follows pattern of place settings.<br>**Social:** Cooperates with other children. May teach younger children to help.<br>**Physical:** Picks up and places objects (small motor coordination). |
| Sitting down to eat | **Physical:** Pours milk, passes the dish (small motor coordination).<br>**Cognitive:** Measures to pour. Understands directions.<br>**Social/Language:** Learns appropriate table conversation and manners. |
| Story time or listening to music | **Cognitive:** Listens and retains information. Follows story line (sequencing) with eyes and/or ears.<br>Recognizes words, pictures, instruments, and rhythms. |
| Finger plays and songs | **Cognitive/Language:** Learns words, gestures, and melody (sequencing, repetition, speech, and listening skills). Follows directions.<br>**Physical:** Coordination (small and large motor) for gestures and finger plays. |
| Dance | **Cognitive/Language:** Listens to music and rhythms. Learns to understand simple movement, directions, and their relationship to music.<br>**Physical:** Coordinates movements (large motor). |
| Climbing/riding | **Cognitive:** May count the rungs to the top of a climbing structure; plans the climb. Maps out direction and distance to ride; watches for others in path.<br>**Physical:** Large motor coordination, balance.<br>**Social:** Takes turns, interacts. |
| Sand play | **Cognitive:** Measures sand and maps out roads (spatial relationships).<br>**Physical:** Pours, dumps, pushes, gathers, scoops, packs (small and large motor).<br>**Social:** Shares, interacts, and cooperates. |
| Putting away toys | **Cognitive:** Sorts toys, follows directions.<br>**Physical:** Places objects on the shelf, replaces lids, opens and shuts doors.<br>**Social:** Takes turns, learns to handle toy carefully. |

From *Growing Smart and Healthy Babies*. Reprinted by permission of Bright from the Start: Georgia Department of Early Care and Learning.

# Wisconsin Model Early Learning Standards
## Appendices

## APPENDIXES   Page

**APPENDIX A:** ALIGNMENT OF WISCONSIN MODEL EARLY LEARNING STANDARDS WITH WISCONSIN ACADEMIC STANDARDS FOR ENGLISH LANGUAGE ARTS AND MATHEMATICS AND WISCONSIN ESSENTIAL ELEMENTS    107

**APPENDIX B:** WISCONSIN MODEL EARLY LEARNING STANDARDS AND IDEA EARLY CHILDHOOD OUTCOMES    114

**APPENDIX C:** REFERENCES AND RESOURCES    116

**APPENDIX D:** EARLY CARE AND EDUCATION RESOURCE LISTING    124

## Appendix A
## Standards in the State of Wisconsin

*Wisconsin's adoption of the Wisconsin Academic Standards provides an excellent opportunity for Wisconsin school districts and communities to define expectations from birth through preparation for college and work. By aligning the existing Wisconsin Model Early Learning Standards (WMELS) with the Wisconsin Academic Standards, expectations can be set from birth through high school completion.*

*Since 2003, the WMELS have influenced all programs serving children under mandatory school age to identify what children from birth through entrance to first grade should know and be able to do. Schools across the state have worked with childcare, Head Start, and other community programs to incorporate the WMELS into their early childhood special education, four-year-old kindergarten, and five-year-old kindergarten programs. The adoption of Wisconsin Academic Standards provides opportunity for alignment between the WMELS and the Wisconsin Academic Standards in the areas of English language arts and mathematics. The WMELS provide developmental expectations for young children from birth through entrance to first grade that are foundational to the Wisconsin Academic Standards for kindergarten through grade 12.*

## Overview of WMELS

The development of the WMELS was guided by research in the field of early education and supported by content experts from institutions of higher education in the state. The WMELS provide a framework for families, professionals, and policymakers to:

- Share a common language and responsibility for the well-being of children from birth to first grade;
- Know and understand developmental expectations of young children; and
- Understand the connection of early childhood with K-12 educational experiences and lifelong learning.

The WMELS specify developmental expectations for children birth through entrance to first grade and address all the domains of a child's learning and development including: Health and Physical Development; Social and Emotional Development; Language Development and Communication; Approaches to Learning; and Cognition and General Knowledge. The developmental domains are highly interrelated. Knowledge and skills developed in one area of development impact the acquisition of knowledge and skills in other areas of development. Each domain is divided into sub-domains, which include developmental expectations, program standards, performance standards, and a developmental continuum, along with samples of children's behavior and adult strategies.

The WMELS are intended to:
- Improve the quality of all early learning environments;
- Guide professional development activities and investments;
- Inform educators and caregivers in their decisions regarding approaches to curriculum development across all early learning environments; and
- Guide communities as they determine local age/grade level learning expectations at the district level. The local age/grade level learning expectations assist to make decisions regarding curriculum and assessment that will determine instruction, interactions, and activities.

## Overview of the Wisconsin Academic Standards

Teachers, content experts, parents, and community leaders collaborated to review the Wisconsin Academic Standards for English Language Arts, Mathematics, and Literacy in All Subjects, and these standards have been adopted by 45 states. Adopted in 2010, the Wisconsin Academic Standards focus on core conceptual understandings and procedures starting in the early grades, enabling teachers to take the time needed to teach core concepts and procedures well—and to give students the opportunity to master them. With students, parents, and teachers working together for shared goals, we can ensure that students make progress each year and graduate from school prepared to succeed in college and in a 21st Century workforce.

Wisconsin's Guiding Principles for Teaching and Learning inform the instructional design and implementation of all academic standards. All educational initiatives are guided and impacted by important and often unstated attitudes or principles for teaching and learning. For information about Wisconsin's Guiding Principles for Teaching and Learning: see *dpi.wi.gov/standards/guiding-principles.*

## Wisconsin Foundations for English Language Arts

- English language arts is an integrated discipline.
- English language arts instruction builds an understanding of the human experience.
- Literacy is an evolving concept, and becoming literate is a lifelong learning process.
- Critical thinking and problem solving, communication, collaboration, and creativity (the 4 C's) are aspects of effective English education and skills of Wisconsin graduates.
- Literacy, language, and meaning are socially constructed and are enhanced by multiple perspectives.

## Wisconsin Foundations for Mathematics

- Every student must have access to and engage in meaningful, challenging, and rigorous mathematics.
- Mathematics should be experienced as coherent, connected, intrinsically interesting, and relevant.
- Problem solving, understanding, reasoning, and sense-making are at the heart of mathematics teaching and learning and are central to mathematical proficiency.
- Effective mathematics classroom practices include the use of collaboration, discourse, and reflection to engage students in the study of important mathematics.

## Connection between WMELS and Wisconsin Academic Standards

The WMELS address expectations for young children from birth through entrance to first grade. The Wisconsin Academic Standards address what students should know and be able to do from kindergarten through grade 12. Since the WMELS and the Wisconsin Academic Standards both address the five-year-old kindergarten level, school districts are encouraged to use both the WMELS and the Wisconsin Academic Standards as they move forward with their standards work in early childhood four-year-old kindergarten, five-year-old kindergarten programs, and the primary school years.

## Overview of Wisconsin Essential Elements

Except under rare circumstances, students with disabilities will access the general education curriculum through the Wisconsin Academic Standards.

However, some students with significant cognitive disabilities cannot meet the general education standards, even with accommodations and modifications. These students are instructed using alternate academic achievement standards, called the Wisconsin Essential Elements. The Wisconsin Essential Elements are descriptions of what students with significant cognitive disabilities are expected to know and be able to do at each grade level from kindergarten through grade 12. When considering the Wisconsin Essential Elements, it is important to note that they are based on the Wisconsin Academic Standards and align with the WMELS.

It is important to practice caution when making determinations about which set of standards a student will access. Except for the very few students with significant cognitive disabilities, kindergarten students with disabilities will access the general education curriculum through the Wisconsin Academic Standards. The decision to use the Wisconsin Essential Elements should be made only after careful consideration of potential long-term impacts such as limiting a student's opportunity to learn and reducing the access to general education curriculum.

**For more information on:**

- Wisconsin Academic Standards contact Connie Ellingson at: connie.ellingson@dpi.wi.gov
- Wisconsin Essential Elements (CCEE) contact Molly Bever at: molly.bever@dpi.wi.gov
- Wisconsin Model Early Learning Standards (WMELS) contact Sherry Kimball at: sherry.kimball@dpi.wi.gov

For more information about the WMELS: *collaboratingpartners.com/wmels-documents.php*

For more information regarding Wisconsin's Academic Standards: *dpi.wi.gov/standards*

For more information about teaching and learning English language arts in Wisconsin and to download and print the Wisconsin Academic Standards for English Language Arts: *https://dpi.wi.gov/ela*

For more information about teaching and learning mathematics in Wisconsin and to download and print the Wisconsin Academic Standards for Mathematics: *dpi.wi.gov/math*

The Wisconsin Essential Element webpage: *dpi.wi.gov/sped/topics/essential-elements*

# Wisconsin Model Early Learning Standards Comparison with Mathematics Strands of Wisconsin Academic Standards
## (Grade K Overview)

| | Wisconsin Academic Standards: Mathematics Domains | | | | |
|---|---|---|---|---|---|
| | **Counting and Cardinality** | **Operations and Algebraic Thinking** | **Number and Operations in Base Ten** | **Measurement and Data** | **Geometry** |
| **Wisconsin Model Early Learning Standards Developmental Domain: V. Cognition and General Knowledge Sub-Domain: B. Mathematical Thinking** | Performance Standard B.EL.1 Demonstrates understanding of numbers and counting | Performance Standard B.EL.2 Understands number operations and relationships | Performance Standard B.EL.2 Understands number operations and relationships | Performance Standard B.EL.5 Understands the concept of measurement<br><br>Performance Standard B.EL.6 Collects, describes and records information using all senses | Performance Standard B.EL.3 Explores, recognizes, and describes shapes and spatial relationships |

## Standards for Mathematical Practice

dpi.wi.gov/math/professional-learning/standards-mathematical-practice

1. Make sense of problems and persevere in solving them.
2. Reason abstractly and quantitatively.
3. Construct viable arguments and critique the reasoning of others.
4. Model with mathematics.
5. Use appropriate tools strategically.
6. Attend to precision.
7. Look for and make use of structure.
8. Look for and express regularity in repeated reasoning.

# Wisconsin Model Early Learning Standards Comparison with English Language Arts Strands of Wisconsin Academic Standards (Kindergarten)

| | Wisconsin Academic Standards: English Language Arts Strands | | | |
|---|---|---|---|---|
| | Reading: Literature | Reading: Informational Text | Reading: Foundational Skills | Writing |
| **Wisconsin Model Early Learning Standards Developmental Domain: III. Language Development and Communication Sub-Domain: C. Early Literacy** | **Performance Standard C.EL.3** Shows appreciation of books and understands how print works | **Performance Standard C.EL.3** Shows appreciation of books and understands how print works | **Performance Standard C.EL.1** Develops ability to detect, manipulate, or analyze auditory parts of spoken language<br><br>**Performance Standard C.EL.2** Understands concept that the alphabet represents the sounds of spoken language and letters of written language<br><br>**Performance Standard C.EL.3** Shows appreciation of books and understands how print works | **Performance Standard C.EL.4** Uses writing to represent thoughts or ideas |

# Wisconsin Model Early Learning Standards Comparison with English Language Arts Strands of Wisconsin Academic Standards
## (Kindergarten)

| | Wisconsin Academic Standards: English Language Arts Strands | |
|---|---|---|
| | **Speaking and Listening** | **Language** |
| Wisconsin Model Early Learning Standards Developmental Domain: III. Language Development and Communication Sub-Domain: A. Listening and Understanding Sub-Domain: B. Speaking and Communicating Sub-Domain: C. Early Literacy | **Performance Standard A.EL.1** Derives meaning through listening to communication of others and sounds in the environment<br><br>**Performance Standard A.EL.2** Listens and responds to communications with others<br><br>**Performance Standard A.EL.3** Follows directions of increasing complexity<br><br>**Performance Standard B.EL.1** Uses gestures and movements (non-verbal) to communicate<br><br>**Performance Standard B.EL.2a** Uses vocalizations and spoken language to communicate (Language Form-Syntax)<br><br>**Performance Standard B.EL.2b** Uses vocalizations and spoken language to communicate (Language Content-Semantics)<br><br>**Performance Standard B.EL.2c** Uses vocalizations and spoken language to communicate (Language Function-Pragmatics) | **Performance Standard B.EL.2a** Uses vocalizations and spoken language to communicate (Language Form-Syntax: rule system for combining words, phrases, and sentences, includes parts of speech, word order, and sentence structure)<br><br>**Performance Standard B.EL.2b** Uses vocalizations and spoken language to communicate (Language Form-Semantics: rule system for establishing meaning of words, individually and in combination)<br><br>**Performance Standard C.EL.4** Uses writing to represent thoughts or ideas |

## Portrait of a Literate Student
dpi.wi.gov/sites/default/files/imce/cal/pdf/portrait-literatestudent.pdf

1. Demonstrate independence.
2. Build strong content and knowledge.
3. Respond to the varying demands of audience, task, purpose, and discipline.
4. Comprehend as well as critique.
5. Value evidence.
6. Use technology and digital media strategically and capably.
7. Come to understand other perspectives and cultures.

# Appendix B
## Wisconsin Model Early Learning Standards and IDEA Early Childhood Outcomes

Child outcomes are defined as the benefits experienced as a result of services and supports provided for a child or family. The fact that a service has been provided does not mean that an outcome has been achieved. Likewise, an outcome is not the same as satisfaction with the services received. The impact that those services and supports have on the functioning of children and families constitutes the outcome. The Federal Individuals with Disabilities Education Act of 2004 (IDEA), instilled heightened awareness of accountability, by requiring states to measure educational results and functional outcomes for children with disabilities. In Wisconsin, we have worked to blend the requirements of the Preschool Outcomes for children with Individualized Education Programs (IEPs), ages 3 through 5 years, and Infant and Toddler Outcomes for children with Individual Family Service Plans (IFSPs), from birth to age 3, into a birth to 6 Child Outcome system.

The outcomes address three areas of child functioning necessary for each child to be an active and successful participant at home, in the community, and in other places like a child care program or preschool. Thinking functionally moves us from single behaviors in domain-specific areas to thinking about how skills and routines are functional and meaningful.

Positive social-emotional skills refer to how children get along with others, how they relate with adults and with other children. For older children, these skills also include how children follow rules related to groups and interact with others in group situations such as a child care center. The outcome includes the ways the child expresses emotions and feelings and how he or she interacts with and plays with other children.

The acquisition and use of knowledge and skills refers to children's abilities to think, reason, remember, problem solve, and use symbols and language. The outcome also encompasses children's understanding of the physical and social worlds. It includes understanding of early concepts (e.g., symbols, pictures, numbers, classification, spatial relationships), imitation, object permanence, the acquisition of language and communication skills, and early literacy and numeracy skills. The outcome also addresses the precursors that are needed so that children will experience success later in elementary school when they are taught academic subject areas (e.g., reading, mathematics).

The use of appropriate behavior to meet needs refers to the actions that children employ to take care of their basic needs, including getting from place to place, using tools (e.g., fork, toothbrush, crayon), and in older children, contributing to their own health and safety. The outcome includes how children take care of themselves (e.g., dressing, feeding, hair brushing, toileting), carry out household responsibilities, and act within their environment to get what they want. This outcome addresses children's increasing capacity to become independent in interacting with the world and taking care of their needs.

The following table shows how the five areas of the Wisconsin Model Early Learning Standards align with the three child outcomes.

## Outcomes

### Positive Social Relationships

**II A. Emotional Development**
- A.EL.1 Expresses a wide range of emotions
- A.EL.2 Understands and responds to others' emotions

**II B. Self-Concept**
- B.EL.1 Develops positive self esteem
- B.EL.2 Demonstrates self awareness

**II C. Social Competence**
- C.EL.1 Demonstrates attachment, trust, and autonomy
- C.EL.2 Engages in social interaction and play with others
- C.EL.3 Demonstrates understanding of rules and social expectations
- C.EL.4 Engages in social problem solving, and learns to resolve conflict

### Knowledge and Skills

**III A. Listening and Understanding**
- A.EL.1 Derives meaning through listening to communications of others and sounds in the environment
- A.EL.2 Listens and responds to communications with others
- A.EL.3 Follows directions of increasing complexity

**III B. Speaking and Communicating**
- B.EL.1 Uses gestures and movements (non-verbal) to communicate
- B. EL.2a Uses vocalizations and spoken language to communicate. Language Form
- B. EL.2b Uses vocalizations and spoken language to communicate. Language Content
- B. EL.2c Uses Vocalizations and spoken language to communicate. Language Function

**III C. Early Literacy**
- C.EL.1 Develops ability to detect, manipulate, or analyze the auditory parts of spoken language
- C.EL.2 Understands the concept that the alphabet represents the sounds of spoken language and the letters of written language
- C. EL.3 Shows appreciation of books and understands how print works.
- C. EL.4 Uses writing to represent thoughts or ideas

**IV A. Curiosity, Engagement, and Persistence**
- A.EL.2 Engages in meaningful learning through attempting, repeating, experimenting, refining, and elaborating on experiences and activities

**IV B. Creativity and Imagination**
- B. EL.1 Engages in imaginative play and inventive thinking through interactions with people, materials, and the environment
- B. EL.2 Expresses self creatively through music, movement and art

**IV C. Diversity in Learning**
- C.EL.1 Experiences a variety of routines, practices, and languages
- C.EL.2 Learns within the context of their family and culture
- C.EL.3 Uses various styles of learning including verbal/linguistic, bodily/kinesthetic, visual/spatial, interpersonal, and intra personal

**V A. Exploration, Discovery, and Problem Solving**
- A.EL.1 Uses multi-sensory abilities to process information
- A.EL.2 Understands new meanings as memory increases
- A.EL.3 Applies problem solving skills

**V B. Mathematical Thinking**
- B.EL.1 Demonstrates an understanding of numbers and counting
- B.EL.2 Understand number operations and relationships.
- B.EL.3 Explores, recognizes and describes shapes and spatial relationships
- B.EL.4 Uses the attributes of objects for comparison and patterning.
- B.EL.5 Understands the concept of measurement
- B.EL.6 Collects, describes and records information using all senses

**V.C. Scientific Thinking**
- C.EL.1 Uses observation to gather information
- C.EL.2 Uses tools to gather information, compare observed objects, and seek answers to questions through active investigation
- C.EL.3 Hypothesizes and makes predictions.
- C. EL.4 Forms explanations based on trial and error, observations and explorations

### Action to Meet Needs

**I A. Physical Health and Development**
- A.EL.1 Demonstrates behaviors to meet 1a-d self-help and physical needs including sleep habits, dressing, toileting, and eating
- A.EL.2 Demonstrates behaviors to meet safety needs
- A.EL.3 Demonstrates a healthy lifestyle

**I B. Motor Development**
- B.EL.1a Moves with strength, control, balance, coordination, locomotion, and endurance Purpose and Coordination
- B.EL.1b Moves with strength, control, balance, coordination, locomotion, and endurance Balance and Strength
- B.EL.2 Exhibits eye-hand coordination, strength, control, and object manipulation
- B.EL.3 Uses senses to take in, experience, integrate, and regulate responses to environment

**I C. Sensory Organization**
- C. EL.1 Uses senses to take in, experience, integrate, and regulate responses to the environment

**II. C. Social Competence**
- C. EL.3 Demonstrates understanding to rules and social expectations
- C. EL.4 Engages in social problem solving and learns to resolve conflicts

**III B. Speaking and Communicating**
- B.EL.1 Uses gestures and movements (non-verbal) to communicate
- B. EL.2a Uses vocalizations and spoken language to communicate. Language Form
- B EL.2b Uses vocalizations and spoken language to communicate. Language Content
- B. EL.2c Uses Vocalizations and spoken language to communicate. Language Function

**IV A. Curiosity, Engagement, and Persistence**
- A.EL.1 Displays curiosity, risk-taking and willingness to engage in new experiences
- A.EL.2 Engages in meaningful learning through attempting, repeating, experimenting, refining, and elaborating on experiences and activities
- A.EL.3 Exhibits persistence and flexibility

**IV B. Creativity and Imagination**
- B.EL.1 Engages in imaginative play and inventive thinking through interactions with people, materials, and the environment
- B.EL.2 Expresses self creatively through music, movement, and art

# Appendix C
## References and Resources

All websites accessed August 2017

### Introduction and Appendix

Harbin, Gloria, Beth Rous, and Mary McLean. 2004, August. *Issues in designing state accountability systems.* Lexington, KY: University of Kentucky, Interdisciplinary Human Development Institute.
http://www.academia.edu/4096177/Issues_in_Designing_State_Accountability_Systems

Minnesota Department of Education, Division of Early Learning Support. 2005. *Early childhood indicators of progress: Minnesota's early learning standards.* Roseville, MN: Author. colheights.k12.mn.us/cms/lib/MN02204243/Centricity/Domain/305/3file2431.pdf

National Association for the Education of Young Children, and National Association of Early Childhood Specialists in State Departments of Education. 2002. *Early learning standards: Creating the conditions for success, a joint position statement of the National Association for the Education of Young Children (NAEYC) and the National Association of Early Childhood Specialists in State Departments of Education (NAECS/SDE).* Washington, DC: Authors.
www.naeyc.org/positionstatements/learning_standards

Scott-Little, Catherine, Sharon Lynn Kagan, and Victoria Stebbins Frelow. 2003, Fall. Creating the conditions for success with early learning standards: Results from a national study of state-level standards for children's learning prior to kindergarten. *Early Childhood Research & Practice (ECRP)* 5 (2). http://ecrp.uiuc.edu/v5n2/little.html

Wisconsin Department of Public Instruction. Wisconsin Academic Standards
dpi.wi.gov/standards

### Performance Standards, Developmental Continuum, Sample Behaviors of Children and Sample Strategies for Adults

Arkansas Division of Child Care and Early Childhood Education. 2004. *Arkansas early childhood education framework handbook: For three and four year old children.* Little Rock, AR: Author.
www.arkansas.gov/childcare/programsupport/pdf/aeceframwork.pdf

Bodrova, Elena, Deborah J. Leong, Diane E. Paynter, and Dmitri Semenov. 2000. *A framework for early literacy instruction: Aligning standards to developmental accomplishments and student behaviors: Pre-K through kindergarten.* Rev. ed. Aurora, CO: Mid-continent Research for Education and Learning.
http://www.gpo.gov/fdsys/pkg/ERIC-ED465183/pdf/ERIC-ED465183.pdf

Bowman, Barbara, and Moore, Evelyn K., eds. 2006. *School readiness and social-emotional development: Perspectives on cultural diversity.* Washington, DC: National Black Child Development Institute.

Bricker, Diane, ed. 2002. *Assessment, evaluation, and programming system (AEPS®) for infants and children, Vol. 1-4.* 2nd ed. Baltimore, MD: Brookes Publishing Company.

Center on the Social Emotional Foundations for Early Learning. 2006. *Inventory of practices for promoting children's social emotional competence.* Nashville, TN: Author.
http://csefel.vanderbilt.edu/

Cohen, Marilyn A., and Pamela J. Gross. 1979. *The developmental resource: Behavioral sequences for assessment and program planning, Vol. 1-2.* New York: Grune & Stratton.

Cooperative Educational Service Agency 10, Curriculum and Instruction Department. 2006. K-5 *reading, writing, and oral language grade level expectations.* Chippewa Falls, WI: Author.

Copa, Annette, Loraine Lucinski, Elizabeth Olsen, and Karen Wollenburg. 1999. *Growing: Birth to three: Development guide.* Rev. ed. Portage, WI: Cooperative Educational Service Agency 5, Portage Project.

Dodge, Diane Trister, Sherrie Rudick, and Kai-Lee Berke. 2006. *The creative curriculum for infants, toddlers & twos.* 2nd ed. Washington, DC: Teaching Strategies, Inc.

Florida Institute of Education, and Florida Partnership for School Readiness. 2002. *Florida school readiness performance standards for three-, four-, and five-year-old children.* Ann Arbor, MI: Pearson Early Learning.
http://eric.ed.gov/?q=Florida+Partnership+for+School+Readiness&id=ED482874

Florida Partnership for School Readiness. 2004. *Florida birth to three learning and developmental standards.* Tallahassee, FL: Author.
www.unf.edu/uploadedFiles/aa/fie/Birthto3%20Standards.pdf

Gronlund, Gaye. 2006. *Make early learning standards come alive: Connecting your practice and curriculum to state guidelines.* St. Paul, MN: Redleaf Press.

Honig, Bill, Linda Diamond, and Linda Gutlohn. 2000. *Teaching reading sourcebook: For kindergarten through eighth grade.* Novato, CA: Arena Press.

Ireton, Harold. 1992. *Child development inventory.* Minneapolis, MN: Behavior Science Systems.

Janke, Rebecca Ann, and Julie Penshorn Peterson. 1995. *Peacemaker's A,B,Cs for young children: A guide for teaching conflict resolution with a peace table.* Marine on St. Croix, MN: Growing Communities for Peace.

Kentucky Department of Education, Division of Early Childhood Development. Rev. 2009. *Building a strong foundation for school success: Kentucky's early childhood standards.* Frankfort, KY: Author. kidsnow.ky.gov/families/readiness/Pages/standards.aspx

Kranowitz, Carol Stock. 2005. *The out-of-sync child: Recognizing and coping with sensory integration dysfunction.* Rev. ed. New York: Perigee Book.

Kranowitz, Carol Stock. 2006. *The out-of-sync child has fun: Activities for kids with sensory processing disorder.* Rev. ed. New York: Berkley Pub. Group.

Larson, Nola et al. 2003. *Portage guide: Birth to six, Vol. 1-2.* Portage, WI: Cooperative Educational Service Agency 5, Portage Project.

Linder, Toni W. et al. 1993. *Transdisciplinary play-based assessment: A functional approach to working with young children.* Rev. ed. Baltimore: P.H. Brookes Pub. Co.

Meisels, Samuel J., Judy R. Jablon, Margo L. Dichtelmiller, Aviva B. Dorfman, and Dorothea B. Marsden. 2001. *Work sampling system.* New York: Pearson Early Learning.

Meisels, Samuel J., Dorothea B. Marsden, Amy Laura Dombro, Donna R. Weston, and Abigail M. Jewkes. 2003. *The ounce scale: Standards for the developmental profiles.* New York: Pearson Early Learning.

Minnesota Department of Education, Early Learning Services. 2005. *Early childhood indicators of progress: Minnesota's early learning standards.* Roseville, MN: Author. http://education.state.mn.us/MDE/StuSuc/EarlyLearn/

National Association for the Education of Young Children. 2005. *NAEYC, where we stand: On responding to linguistic and cultural diversity.* Washington, DC: Author. www.naeyc.org/files/naeyc/file/positions/diversity.pdf

New Hampshire Early Learning Guidelines Task Force. 2005. *New Hampshire early learning guidelines.* Concord, NH: New Hampshire Department of Health and Human Services, Child Development Bureau.

Parks, Stephanie. 1999. *Inside HELP: Administration and reference manual for HELP (the Hawaii Early Learning Profile) birth – 3 years.* Palo Alto, CA: VORT Corporation.

Rhode Island Department of Education. 2013. *Rhode Island early learning standards.* Providence, RI: Author.

Schmidt, Fran, and Alice Friedman. 1993. *Peace-making skills for little kids.* Miami, FL: Grace Contrino Abrams Peace Education Foundation, Inc.

Teaching Tolerance. 1997. *Starting small: Teaching tolerance in preschool and the early grades.* Montgomery, AL: Southern Poverty Law Center.

Department of Children and Families. 2009 DCF 251, Licensing Rules for Group Child Care Centers. Madison, WI: Author. dcf.wisconsin.gov/publications/pdf/0205.pdf

**Interest Areas: Children Learn From Play**

Wisconsin Department of Public Instruction, Office of Early Learning. 2017. *Early Childhood: Developmentally Appropriate Practices.* Retrieved from dpi.wi.gov/early-childhood/devel-approp

Wisconsin Department of Public Instruction, Office of Early Learning. 2017 *Play is the Way!* [Video File]. Retrieved from dpi.wi.gov/early-childhood/devel-approp

# Resources

## Determining Curriculum and Assessment

Copple, Carol, and Sue Bredekamp, 2006. *Basics of developmentally appropriate practice: An introduction for teachers of children 3 to 6.* 3rd ed.Washington, DC: National Association for the Education of Young Children.

Copple, Carol, and Sue Bredekamp, 2009. *Developmentally appropriate practice in early childhood programs serving children from birth through age 8.* Rev. ed. 3rd ed. Washington, DC: National Association for the Education of Young Children.

Epstein, Ann S. 2015. *The intentional teacher: Choosing the best strategies for young children's learning.* Rev. ed. Washington, DC: National Association for the Education of Young Children.

Gronlund, Gaye, and Marlyn James. 2013. Focused observations: How to observe young children for assessment and curriculum planning. 2nd ed. St Paul, MN: Redleaf Press.

Hemmeter, Mary Louise, Gail E. Joseph, Barbara J. Smith, and Susan Sandall. 2001. DEC recommended practices: Program assessment: Improving practices for young children with special needs and their families. Denver, CO: Division for Early Childhood of the Council for Exceptional Children; and Longmont, CO: Sopris West.

Jablon, Judy R., Amy Laura Dombro, and Margo L. Dichtelmiller. 2007. *The power of observation.* 2nd ed. Washington, DC: Teaching Strategies.

National Association for the Education of Young Children, and National Association of Early Childhood Specialists in State Departments of Education. 2009. *Where we stand on curriculum, assessment, and program evaluation.* Washington, DC: National Association for the Education of Young Children. www.naeyc.org/files/naeyc/file/positions/StandCurrAss.pdf

Neuman, Susan B., Carol Copple, and Sue Bredekamp. 2000. *Learning to read and write: Developmentally appropriate practices for young children.* Washington, DC: National Association for the Education of Young Children.

Seefeldt, Carol. 2005. *How to work with standards in the early childhood classroom.* New York: Teachers College Press.

Shonkoff, Jack P., and Deborah A. Phillips, eds. 2000. *From neurons to neighborhoods: The science of early childhood development.* Washington, DC: National Academy Press.

Wien, Carol Anne. 2004. *Negotiating standards in the primary classroom: The teacher's dilemma.* New York: Teachers College Press.

Wisconsin Early Childhood Collaborating Partners. Curriculum and Assessment: Resources. http://www.collaboratingpartners.com/curriculum-assessment-resources.php

## Guidelines and Standards

Brown, Christopher P. 2007, Spring. It's more than content: Expanding the conception of early learning standards. *Early Childhood Research & Practice (ECRP)* 9 (1). http://ecrp.uiuc.edu/v9n1/brown.html

Emig, Carol, Amber Moore, and Harriet J. Scarupa, eds. 2001, October. School readiness: Helping communities get children ready for school and schools ready for children. Child Trends Research Brief. Washington, DC: Child Trends. https://www.childtrends.org/wp-content/uploads/2001/10/schoolreadiness.pdf

Gronlund, Gaye. 2014. *Make early learning standards come alive: Connecting your practice and curriculum to state guidelines.* 2nd ed. St. Paul, MN: Redleaf Press.

Gronlund, Gaye, and Marlyn James. 2007. *Early learning standards and staff development: Best practices in the face of change.* St. Paul, MN: Redleaf Press.

Harbin, Gloria, Beth Rous, and Mary McLean. 2004, August. *Issues in designing state accountability systems.* Lexington, KY: University of Kentucky, Interdisciplinary Human Development Institute. http://www.academia.edu/4096177/Issues_in_Designing_State_Accountability_Systems

Koralek, Derry G., Laura J. Colker, and Diane Trister Dodge. 1995. *The what, why, and how of high-quality early childhood education: A guide for on-site supervision.* Rev. ed. Washington, DC: National Association for the Education of Young Children.

Marzano, Robert J., and John S. Kendall. 1996. *A comprehensive guide to designing standards-based districts, schools, and classrooms.* Alexandria, VA: Association for Supervision and Curriculum Development.

Minnesota Department of Education, Division of Early Learning Support 2005. *Early childhood indicators of progress: Minnesota's early learning standards.* Roseville, MN: Author. colheights.k12.mn.us/cms/lib/MN02204243/Centricity/Domain/305/3file2431.pdf

National Association for the Education of Young Children. 2005. *NAEYC early childhood program standards and accreditation criteria: The mark of quality in early childhood education.* Washington, DC: Author. www.naeyc.org/academy/

National Association for the Education of Young Children, and National Association of Early Childhood Specialists in State Departments of Education. 2002. *Early learning standards: Creating the conditions for success, a joint position statement of the National Association for the Education of Young Children (NAEYC) and the National Association of Early Childhood Specialists in State Departments of Education (NAECS/SDE).* Washington, DC: Authors.
www.naeyc.org/files/naeyc/file/positions/position_statement.pdf

Ramey, Craig T., and Sharon L. Ramey. 2002. Early childhood education: From efficacy research to improved practice. Paper presented at A Summit on Early Childhood Cognitive Development, 30 April, Little Rock, AR.
http://www2.ed.gov/teachers/how/early/cognitivedevsummit02/page_pg2.html

Schumacher, Rachel, Kate Irish, and Joan Lombardi. 2003, August. *Meeting great expectations: Integrating early education program standards in child care.* Washington, DC: CLASP (Center for Law and Social Policy).
www.clasp.org/admin/site/publications/files/0145.pdf

Scott-Little, Catherine, Sharon Lynn Kagan, and Victoria Stebbins Frelow. 2003. Creating the conditions for success with early learning standards: Results from a national study of state-level standards for children's learning prior to kindergarten. *Early Childhood Research and Practice* 5 (2).
http://ecrp.uiuc.edu/v5n2/little.html

Spicer, Scott. 2002, January 10. States try to specify what young children should learn. *Education Week* 21 (17): 30.

U.S. Department of Education. 2002. Procedures to facilitate the creation of guidelines or standards. Paper presented at the Early Childhood Educator Academy of the U.S. Department of Education, 3-4 December, St. Louis, MO.

U.S. Department of Health and Human Services, Administration for Children and Families, Head Start Bureau. 2003, Summer. *The Head Start path to positive child outcomes: The Head Start child outcomes framework.* Washington, DC: Author.
researchconnections.org/childcare/resources/3469/pdf

Wisconsin Department of Public Instruction Wisconsin Academic Standards. https://dpi.wi.gov/standards

Wisconsin Department of Public Instruction. 2006. Wisconsin's model academic standards: Raising the bar for all students.
http://pubsales.dpi.wi.gov/pbsa_stndrd

Wisconsin Early Learning Standards Steering Committee and Dianne Jenkins. 2013 4th Ed., November. *Wisconsin model early learning standards.* Madison, WI: Wisconsin Department of Public Instruction. http://www.collaboratingpartners.com/wmels-documents.php

## Information for Teachers and Parents

### General Information

Center on the Social and Emotional Foundations for Early Learning *http://csefel.vanderbilt.edu/*
This national resource center promotes positive social emotional outcomes and enhanced school readiness of low-income children birth to age 5.

Child Abuse & Neglect Prevention Board
*https://preventionboard.wi.gov*
Coordinates projects and publishes brochures for child abuse prevention including the Strengthening Families Initiative and Shaken Baby Syndrome prevention training.

Child Care Resources Inc. – Tip Sheets for Child Care Professionals
*http://www.childcareresourcesinc.org/publications-and-multimedia/tip-sheets/tip-sheets-for-child-care-professionals*
Information, ideas and tips on a variety of child care topics available for download in PDF format.

eXtension Alliance for Better Child Care (EABCC)
*http://articles.extension.org/child_care*
Practical information about children and child care, sponsored by the Cooperative Extension System.

Head Start Early Childhood Learning & Knowledge Center (ECLKC)
*https://eclkc.ohs.acf.hhs.gov/hslc/tta-system/teaching*
Information about early childhood development, teaching and learning in any early childhood setting.

National Association for the Education of Young Children (NAEYC). This is a membership organization dedicated to improving the quality of educational and developmental services for all children from birth through age eight. Its website provides much useful information on early childhood practice, policy, and research. *www.naeyc.org*

Search Institute *http://www.search-institute.org/*
This organization promotes developmental assets, which are positive experiences and personal qualities that young people need to grow up healthy, caring, and responsible.

Strengthening Families
*www.cssp.org/reform/strengthening-families*
Strengthening Families is a proven, cost-effective strategy to prevent child abuse and neglect. The effort encourages and supports child care providers as they strengthen families and help prevent abuse through their daily contact with parents and children.

Supporting Families Together Association (SFTA)
*http://supportingfamiliestogether.org*
SFTA coordinates Wisconsin's Child Care Resource and Referral Agencies in building systems and supporting quality care, resources, and education to enrich the lives of children.

Wisconsin Child Care Information Center (CCIC)
*https://ccic.wi.gov*
Mail order lending library and information clearinghouse for Wisconsin child care teachers.

Wisconsin Early Childhood Association (WECA)
*www.wisconsinearlychildhood.org*
Professional association whose members care for and educate Wisconsin's children, aged birth to eight. An affiliate of the National Association for the Education of Young Children (NAEYC).

Wisconsin Early Childhood Collaborating Partners
*www.collaboratingpartners.com*
WECCP represents many public and private agencies, associations, and individuals. It coordinates their collaborations around Wisconsin Model Early Learning Standards, early childhood special education, professional development, 4-year-old kindergarten, and community collaborations. WI Early Childhood Career Guide www.collaboratingpartners.com/professional-guidance-career-guide.php

YoungStar
*dcf.wisconsin.gov/youngstar*
YoungStar is Wisconsin's child care quality rating and improvement system. Its website has many information resources for parents and providers.

## Free Online Magazines and Newsletters

*Earlychildhood NEWS   www.earlychildhoodnews.com*
Articles, ideas, and crafts for teachers and parents of young children, infants to age eight.

*ExchangeEveryDay        www.childcareexchange.com/eed*
Child Care Information Exchange emails this short, free, electronic newsletter five days a week with a news story, success story, solution, trend report, or other useful item.

*FPG eNews*
*http://fpg.unc.edu/subscribe-enews*
News and resources from the Frank Porter Graham Child Development Institute at the University of North Carolina.

*HealthyChildren.org E-Newsletter*
*https://www.healthychildren.org/English/tips-tools/newsletters/Pages/default.aspx*
Bi-weekly news about health and safety from the American Academy of Pediatrics.

NPPS News and Updates
*www.playgroundsafety.org/news/archive*
Articles from the National Program for Playground Safety tell how to make child care, elementary school, and residential playgrounds safe.
*Texas Child Care Quarterly http://www.childcarequarterly.com/*

*Texas Child Care Quarterly*
*www.childcarequarterly.com/*
This excellent training journal for child care providers and early childhood education teachers gives information on how children develop and how teachers can help children grow and learn.  Most issues contain articles to download in PDF format.

## Classroom Activity Ideas

Discount School Supply: Free Activities
*http://www.discountschoolsupply.com/community/MyCommunityResources.aspx*

eXtension Alliance for Better Child Care - Database of Hands-On Activities for Child Care
*http://articles.extension.org/pages/25442/hands-on-activities-for-child-care*

Gryphon House: Free Activities
*www.gryphonhouse.com/activities/index.asp*

Teacher QuickSource   *www.teacherquicksource.com*

Teaching Our Youngest: A Guide for Preschool Teachers and Child Care and Family Providers *www2.ed.gov/teachers/how/early/teachingouryoungest/index.html*

WISELearn Resources
*https://wlresources.dpi.wi.gov/home.do*

## Infant and Toddler Care

Healthy Child Care America Back to Sleep Campaign (SIDS prevention)
*www.healthychildcare.org/sids.html*

*National Center on Shaken Baby Syndrome*
*www.dontshake.org*

Program for Infant/Toddler Caregivers
*www.pitc.org/pub/pitc_docs/resources.html*
The PITC Online Library houses an extensive collection of multimedia resources related to infant/toddler care. It includes many interesting PowerPoint presentations to download.

Zero to Three   *www.zerotothree.org*
Supports the healthy development and well-being of infants, toddlers, and their families. Its website has information for professionals, parents, and policymakers. Click on Key Topics.

## Health and Safety

American Academy of Pediatrics
*www.healthychildren.org*
Information on child development and health for parents and professionals from an organization of 60,000 pediatricians.

ECELS - Healthy Child Care Pennsylvania
*www.ecels-healthychildcarepa.org*
Fact sheets and other information for early education and child care providers.

*National Center on Early Childhood Health and Wellness (NCECHW)*
*https://eclkc.ohs.acf.hhs.gov/hslc/tta-system/health*
The NCECHW portal shares resources and best practices with early childhood educators, health care professionals, and families.

*National Program for Playground Safety*
*www.playgroundsafety.org/*
Safety tips and standards for child care, elementary school, residential, and park playgrounds.

*National Resource Center for Health and Safety in Child Care and Early Education*
*http://nrckids.org*
The full, updated set of National Health and Safety Performance Standards, Guidelines for Early Care and Education Programs in a searchable online database.

*U.S. Consumer Product Safety Commission*
*www.cpsc.gov*
Safety and recall information about consumer products that could cause serious injury or death.

*Wisconsin Department of Health Services Childhood Communicable Diseases*
*https://www.dhs.wisconsin.gov/disease/childhood-communicable-diseases.htm*
For those responsible for the care of children and teens in group settings, charts show how diseases are spread, incubation period, signs and symptoms, when contagious, exclusion criteria.

## Children with Special Needs

CESA #7 Special Education Services *www.specialed.us*
Special Education in Plain Language in English and Spanish, autism information for staff, and many other helpful resources.

ECTA Center (Early Childhood Technical Assistance Center)
*http://ectacenter.org*
The Center organizes papers and presentations on inclusion, early intervention, and early childhood special education in order to improve systems, practices, and child outcomes.

Frank Porter Graham Child Development Institute
*http://fpg.unc.edu*
FPG generates knowledge, informs policies and supports practices to promote positive developmental and educational outcomes for children of all backgrounds and abilities from the earliest years.

National Center on Birth Defects and Developmental Disabilities (NCBDDD)
*www.cdc.gov/ncbddd/index.html*
Information on identifying developmental disabilities and acting early to make sure young children get the help they need to reach their full potential.

YoungStar – Early Childhood Inclusion
*https://dcf.wisconsin.gov/youngstar/eci*
Information, helpful tips, and relevant resources for child care providers and families.

## Wisconsin Regulations

Supporting Families Together Association (SFTA)
*http://supportingfamiliestogether.org*
SFTA coordinates Wisconsin's Child Care Resource and Referral Agencies in building systems and supporting quality care, resources, and education to enrich the lives of children.

Wisconsin Department of Children and Families (DCF)
*https://dcf.wisconsin.gov/childcare*
The DCF Division of Early Care and Education (DECE) regulates child care programs serving Wisconsin families and supports program quality improvement and improved access to affordable high-quality child care. This website has a wealth of information for families and child care programs in a variety of settings.

Wisconsin Department of Public Instruction
*https://dpi.wi.gov/early-childhood/office-of-early-learning*
DPI regulates public schools and administers the Child and Adult Care Food Program in Wisconsin. This website covers a variety of early childhood topics.

# Information Especially for Parents
*All websites accessed August 2017

### . . . about how to choose child care

**Child Care Aware**
www.childcareaware.org
Information in English and Spanish on choosing child care and other aspects of parenting.

**Supporting Families Together Association**
https://supportingfamiliestogether.org/families
Ten community-based Child Care Resource and Referral Agencies (CCR & R) agencies in Wisconsin help parents find child care.

**Wisconsin Child Care Finder**
http://childcarefinder.wisconsin.gov
Parents can search this website by location to compare child care programs' YoungStar quality ratings and regulatory compliance records to choose the best program for their children.

**Wisconsin Department of Children and Families**
https://dcf.wisconsin.gov/youngstar/parents
DCF regulates licensed family and group child care programs and day camps; administers the Wisconsin Shares Child Care Subsidy Program, the YoungStar Quality Rating and Improvement System, and child welfare programs; and in cooperation with counties regulates certified family child care homes.

### . . . about children with special needs

**Wisconsin FACETS**
(Wisconsin Family Assistance Center for Education, Training, and Support)
www.wifacets.org
This nonprofit organization was founded in 1995 by parents who believed that parents are the best advocates for their children. Wisconsin FACETS' parent centers around the state offer free education and support services to children and adults with disabilities and their families.

**Wisconsin First Step**
http://www.mch-hotlines.org/mch-hotlines/wisconsin-first-step
Information and referral hotline for children and youth from birth to age 21 with special needs. Serves families and professionals. Website includes an On-line Resource Directory searchable by location and agency or service needed.

## . . . about family activities and child rearing

### Child Care Resource Center (CCRC):
Online resource for families providing information about child care and early education. *http://www.ccrcca.org/parents*

### Child Care Resources Inc. – Tip Sheets for Parents and Families
*http://www.childcareresourcesinc.org/publications-and-multimedia/tip-sheets/tip-sheets-for-parents-and-families*

Information, ideas and tips on a variety of parenting and child development topics available for download in PDF format.

### Family Resource Centers
*https://supportingfamiliestogether.org/family-resource-centers*

10 family resource centers around Wisconsin offer parent education and support. All focus on family strengths and building self-esteem and confidence within families.

### Parenting Counts
Research-based resource site developed to support parents and caregivers in raising socially and emotionally healthy children. Includes over 250 articles and 60-second videos about child development from birth to age five. In English or Spanish. *www.parentingcounts.org*

### Prevent Child Abuse Wisconsin: Family Fun Calendar
*www.chw.org/childrens-and-the-community/child-abuse-prevention/prevent-child-abuse-wisconsin*

A calendar with a fun activity idea for each day of the year and helpful tips and resources for creating character in ourselves and in our children. In English or Spanish.

### U.S. Department of Education – Early Learning: Information and Resources for Families
*https://www2.ed.gov/about/inits/ed/earlylearning/families.html*

Recommended resources from the Department of Education, other agencies and organizations.

### YoungStar Resources for Parents
*https://dcf.wisconsin.gov/youngstar/parents/resources*

What to look for when selecting a child care provider; information on early childhood education, nutrition and healthy learning environments; activities that promote children's healthy brain development.

### Zero to Three – Parent Favorites
*https://www.zerotothree.org/resources/series/parent-favorites*

An extensive collection of articles and videos designed to help parents of infants and toddlers tune in to what makes their child tick and to guide them in thinking about the best way to meet their child's individual needs.

## Appendix D
## Early Care and Education Resource Listing

All websites accessed June 2017

**Birth to 3 Early Intervention Program**
Wisconsin Department of Health Services
1 W. Wilson Street, P.O. Box 7851
Madison, WI 53707-7851
Phone: 608-266-8276, Fax: 608-261-8884
*http://dhs.wisconsin.gov/birthto3/*

Birth to 3 is Wisconsin's early intervention program for infants and toddlers with developmental delays and disabilities and their families. A federal law, the Individuals with Disabilities Education Act (IDEA), provides a framework for a comprehensive program and coordinates developmental, health and social services within a community. The Department of Health Services oversees the Birth to 3 Program in Wisconsin. The Birth to 3 Program is for children ages birth to 36 months. Eligibility is based on a diagnosed disability or significant delay in one or more areas of development. The team will evaluate the child's ability to learn (cognitive development); move, see and hear (physical/motor development); communicate and understand others' communication (speech and language development); respond to and relate with others' (social and emotional development); and eat, dress and care for daily living needs (adaptive development). A Birth to 3 service coordinator helps the family understand and participate in the evaluation process.

**Child Abuse & Neglect Prevention Board**
110 E. Main Street, Suite 810
Madison, WI 53703
Phone: 608-266-6871, Fax: 608-266-3792
*https://preventionboard.wi.gov/pages/homepage.aspx*

The Child Abuse & Neglect Prevention Board (formerly the Children's Trust Fund) promotes the development of a sustainable, comprehensive prevention infrastructure that reflects research and promising practices in child abuse and neglect prevention. Through strategic partnerships and investments, the Board supports Wisconsin communities in the provision of services to prevent child abuse and neglect. Best-practice guidelines, comprehensive training, and tools for collecting uniform outcome-based evaluation data measuring the effectiveness of prevention programs are provided to funded organizations.

**Child and Adult Care Food Program (CACFP)**
Wisconsin Department of Public Instruction, Community Nutrition Programs
P.O. Box 7841
Madison, WI 53707
Phone: 608-267-9129, Fax: (800) 441-4563
*http://dpi.wi.gov/community-nutrition/cacfp*

The Wisconsin Department of Public Instruction (DPI) administers the U.S. Department of Agriculture (USDA) Child and Adult Care Food Program (CACFP) in Wisconsin. The CACFP helps provide funding for nutritious meals and snacks served to children and adults receiving day care. The CACFP also provides funding for meals served to children and youth residing in homeless shelters and for snacks provided to youth participating in eligible afterschool care programs. The CACFP promotes healthy and nutritious meals for children and adults in day care by reimbursing participating day care operators for their meal costs. A resource library is available on the USDA Team Nutrition website at:
*http://www.fns.usda.gov/tn/resource-library*

**Child Care Information Center (CCIC)**
2109 S. Stoughton Road
Madison, WI 53716
Phone: 608-224-5388 or 1-800-362-7353, Fax: 608-224-6178
E-mail: ccic@wi.gov
*http://ccic.wi.gov*

The Department of Children and Families supports the CCIC mail-order lending library and information clearinghouse serving anyone in Wisconsin working in the field of child care and early childhood education. CCIC offers educators statewide free written materials, help in planning individualized and group trainings, and loan of books and videos from a specialized collection in the DPI Resources for Libraries and Lifelong Learning. Staff will search for information as requested and mail it out in customized packets. CCIC has materials on numerous topics including:
1) child care, early childhood, and school-age care; 2) early childhood curriculum and assessment; 3) health and safety; 4) Wisconsin Model Early Learning Standards (books, posters, bookmarks, and training materials); 5) multicultural awareness;
6) inclusion of children with disabilities in child care programs;
7) brochures and other information providers need to meet regulatory requirements; and 8) materials in Spanish and Hmong.

### Child Care Licensing and Certification
Wisconsin Department of Children and Families, Bureau of Early Care Regulation
201 E. Washington Avenue - Room E200, P.O. Box 8916
Madison, WI 53708
Phone: 608-266-9314, Fax: 608-267-7252
*https://dcf.wisconsin.gov/ccregulation*

Child care programs that provide care for 4 or more children under age 7 who are unrelated to the provider are required to be licensed. There are 5 regional and 3 district offices around the state that issue licenses, monitor programs for compliance with the licensing rules, and investigate complaints.

The licensing offices maintain a file on each facility that includes copies of the center's complaint and compliance history. Information on a center's complaint and compliance history is available by phone, mail, in-person review, or on the Child Care Search website at: http://childcarefinder.wisconsin.gov. Packets that provide information on how to become licensed are available for $25 from the Northern Regional Office.

A child care provider who provides care for 3 or fewer children under the age of 7 years who are unrelated to the provider may voluntarily become certified. The county/tribal human services departments are required to certify providers who serve children subsidized by the Wisconsin Shares Child Care Subsidy Program.

In Milwaukee County, the Bureau of Early Care Regulation Southeastern Regional Office is responsible for certification. The certifying agency may make certification available to all providers, whether or not public funding is involved. DCF promulgates the certification rules in chapter DCF 202. There are 71 counties and 8 tribes throughout Wisconsin that administer certification programs; monitor providers for compliance with the certification rules, and investigate complaints. Certification in Milwaukee County is done by DCF's Milwaukee Early Care Administration. Certification agencies maintain a file on each provider that includes copies of the provider's complaint and compliance history. Information on a provider's complaint and compliance history is available by phone, mail, or in-person review. The listing of certification agencies is posted at: http://dcf.wisconsin.gov/childcare/certification/pdf/certifiers.pdf

### Child Care Resource & Referral (CCR&R) Agencies
Contact Information:
*https://supportingfamiliestogether.org/child-care-resource-referral-agencies/*

Wisconsin's Child Care Resource & Referral Agencies work within eight regions of the state, serving all 72 counties and 11 tribes to ensure that Wisconsin's youngest children have high quality early childhood experiences. CCR&Rs have something to offer everyone: families looking for care or supports, early care and education providers in need of professional development opportunities or communities looking for information, data or solutions.

- For Families: educating families, as consumers of child care, so that they can make the most informed choice that is best for their family, providing a list of referred providers based on their needs and priorities, and connecting them with other community resources or supports so that they are prepared to be successful in raising their family.
- For Early Care and Education Professionals: delivering high quality training on a range of content areas from developmentally appropriate practices to Strengthening Families, providing customized technical consultation to potential and current early care and education providers through programs like Licensing Preparation, Active Early & YoungStar, and collecting and annually updating business information to maximize referrals to their programs.
- For Communities: educating stakeholders about what quality early care and education is and how to support it in communities, compiling data and producing reports regarding the local child care industry and convening stakeholders to advocate for the best possible outcomes for Wisconsin's youngest children.

### Children and Youth with Special Health Care Needs Program (CYSHCN)
Wisconsin Department of Health Services, Division of Public Health, Bureau of Family and Community Health
Phone: 608-266-3674 Fax: 608-267-3824
*https://www.dhs.wisconsin.gov/cyshcn/index.htm*

The Wisconsin CYSHCN Program funds 5 Regional Centers which provide direct service to families and providers. The CYSHCN Program philosophy is that children are best served within their families.

- Children and families are best supported within the context of their community.
- Families will have convenient access to care coordinators.
- Collaboration is the best way to provide comprehensive services.
- Family perspectives and presence must be included in all aspects of the system.

*The Wisconsin CYSHCN Program directs projects and programs, provides leadership and technical assistance to support the efforts of agencies, provides education and training opportunities for staff and service providers and coordinates a statewide system of nutrition services. The CYSHCN Program provides grants to promote care for Wisconsin children and youth with special health care needs and their families. It publishes Finding Your Way: A Navigation Guide for Wisconsin Families Who Have*

*Children and Youth with Special Health Care Needs and Disabilities*, available in English or Spanish at: *http://www.waisman.wisc.edu/connections*

**Cooperative Educational Service Agency (CESA)**
*CESA Contact Information:*
*http://dpi.wi.gov/cesa*

CESAs provide leadership and coordination of services for school districts, including curriculum development assistance; school district management development; coordination of vocational education; and exceptional/special education, research, human growth and development, data collection processing and dissemination, and in-service programs. CESAs work in partnership with school districts to provide leadership and to help facilitate change and continuous improvement in schools so that all children will achieve educational excellence. Twelve agencies across Wisconsin provide statewide service delivery.

**Early Childhood Kindergarten**
Wisconsin Department of Public Instruction
125 S. Webster Street
Madison, WI 53707
Phone: (608) 267-9652, Fax: (800) 441-4563
*https://dpi.wi.gov/early-childhood/kind*

*4K: http://dpi.wi.gov/early-childhood/4k*

*4K Community Approach (4KCA):*
*http://dpi.wi.gov/early-childhood/kind/4k/4kca*

*5K: http://dpi.wi.gov/early-childhood/kind/5k*

All Public elementary schools include 5-year-old kindergarten and may include 4-year-old kindergarten programs. Recently, 4-year-old kindergarten programs have seen a dramatic increase. Typically, these programs have been in public school buildings. An increased number of school districts have initiated community-based approaches through partnerships that bring 4- and 5-year-old kindergarten programs into child care, preschool, or Head Start center settings. In these locations, licensed teachers may still have separate kindergarten classrooms, may team-teach in a blended program, or teach through other arrangements. As of the 2016-17 school year, 97.6 percent of public school districts were offering 4K, serving 48,764 students.

**Early Childhood Special Education (ECSE)**
Wisconsin Department of Public Instruction
125 S. Webster Street
Madison, WI 53707-7841
Phone: (608) 267-9172, Fax: (608) 267-1052
*http://dpi.wi.gov/sped/early-childhood*

Each of Wisconsin's 422 school districts provides special education services to children with identified disabilities, ages three to 21. Programs serving children from three to five years of age are called Early Childhood Special Education (ECSE) programs. Services are provided in the least restrictive environment within a range of settings including the home, child care, Head Start, kindergarten, and early childhood special education programs. When children are served in general education, consultation and support services are available to teachers and other staff. Each school district is responsible to provide a continuum of special education and related services to children with disabilities who need special education. Children are evaluated to determine if they meet state eligibility criteria.

**Early Childhood Systems**
Wisconsin Department of Health Services – Wisconsin Maternal & Child Health Program
Phone: 608-266-3674, Fax: 608-267-3824
*https://www.dhs.wisconsin.gov/mch/earlychildhoodsystems/index.htm*

Wisconsin Healthiest Families initiative focuses on networks of services addressing family supports, child development, mental health, and safety and injury prevention. The Keeping Kids Alive objective includes Child Death Review and Fetal Infant Mortality Review with the goal to establish a sustainable, coordinated system to identify causes of all fetal, infant and child deaths, resulting in preventive strategies for community action.

**Early Dual Language Learner Initiative (EDLLI)**
Wisconsin Department of Public Instruction
125 S. Webster Street
Madison, WI 53707
Phone: (608) 267-9625
*http://dpi.wi.gov/early-childhood/diversity/dual-language-learners*

The Early Dual Language Learner Initiative (EDLLI) provides resources, professional development, and technical assistance to community partners regarding culturally and linguistically responsive practices for young children, birth through 5. The EDLLI cross sector group collaborates with other state initiatives in order to include the strengths and needs of dual language learners and their families in different statewide trainings such as those provided by Wisconsin Model Early Learning Standards, Preschool Options, and Wisconsin Pyramid Model for Social Emotional Competence.

**Governor's Early Childhood Advisory Council (ECAC)**
Wisconsin Department of Children and Families
201 E. Washington Avenue, P.O. Box 8916
Madison, WI 53708-8916
Phone: 608-266-9314, Fax: 608-267-7252
*http://dcf.wisconsin.gov/ecac*

The ECAC was established in December 2008. The mission of the Council is to help ensure that all children and families in Wisconsin have access to quality early childhood programs and services. It continues work dedicated to building a comprehensive, sustainable early childhood system in Wisconsin.

**Great Lakes Inter-Tribal Council, Inc. (GLITC)**
2932 Highway 47 N., P.O. Box 9
Lac du Flambeau, WI 54538
Phone: 715-588-3324, Fax: 715-588-7900
http://www.glitc.org

The Great Lakes Inter-Tribal Council (GLITC) provides services to Native Americans in Wisconsin, Michigan, and Minnesota. GLITC supports member tribes in expanding self-determination efforts by providing services and assistance. Member tribes of GLITC are: Bad River Band of the Lake Superior Tribe of Chippewa Indians, Lac Vieux Desert Band of Lake Superior Chippewa Indians, Menominee Indian Tribe of Wisconsin, Oneida Nation, Red Cliff Band of Lake Superior Chippewa Indians, Sokaogon Chippewa Community, Saint Croix Chippewa Indians of Wisconsin, Stockbridge-Munsee Community, Forest County Potawatomi Community, Ho-Chunk Nation, Lac Courte Oreilles Band of Lake Superior Chippewa Indians of Wisconsin, Lac du Flambeau Band of Lake Superior Chippewa

**The Registry**
2908 Marketplace Drive, Suite 103
Fitchburg, WI 53719
Phone: 608-222-1123, Fax: 608-222-9779
E-mail: support@the-registry.org
www.the-registry.org

The Registry is a career level system which awards a certificate verifying that an individual has met all State of Wisconsin, Department of Children and Families entry-level training and is qualified for the position that s/he holds. Additional credit-based training is categorized by core knowledge areas as defined by the National Association for the Education of Young Children. The Registry encourages professional development by defining set goals and recognizes the attainment of those goals by individuals. The Registry has developed highly specialized professional credentials and awards completion of the credential to those individuals who have met all prescribed goals. Resource and support materials related to the Registry services are available at: http://the-registry.org/ResourceCenter.aspx

**R.E.W.A.R.D Wisconsin Stipend Program (Rewarding Education with Wages And Respect for Dedication)**
Wisconsin Early Childhood Association (WECA)
Madison Office
2908 Marketplace Dr., Suite 101
Fitchburg, WI 53719
Phone: 800-783-9322
Office: 608-240-9880

Milwaukee Office
316 N. Milwaukee St., Suite 410
Milwaukee, WI 53202
Office: 414-278-9322
http://wisconsinearlychildhood.org/programs/reward/

The R.E.W.A.R.D Wisconsin Stipend Program is a compensation and retention initiative for members of the early care and education workforce who are at Registry Level 7 or higher. Incremental yearly salary supplements are awarded based on one's educational attainments and longevity in the field. This program encourages increased education and retention through increased compensation.

**Supporting Families Together Association (SFTA)**
700 Rayovac Drive, Suite 6
Madison, WI 53711
Phone: 1-888-713-KIDS or 608-443-2490,
Fax: 608-441-5399
E-mail: info@supportingfamiliestogether.org
http://www.supportingfamiliestogether.org

Supporting Families Together Association envisions an environment in which all children have the opportunity to reach their highest potential and all adults understand their roles and responsibilities to children. To make this happen, SFTA supports and sustains an effective network of family support and early care and education systems through statewide membership of Child Care Resource & Referral Agencies, Family Resource Centers, and other organizations and individuals committed to early childhood. SFTA focuses efforts on four early childhood priorities:

- Quality Early Care and Education: SFTA is committed to working with its community-based organizations to advocate, educate and build Wisconsin's capacity to deliver high-quality early care and education experiences to all of Wisconsin's children. This is supported through programming like YoungStar, Training & Technical Assistance and Child Care Resource & Referral services.
- Strong Families: SFTA provides concrete support to families in a strengths-based and evidence-informed manner in order to prevent child abuse and neglect. This is supported through child abuse and neglect prevention efforts and training, including Strengthening Families, Stewards of Children and SFTA's annual Small Change Makes a Big Difference Campaign.
- Healthy Children: SFTA is actively engaged in a broad range of health promotion efforts that are designed to create better health outcomes for all of Wisconsin's children. This is supported through efforts to promote The Pyramid Model of Social Emotional Competence and obesity prevention initiatives like Active Early.
- Responsive Systems: SFTA builds systems and supports to early childhood that result in opportunities for all children to reach their highest potential. This is integrated into all programming at SFTA, including the radio program Apoyando Familias, Aprendiendo Juntos and intentional supports for Wisconsin's 11 Tribes.

**T.E.A.C.H. Early Childhood® Wisconsin Scholarship Program (Teacher Education And Compensation Helps)**
Wisconsin Early Childhood Association (WECA)
Madison Office
2908 Marketplace Dr., Suite 101
Fitchburg, WI 53719
Phone: 800-783-9322
Office: 608-240-9880
Fax: 877-432-7567

Milwaukee Office
316 N. Milwaukee St., Suite 410
Milwaukee, WI 53202
Office: 414-278-9322
Fax: 877-432-7567
*http://wisconsinearlychildhood.org/programs/teach*

T.E.A.C.H. Early Childhood® Wisconsin is a statewide scholarship program designed to help teaching staff in child care centers and after-school programs, Head Start teachers, family child care providers, and center directors and administrators advance their educational qualifications while continuing their current employment in regulated early childhood and school age care settings. A variety of scholarship models meet the diverse needs of the workforce. All models support credit-based education in Wisconsin institutions of higher education. By working in partnership with programs and scholarship recipients, T.E.A.C.H. pays the largest share of expenses related to the completion of an educational path towards a credential, degree, or coursework related to improving a YoungStar rating. T.E.A.C.H. provides counseling and administrative support as well, plus a bonus upon contract completion.

**UMOS Migrant Child Care Program**
2701 S. Chase Avenue, Suite B
Milwaukee, WI 53207
Other UMOS office locations:
*http://www.umos.org/corporate/locations.html*

Phone: 414-389-6000 or 1-800-279-8667, Fax: 414-389-6047
*Website: http://www.umos.org/childhood/migrant_child_care.html*

UMOS services enhance the overall development of children from migrant farmworker parents through the consolidation and allocation of administration and social service migrant child care funds. The overall goal of the UMOS Migrant Child Care Program is to collaboratively provide quality educational and supportive services to eligible migratory children, addressing their special needs and empowering them to achieve to high standards.

**Waisman Center**
1500 Highland Avenue
Madison, WI 53705-2280
Phone: 608-263-5776
Fax: 608-263-0529
*http://www.waisman.wisc.edu*

One of 14 national centers dedicated to the advancement of knowledge about human development, developmental disabilities, and neurodegenerative diseases through research and practice, the Waisman Center shares its resources in many ways: through public lectures and seminars; through consultation to physicians, educators, and other professionals; through articles in professional journals, books, and other publications; and through an internet website and resource center related to developmental disabilities in early childhood: http://www.waisman.wisc.edu/cedd/early.php

**Wisconsin AfterSchool Association (WAA)**
E. Capitol Drive
Milwaukee, WI 53211
Phone: 608-276-9782
E-mail: waa.organization@gmail.com
*http://www.waaweb.org*

The National AfterSchool Association's mission is to be the leading voice of the afterschool profession dedicated to the development, education, and care of children and youth during their out-of-school hours. The Wisconsin AfterSchool Association is the state affiliate of the national organization. It hosts a statewide conference, administers the Wisconsin Afterschool and Youth Development Credential, publishes a quarterly newsletter, and supports public policy development at state and national levels. It provides a professional network for all providers of out-of-school time programs serving the diverse needs of Wisconsin's children and families.

**Wisconsin Alliance for Infant Mental Health (WI-AIMH)**
133 S. Butler Street, Suite 340
Madison, WI 53703-5606
Phone: 608-442-0360 Fax: 608-441-8920
*http://wiaimh.org/*

The WI-AIMHis focused on promoting healthy social and emotional development of all Wisconsin children birth through age five. The Wisconsin Infant and Early Childhood Mental Health Plan presents a blueprint for a comprehensive system of care that includes prevention, early intervention, and treatment. The goal of the initiative is to weave infant and early childhood principles into the fabric of all systems that touch the lives of young children. The developing infant and early childhood system of care in Wisconsin includes the critical components of public awareness, training, service delivery, and policy.

**Wisconsin Child Care Administrator's Association (WCCAA)**
http://www.wccaa.org/
The Wisconsin Child Care Administrators Association was founded in 1976 to help child care administrators in Wisconsin network with each other, spread the news about issues affecting them, take joint action on advocacy issues, and help administrators find out about classes and training specifically designed to meet their needs. WCCAA plays a critical role in directing the future of professionalism in child care in Wisconsin by working with local, state, and federal government officials to educate them about WCCAA, its members, and its commitment to professionalism and excellence in child care.

**WI Council on Children and Families:**
**NEW NAME: Kids Forward**
555 W. Washington Avenue, Suite 200
Madison, Wisconsin 53703
Phone: 608-284-0580, Fax: 608-284-0583
E-mail: info@kidsforward.net
*http://kidsforward.net/*

Kids Forward (formerly the Wisconsin Council on Children and Families) is a nonprofit, multi-issue child and family advocacy agency. Headquartered in Madison, its mission is to promote the well-being of children and families in Wisconsin by advocating for effective and efficient health, education, and human service delivery systems. Kids Forward accomplishes this through publications, educational conferences, and ongoing projects like Wisconsin Budget Project, and WisKids Count.

Its early education efforts focus on quality early learning experiences for Wisconsin's children ages birth to five. The intent is that all early education – no matter what the setting – meets critical standards of quality. Kids Forward sees early education as a linchpin for children's educational success in Wisconsin.

**Wisconsin Department of Children and Families (DCF) – Quality Initiatives**
Bureau of Early Learning and Policy (BELP), Quality Initiatives Section
201 E. Washington Avenue, P.O. Box 8916
Madison, WI 53708-8916
*Quality Initiatives:*
*http://dcf.wisconsin.gov/childcare/quality/*

The Department of Children and Families, Bureau of Early Learning and Policy has lead planning responsibility for quality improvement efforts and delivery of resources and support to child care programming. The Bureau, in cooperation with the early childhood community, provides knowledgeable leadership, guidance, and joint planning to achieve this vision. Additionally, the Bureau directs the YoungStar Quality Rating and Improvement System for child care programs, the Scholarship and Bonus Initiatives administered through the Wisconsin Early Childhood Association, the Child Care Resource and Referral Contract administered through the Supporting Families Together Association, and the quality contracts for training and technical assistance delivery for quality programming and planned supply of child care and early education services.

**Wisconsin Department of Children and Families (DCF) – Wisconsin Shares Child Care Subsidy Program/ Fraud Detection and Investigation**
201 E. Washington Avenue, P.O. Box 8916
Madison, WI 53708-8916
Bureau of Early Learning and Policy (BELP), Shares Policy Section
*Wisconsin Shares: http://dcf.wisconsin.gov/wishares*

**Bureau of Program Integrity, Fraud Detection and Investigation**
Phone: 1-877-302-FRAUD (3728)
E-mail: dcfmbchildcarefraud@wisconsin.gov
Report Fraud: https://dcf.wisconsin.gov/reportfraud
*Program Integrity: http://dcf.wisconsin.gov/progintegrity*

The Wisconsin Shares Child Care Subsidy supports low-income working families by subsidizing a portion of the cost of child care while the parents or caregivers are working or participating in another approved activity. Wisconsin Shares is implemented locally by counties and tribes. The Department of Children and Families, Bureau of Early Learning and Policy (BELP) provides effective management, development, and coordination of Wisconsin Shares. The Bureau of Program Integrity prevents, detects, and recovers fraudulent Wisconsin Shares payments.

**Wisconsin Division for Early Childhood**
*http://www.dec-sped.org/wi*

*WDEC Pinterest Page: https://www.pinterest.com/wdec*

*WDEC Facebook Page: https://www.facebook.com/pages/Wisconsin-Division-for-Early-Childhood-WDEC/489375867751254*

WDEC is a state chapter of the Division for Early Childhood (DEC) of the Council for Exceptional Children (CEC), the largest international professional organization dedicated to improving educational outcomes for individuals with exceptionalities, students with disabilities, and/or the gifted. DEC is especially for individuals who work with or on behalf of children with special needs, birth through age eight, and their families. Founded in 1973, DEC promotes policies and advances evidence-based practices that support families and enhance the optimal development of young children (0-8) who have or are at risk for developmental delays and disabilities.

WDEC established the Jenny Lange Scholarship Fund through UW-Whitewater and is a co-sponsor of the annual WI Early Childhood Education and Care Conference and the biennial JoLyn Beeman Memorial Lecture Series. Membership in WDEC provides reduced fees at these conferences; a state e-newsletter, and the quarterly journal Young Exceptional Children.

**Wisconsin Early Care and Education Career Guide**
*http://www.collaboratingpartners.com/professional-guidance-career-guide.php*

The intent of the Wisconsin Career Guide is to support individuals in identifying career paths within the field of early care and education. Links are provided to connect individuals to the organizations with which they may be interested in seeking employment. Links are also provided to sites with information on educational and degree requirements. Resources are identified to support individuals seeking to further their education through credit-based coursework.

**Wisconsin Early Childhood Association (WECA)**
Madison Office
2908 Marketplace Dr., Suite 101
Fitchburg, WI 53719
Phone: 800-783-9322
Office: 608-240-9880
Fax: 608-663-1091

Milwaukee Office
316 N. Milwaukee St., Suite 410
Milwaukee, WI 53202
Milwaukee Office: 414-278-9322
Fax: 414-278-9336
*http://wisconsinearlychildhood.org/*

WECA is a statewide, nonprofit organization serving as a professional association whose members care for and educate Wisconsin's children, ages birth to eight. WECA is an affiliate of the National Association for the Education of Young Children (NAEYC). WECA advocates for the child care profession, offers training and professional development, sponsors a Child Care Food Program, and administers the T.E.A.C.H. Early Childhood® Wisconsin Scholarship Program which offers scholarship opportunities to teachers, family child care providers, center directors and administrators for credit-based education. WECA also administers the REWARD Wisconsin Stipend Program, a statewide compensation initiative that awards stipends directly to family child care providers, center teachers, and program directors based on attained levels of education. WECA offers a free statewide Professional Development Counseling Service over the phone to anyone employed in early childhood education who wants to hear about the options for training and education available in Wisconsin. It co-sponsors a statewide conference annually.

**Wisconsin Early Childhood Collaborating Partners (WECCP)**
E-mail: Catherine Daentl at daentlc@cesa5.org
*http://www.collaboratingpartners.com*

WECCP was started in 1994 and focuses on collaboration among diverse early childhood partners, including the Wisconsin Departments of Children and Families (DCF), Public Instruction (DPI), and Health Services (DHS), and related early childhood organizations and agencies. The WECCP website serves as the collaborative source of information on issues of cross sector interest, state initiatives, and research-based practices. Regional Collaboration Coaches have been in place since 2004 to connect, build, and sustain cross sector systems around state and regional early childhood priority areas. WECCP's goal is for Wisconsin communities, agencies, associations, and state government to work together as a system of high quality comprehensive early childhood services for all children and families. Essential content areas for collaboration are: professional guidance; child development; Wisconsin Model Early Learning Standards; Wisconsin Pyramid Model for Social and Emotional Competence; curriculum and assessment; literacy, math, and other content areas; health and wellness; diversity; Child Find and screening; children with disabilities; family partnerships; 4K community approaches; and councils and partnerships.

The WECCP listserv - *http://www.collaboratingpartners.com/docs/listserv-weccp.pdf* - is designed to facilitate interactive, electronic communication among agencies, associations, and individuals providing services to Wisconsin's young children (birth to age 8) and their families. The focus of this listserv is on state, community and interagency efforts to improve service delivery approaches for young children and their families.

WECCP information on community approaches to serving children is available at: *http://www.collaboratingpartners.com/4k-community-approaches-about.php*.
WECCP professional development resources – including the Wisconsin Core Competencies for Professionals Working with Young Children & Their Families and the Wisconsin Training and Technical Assistance Professional (T-TAP) Competencies for Early Childhood and Related Professionals Working with Adults – are available at: *http://www.collaboratingpartners.com/professional-guidance-about.php*

**Nutrition, Physical Activity and Obesity: Early Care and Education (Early Childhood) Initiatives**
Wisconsin Department of Health Services
1 W. Wilson Street
Madison, WI 53703
Phone: 608-266-1865, Fax: 608-267-3824
*https://www.dhs.wisconsin.gov/physical-activity/childcare.htm*

The Wisconsin Nutrition, Physical Activity and Obesity: Early Care and Education (Early Childhood) Initiative The health and well-being of Wisconsin's children are directly related to the development and strengthening of their large and small muscles, involvement in sensory experiences, and practicing of healthy behavior. The Department of Health Services, Nutrition and Physical Activity Obesity Prevention Program supports the developmental expectation that children in Wisconsin will be physically healthy and will be able to effectively care for their own physical needs. This site contains information and tools to support child care, preschool, Head Start, early childhood special education and kindergarten programs for four- and five-year-olds to provide developmentally appropriate, increasingly complex and diverse opportunities for children to understand and care for their physical well-being.

**Wisconsin Family Assistance Center for Education, Training & Support, Inc. (WI FACETS)**
600 W. Virginia Street, Suite 501
Milwaukee, WI 53204
Phone: 877-374-0511 or 414-374-4645
*http://www.wifacets.org*

WI FACETS is a nonprofit organization serving Wisconsin children and adults with disabilities, their families and those who support them. Services provided include: public awareness, parent education, specialized workshops, parent support, parent leadership, and promotion of partnership activities between parents and professionals. All services are free of charge.

**Wisconsin Family Child Care Association (WFCCA)**
*http://www.wisconsinfamilychildcare.org/*

The Wisconsin Family Child Care Association, WFCCA, is a statewide organization of family child care providers and their supporters, formed to provide support, involvement, and communication with others in the profession. The goal of the Association is to help maintain the high quality of care that promotes the physical, intellectual, emotional, and social development of children by:
- Promoting the awareness of family child care as a viable choice in child care.
- Promoting awareness of the professionalism of family child care.
- Providing an opportunity for input into laws concerning children.
- Providing a statewide information/assistance network.
- Providing an opportunity for involvement, support, and communication with others.

**Wisconsin First Step**
Hotline: 1-800-642-7837
*http://www.mch-hotlines.org/wisconsin-first-step*

Wisconsin First Step is a statewide Information and Referral hotline that serves families with children who have special health care needs. The line is operational 24 hours per day, 7 days a week. Parent Specialists with specialized disability expertise and having a child with a special need answer the line Monday through Friday 8 a.m. to 4 p.m. Wisconsin First Step has two components. It serves as a central online resource directory of public health services, including Wisconsin's Birth to Three Program. This statewide program provides supports and services to infants and toddlers with developmental disabilities and their families. Another component to First Step is to serve as the Information and Referral hotline for the Children and Youth with Special Health Care Needs (CYSHCN) Regional Centers. In addition to providing referrals to disability-related resources, Parent Specialists provide direct linkages to the closest CYSHCN Regional Center. The Regional Centers provide information and referral, service coordination, and parent networking for families of children ages 0-21 with special health care needs.

**Wisconsin Head Start Association (WHSA)**
5250 E. Terrace Drive, Suite 110 D
Madison, WI 53718
Phone: 608-442-6879 Fax: 608-442-7672
*http://www.whsaonline.org/*

The Wisconsin Head Start Association (WHSA) is a private, not-for-profit, membership organization representing over 16,000 young children and their families and over 4,000 staff composing 66 Head Start/Early Head Start programs – including American Indian and Migrant/Seasonal programs – in Wisconsin. WHSA is an association of leaders dedicated to assuring the availability of comprehensive, top quality services for children and families in our state. They accomplish this through advocacy, the delivery of professional development services, and the creation of unique resources for people and organizations committed to families.

**Wisconsin Model Early Learning Standards (WMELS)**
*http://www.collaboratingpartners.com/wmels-about.php*

The Wisconsin Model Early Learning Standards are derived from research in all the domains of the child's early learning and development and apply to all settings in which children receive care and education from birth through entrance to 1st grade. They were developed by the Wisconsin Model Early Learning Standards Steering Committee, composed of representatives from the state Departments of Public

Instruction, Health Services, and Children and Families; the Head Start State Collaboration Office; and Wisconsin Early Childhood Collaborating Partners. The Standards include developmental expectations, performance standards, developmental continuum, example behaviors of children, and example strategies for adults. They provide a shared framework for understanding and communicating expectations for young children's development. They are a guide for parents, early care and education professionals, and policy makers, all of whom share responsibility for the well-being of young children. A copy of the Wisconsin Model Early Learning Standards can be downloaded at the link listed above. The Frequently Asked Questions section lists commonly asked questions regarding the development and intended use of the standards.

Training for Wisconsin Model Early Learning Standards takes place throughout Wisconsin for educators, child care providers and families who want to continue to improve the quality of early education and care for children birth to first grade.

**Wisconsin Pyramid Model for Social and Emotional Competence**
*http://www.collaboratingpartners.com/wi-pyramid-model-about.php*

The Wisconsin Pyramid Model for Social and Emotional Competence in Young Children is a developmentally appropriate, evidence-based framework designed to promote social and emotional competence and address challenging behaviors in young children ages birth to 5. An implementation grant from the Center on the Social and Emotional Foundations for Early Learning (CSEFEL) at Vanderbilt University allowed Wisconsin to establish demonstration sites and adapt the curriculum for child care staff into an 8-part training series. Pyramid Model materials are available at:
*http://csefel.vanderbilt.edu/index.html*

**YoungStar – Wisconsin's Child Care Quality Rating and Improvement System**
Wisconsin Department of Children and Families, Bureau of Early Learning and Policy (BELP)
201 E. Washington Avenue
Madison, WI 53708
*http://dcf.wisconsin.gov/youngstar*

YoungStar, Wisconsin's Child Care Quality Rating and Improvement System, sets a five-star rating system for child care providers based on four quality components: the provider's education and training, the learning environment and curriculum, the program's business and professional practices, and the children's health and well-being. Through this rating system the state is addressing several key issues in Wisconsin's child care system. It is:
1. Improving the overall quality of child care.
2. Giving parents a clear, understandable tool to compare their child care options and choose high quality care.
3. Creating tools, training, and incentives for providers to improve services, particularly for low-income children.
4. Establishing a connection between child care quality and the rate of Wisconsin Shares payments, and helping prevent fraud in the Wisconsin Shares system.

*Supporting Families Together Association (SFTA) is the contracted agency for the delivery of YoungStar services. It supports early education programs as they demonstrate the quality of care they offer to Wisconsin's youngest children. Local administration of YoungStar occurs through 14 Local YoungStar Offices. Contact information is available at: https://dcf.wisconsin.gov/youngstar/program/localoffice*

*The YoungStar Quality Indicator Point Detail documents for Family Child Care, Group Child Care, School-Age Care, and Licensed Day Camps are available at: https://dcf.wisconsin.gov/youngstar/providers/point-detail*

*The Star ratings of child care programs may be seen on the Regulated Child Care and YoungStar Public Search at: http://childcarefinder.wisconsin.gov*

## NATIONAL RESOURCES

**American Academy of Pediatrics (AAP) – Healthy Children.org**
141 Northwest Point Boulevard
Elk Grove Village, IL 60007-1098
847-434-4000 (tel)
800-433-9016 (toll-free tel)
847-434-8000 (fax)
*http://www.aap.org and https://healthychildren.org*

AAP is committed to the attainment of optimal physical, mental, and social health and well-being for all infants, children, adolescents, and young adults. Its HealthyChildren.org website provides information on health-related and child-rearing topics, AAP programs, policies, and publications, and many other child health resources.

**Center on the Social and Emotional Foundations for Early Learning (CSEFEL)**
Mary Louise Hemmeter, Principal Investigator
Vanderbilt University, Department of Special Education
Box 328 GPC
Nashville, TN 37203
Phone: 615.322. 8150 or 866.433.1966
Fax: 615-343-1570
E-mail: ml.hemmeter@vanderbilt.edu
*http://csefel.vanderbilt.edu*

CSEFEL is a national center focused on strengthening the capacity of child care and Head Start programs to improve the social and emotional outcomes of young children. The Center develops and disseminates evidence-based, user-friendly information to help early childhood educators meet the needs of the growing number of children with challenging behaviors and mental health challenges in child care and Head Start programs. The Center has also developed What Works Briefs that provide summaries of effective practices for supporting children's social-emotional development and preventing challenging behaviors. Each Brief describes practical strategies, provides references to more information about the practice, and includes a one-page handout that highlights the major points of the Brief.

**eXtension Alliance for Better Child Care**
c/o Bryan Cave LLP
One Kansas City Place
1200 Main Street, Suite 3800
Kansas City, MO 64105-2122
http://www.extension.org/child_care

This interactive learning environment, sponsored by the Cooperative Extension System, is an excellent place to find research-based, practical information about children and child care.

**Head Start Early Childhood Learning and Knowledge Center (ECLKC)**
Phone: 1-866-763-6481
HeadStart@eclkc.info
https://eclkc.ohs.acf.hhs.gov/hslc

The Administration for Children and Families' (ACF) Office of Head Start and Office of Child Care collaborate to provide on this website effective, evidence-based resources and teaching practices for early childhood care and education.

**National Association for the Education of Young Children (NAEYC)**
1313 L Street NW, Suite 500
Washington, DC 20005
Phone: 202-232-8777 or 1-800-424-2460 or
1-866-NAEYC-4U
http://www.naeyc.org

The nation's largest professional association for early childhood educators, NAEYC membership includes a subscription to the magazine of your choice – Young Children or Teaching Young Children – access to digital content, discounts on books and conference registrations, an Action Center for advocates, and other benefits. Members of the Wisconsin Early Childhood Association (WECA) are members of NAEYC. NAEYC works to raise the quality of programs for all children from birth through age eight. A major part of NAEYC's efforts to improve early childhood education is through different systems of accreditation for programs that are committed to meeting national standards of quality.

**National Association for Family Child Care (NAFCC)**
1743 W. Alexander Street, Suite 201
Salt Lake City, UT 84119
Phone: 801-886-2322
E-mail: nafcc@nafcc.org
http://www.nafcc.org

The mission of NAFCC is to support the profession of family child care and to encourage high-quality care for children. NAFCC promotes high-quality family child care through accreditation, leadership training, technical assistance, public education, and policy initiatives. NAFCC holds an annual national conference and publishes a quarterly newsletter.

**National Institute for Early Education Research (NIEER)**
1743 W. Alexander Street, Suite 201
Salt Lake City, UT 84119
Phone: 848-932-4350, Fax: (732) 932-4360
E-mail: info@nieer.org
http://nieer.org

NIEER supports early childhood education initiatives by providing objective, nonpartisan information based on research.

**Strengthening Families: Center for the Study of Social Policy (CSSP)**
https://www.cssp.org/about

The Center for the Study of Social Policy (CSSP) works to secure equal opportunities and better futures for all children and families, especially those most often left behind.

**Zero to Three**
ZERO TO THREE: National Center for Infants, Toddlers and Families
1255 23rd Street NW, Suite 350
Washington, DC 20037
Phone: 202-638-1144 or 1-800-899-4301
http://www.zerotothree.org

Zero to Three is a national, nonprofit, multidisciplinary organization that advances the mission to inform, educate, and support adults who influence the lives of infants and toddlers. Its mission is to ensure that all babies and toddlers have a strong start in life.